The Dog as Guide,
Guard and Healer

"Dogs in Our World" Series

Be Your Dog's Best Friend: The Benefits of Mutual Bonding and Relationship Building (Katya Lidsky, 2025)

Canine Agility and the Meaning of Excellence (Beth A. Dixon, 2025)

Canine Crania: Your Dog's Head and Why It Looks That Way (Bryan D. Cummins with Kaelyn Racine, 2025)

The Dog as Guide, Guard and Healer: A Journey with People Since Ancient Times (Cinde L. Bauer, 2025)

Dogs of the Railways: Canine Guardians, Companions and Mascots Since the 19th Century (Jill Lenk Schilp, 2024)

The Force-Free Dilemma: Truth and Myths in Modern Dog Training (Nicola Ferguson, 2024)

I Know Your Dog Is a Good Dog: A Trainer's Insights on Reactive, Aggressive or Anxious Behavior (Linda Scroggins, 2024)

My Broken Dog: Living with a Handicapped Pet (Sandy Kubillus, 2024)

The Peace Puppy: A Memoir of Caregiving and Canine Solace (Susan Hartzler, 2024)

Police Dogs of Trinidad and Tobago: A 70-Year History (Debbie Jacob, 2024)

We Saved Each Other (Christopher Dale, 2024)

Horror Dogs: Man's Best Friend as Movie Monster (Brian Patrick Duggan, 2023)

The Most Painful Choice: A Dog Owner's Story of Behavioral Euthanasia (Beth Miller, 2023)

Your Service Dog and You: A Practical Guide (Nicola Ferguson, 2023)

Dog of the Decade: Breed Trends and What They Mean in America (Deborah Thompson, 2022)

Laboratory Dogs Rescued: From Test Subjects to Beloved Companions (Ellie Hansen, 2022)

Beware of Dog: How Media Portrays the Aggressive Canine (Melissa Crawley, 2021)

I'm Not Single, I Have a Dog: Dating Tales from the Bark Side (Susan Hartzler, 2021)

Dogs in Health Care: Pioneering Animal-Human Partnerships (Jill Lenk Schilp, 2019)

General Custer, Libbie Custer and Their Dogs: A Passion for Hounds, from the Civil War to Little Bighorn (Brian Patrick Duggan, 2019)

Dog's Best Friend: Will Judy, Founder of National Dog Week and Dog World Publisher (Lisa Begin-Kruysman, 2014)

Man Writes Dog: Canine Themes in Literature, Law and Folklore (William Farina, 2014)

Saluki: The Desert Hound and the English Travelers Who Brought It to the West (Brian Patrick Duggan, 2009)

The Dog as Guide, Guard and Healer

A Journey with People Since Ancient Times

CINDE L. BAUER

DOGS IN OUR WORLD
Series Editor Brian Patrick Duggan

McFarland & Company, Inc., Publishers
Jefferson, North Carolina

LIBRARY OF CONGRESS CATALOGING-IN-PUBLICATION DATA

Names: Bauer, Cinde L., 1953– author
Title: The dog as guide, guard and healer : a journey with people since ancient times / Cinde L. Bauer.
Description: Jefferson, North Carolina : McFarland & Company, Inc., Publishers, 2025 | Series: Dogs in our world | Includes bibliographical references and index.
Identifiers: LCCN 2025030343 | ISBN 9781476695150 paperback ∞
 ISBN 9781476656311 ebook
Subjects: LCSH: Dogs—History | Human-animal relationships | Dogs—Behavior
Classification: LCC SF422.5 .B38 2025
LC record available at https://lccn.loc.gov/2025030343

ISBN (print) 978-1-4766-9515-0
ISBN (ebook) 978-1-4766-5631-1

© 2025 Cinde L. Bauer. All rights reserved

No part of this book may be reproduced or transmitted in any form or by any means, electronic or mechanical, including photocopying or recording, or by any information storage and retrieval system, without permission in writing from the publisher.

Front cover image: © Everett Collection/Shutterstock.

Printed in the United States of America

McFarland & Company, Inc., Publishers
 Box 611, Jefferson, North Carolina 28640
 www.mcfarlandpub.com

To Mr. Murphy:
My Guide, Guard, and Healer

Table of Contents

Preface	1
Introduction: Within the Spheres of Mind, Culture and Nature	3
1. Links Between Dog Domestication and Comparative Mythology	9
Shared Themes and Different Perspectives	12
People and Prehistoric Dogs: Theories on Interactions	16
The Evolutionary Path of Dog Domestication	21
2. Contemporary Research: New Methods and Old Discoveries	26
Ancient Cultures and Mythologies: Roles of Dogs in Life and Death	28
Dog Burial Practices: Insights from Archaeological Discoveries	33
Ancient Clues Lead to New Perspectives	37
3. Journey from Antiquity to Victorian Parlors	41
Connections: Migration Paths through History	44
Early Civilizations and New Roles	46
Classical Breeds: Roles and Attributes	50
Ancient Breeds and Familiar Faces	53
4. Genetics, Breeds and Antiquity	57
Genetic Clusters and Breed Groups	58
Mutual Gaze and Facial Features	60
Breed Groups and Working Styles	64
Links Between Breeds and Roles	69
5. The Nature of Dog Archetypal Images	72
Celestial Dogs in the Starry Sky	74
Mythical Messages Framed Within Nature	77
Avenging Hounds and Guides at the Crossroads	80
Guards at the Gates	83

Table of Contents

6. Ancient Roles: Spiritual and Physical Spaces — 90
   - Loyalty and Devotion: Links from Past to Present — 95
   - Sanctuaries and Rituals — 99
   - Healing Practices and Dog Residents — 103
7. Psychological Journeys: Bridges Between the Past and Present — 107
   - Archetypal Imagery and the Theories of Jung — 109
   - Animals, Nature and Soul Through the Perspectives of Hillman — 114
   - Synchronicity and the Network of Dog Archetypal Images — 119
8. Social Skills: Impacts of Awareness and Intentions — 124
   - Interactive Aspects Within a Unique Niche — 126
   - Mechanisms of Social Learning — 127
   - Signals and Senses — 130
   - Vocal and Visual Patterns — 133
9. Observations, Communications and Viewpoints: A Two-Way Street — 140
   - Pathways to Shared Communication — 143
   - Canine Perspectives and Human Viewpoints — 145
   - Dogs and Guesser-Knower Tasks — 147
   - Aspects of Referential Gestures — 150
10. Interactions: Aspects of Emotion and Empathy — 155
    - Perspectives Concerning Emotions and Empathy — 159
    - Emotional Contagion and Emphatic Responses — 163
    - Facial Expressions and Emotional Intentions — 166
    - Companionship Within Individual and Social Environments — 170
11. Links Between Motivation, Companionship and Social Capital — 174
    - Aspects of Companionship — 177
    - Characteristics of Attachments: Similarities Between People and Dogs — 180
    - Relationships and Rating Scales — 185
    - Dogs, People and Social Capital — 189
12. The Journey: Framed by Aspects of Past, Present and Future — 192

Bibliography — 195

Index — 201

Preface

People and dogs are the world's oldest companions and since ancient times have traveled a long journey together. This book utilizes three disciplines—psychology, comparative mythology, and dog ethology—to examine aspects of this journey. Along this path, the spheres of mind (psychology), culture (comparative mythology), and nature (dog ethology) provide new insights into the evolution and significance of the human/dog bond. The chapters reinforce intertwined aspects of these spheres, weaving dog archetypal characteristics of guide, guard, and healer throughout the pages.

As a landscape architect, I love design, nature, and mythology. I have also always loved dogs. Recently, I received a doctorate degree in Mythological Studies with Emphasis in Depth Psychology from Pacifica Graduate Institute. Early on, I realized I wanted to write a book about dog archetypal characteristics of guide, guard, and healer. I especially wished to frame my concepts in the perspectives of past philosophers, psychologists, and dog ethological research. This book contains selected scientific studies with primary source materials which offer context and insights for this work. Along the way, I also propose questions for the reader's consideration concerning the nature of dog archetypal characteristics in the human/dog bond.

Dogs possess both a unique *psychological essence* as well as *physical presence* within the human/dog bond. Dogs as guides, guards, and healers share individual relationships couched in the present and framed by universal influences extending from the ancient past until now. The human/dog bond exists at the nucleus of all these influences. Two of the most important influences in history revolve round the questions of *how* and *why*. This book takes the reader on their own journey of discovery concerning how and why the characteristics of guide, guard, and healer resonate within relationships between people and dogs.

Introduction:
Within the Spheres of Mind, Culture and Nature

Thousands of years ago, humans and prehistoric dogs shared the protection and warmth in camps, and they share hearths in homes today. People and dogs are social species. They gather together, in part, because they want to be together. Since ancient times, long before recorded history, but revealed by archaeological findings, humans and dogs have traveled a journey together. The bond between these two species began in these early times—a journey that continues to evolve shaped by interactions within their intertwined destinies.

Dogs and people share a unique bond couched within nature, framed by social intention and cognitive skills, attachment, and communication. These influences exist within cultures throughout history, individual relationships, and interactions within larger societies. Dogs and people share a fascinating and complex journey, two species united by influences involving mind, culture, and nature.

Along this path, the spheres of mind (psychology), culture (comparative mythology), and nature (dog ethology) provide insights into the evolution and significance of the human/dog bond. The influences of these spheres do not function independently but rather are interconnected through temporal time within nature and mythopoetically within the archetypal realms of mind and culture. Within these spheres, dogs as guides, guards, and healers share individual relationships with their human companions. The human/dog bond exists at the nucleus of all these influences, couched in the present and framed by universal influences extending from the ancient past until now.

In what ways do dogs interact with people as guides, guards, and healers within the contexts of mind, culture, and nature? How have these influences impacted the intertwined destinies of humans and dogs? This

Introduction

book explores four central influences revolving around longevity, connection, and communication that weave throughout the human/dog bond. These influences include (a) the continuing evolution of the human/dog bond since the dog's domestication; (b) cultural and archetypal characteristics, both individual and universal, of this relationship; (c) different types and methods of communication between people and dogs; and (d) aspects of attachment, emotion, and motivation within the human/dog bond. All of these influences impact the unique nature of the relationship between these two species and contribute to the story of their journey together. The following pages provide examples of these influences, highlighted by the perspectives of scholars and selected scientific research studies. In this process, guideposts and crossroads framed by longevity, connection, and communication unfold.

This journey begins with domestication and the longevity of the bond between people and dogs. Dogs and people have shared a destiny for a long, long time. On the earth there are many species of mammals, fish, fowl, and plants. During prehistoric times this is also true. Of all the species inhabiting nature, the dog is the first specie domesticated by humans (Stahl 52). Dog morphology and archaeological findings provide insights concerning the influences of dog domestication on the development of the human/dog bond. These findings reveal the earliest interactions of people and prehistoric dogs that create the foundations of the bond between these two species.

From ancient times, philosophers, historians, and storytellers consider both the individual and universal aspects of the bond between people and dogs. Throughout human history, dogs serve as guides, guards, and healers, sometimes *simultaneously*. Stories within comparative mythology illustrate the importance of canine characteristics of guide, guard, and healer and the archetypal imagery associated with dogs and humans and dogs and gods.

Within the human/dog bond, dog archetypal images unfold framed by psychological and cultural influences. What are dog archetypal images and how do they impact interactions between dogs and people? Dogs and humans share a significant bond, in part due to the archetypal nature of their relationship. This presence exists archetypally as guard, guide, and healer imagery within the interactions between dogs and people as well as in the physical characteristics of dogs in their relationships with people. Dogs possess both a *psychological essence* as well as a *physical presence* which influences the human/dog bond.

Archetypal imagery connects dogs to people along their journey,

Introduction

weaving throughout the spheres of mind, culture, and nature. Stories from comparative mythology illustrate how dog archetypal images provide psychological and spiritual guideposts for the individual's journey and how they have done so throughout history. For instance, Egyptian, Greek, Roman, and Iranian archeological discoveries highlight both the mythological and practical importance of dogs within ancient cultures. Findings reflect the impact of dogs concerning the human journey of life through death and in the struggles and successes of human history. From earliest times, people and dogs have shared companionship in both spiritual and physical transitions. In many mythologies, dogs exist at the liminal crossroads between the earthly and supernatural realms. Stories of both mythological and earthly dogs' importance in healing rituals illustrate their significance.

The dog serves as a *psychopomp*, creating a mirror to the past, the present, and potential for the future within the human psyche. The dog, as guide and sometimes guard, leads the individual through a journey that is never static, often unpredictable, often opening the individual to unforeseen numinous experiences.

The influences of psychology and attachment weave throughout the communications between people and dogs. Depth and humanistic psychologies provide some perspectives on these influences. For example, C.G. Jung and James Hillman offer insights applicable to these interactive communications. Aspects of humanistic psychology and attachment theory also provide insight into the ways people interact with dogs and the importance of these relationships. For instance, Abraham Maslow presents a humanistic psychology involving a "Theory of Motivation," which presents five basic needs with ascending order of strength and priority ("Theory" 12). Included in this hierarchy are the needs for safety, love, a sense of belonging, and esteem.

Relationships between humans and dogs enhance the sense of belonging and self-esteem within people. Numerous scholars note that "the sense of being needed" is one of the reasons that the human/animal bond is established (Fine and Beck 6). The desire to be needed provides a sense of purpose in relationships between dogs and people. Companionship and attachment between individuals and dogs lie at the center of the human/dog bond, framed within psychological and social parameters. Dog archetypal characteristics of guide and healer are manifested in these interactions. The following pages explore *how* and *why* these characteristics occur and their significance in the human/dog bond.

Scientific research has determined that "Domestic dogs are especially

Introduction

skillful at understanding human forms of communication" (Kaminski and Piotti 322). Evidence suggests these skills have resulted from adaptation to life with humans and the selection process during domestication. Both mythologies of past cultures, as well domestication, have impacted these developments. Studies on dog cognition and social skills reveal that dogs possess specialized skills for reading not only communicative behavior but also social behavior of humans. How are these studies pertinent to the interconnected spheres of mind, culture, and nature within the human/dog bond? This book utilizes specific research studies, with primary source materials, to explore these questions.

Communication framed by psychology and dog ethology exists at the nexus of scientific research concerning the human/dog bond. For example, "Dogs have occupied a central place in modern comparative cognition" studies concerning how dog's problem solving abilities differ from those of related species (Miklósi and Kubinyi 300). Research also suggest that dogs can comprehend some aspects of empathy and emotional intents behind cues they both *provide* and *receive* from their human companions (Pongrácz et al. 228–229). These cues deal with cognitive ideas not associated with physical interactions such as requests to seek objects, to protect and guard people and property, and to assist in hunting activities. Empathetic responses are grounded in many ways which include the influences of dog archetypal imagery such as guide, guard, and healer.

The social skills of dogs also create opportunities for larger groups to experience these characteristics within the human/dog bond. For instance, "dogs are often perceived as charismatic, gregarious, social animals" (Arkow 44). Dogs help facilitate positive social capital including descriptions such as social lubricants, ice breakers, and instigators of walks and play in social interactions with people (Wood et al. 2).

The abilities of dogs to problem solve, inform, and cooperate create a foundation for the human/dog bond. Dogs possess amazing abilities to adapt, interact, and communicate with people. These interspecies communications possess an elasticity, moving back and forth between dogs and people. Dogs communicate with physical, visual, and vocal skills, often informed with aspects of social cognition and intention. The following pages consider some of the ways these interactions unfold.

The elasticity of dog communication with humans and the types of communication between dogs and humans reside at the nucleus of these interactions. Humans and dogs communicate between each other with different patterns, movements, and sounds, and are linked with a connective energy framed by nature and the psyche. These connections between

Introduction

people and dogs create added meaning in life. People experience these communications with dogs and they, in turn, reciprocate. Reciprocity is a central link in these communications and resides at the heart of these interactive connections.

Dog archetypal characteristics of guide, guard, and healer weave throughout these interactions. Psychological disciplines and dog ethological research offer pathways to reveal these forms of interaction and communication which extend from prehistory until now. In this context, the following pages explore how the shared journey of people and dogs unfolds shaped by the spheres of mind, culture, and nature. The story of the intertwined destinies of these two species begins in prehistory, couched in the desire for survival, in domestication, and mythology.

1

Links Between Dog Domestication and Comparative Mythology

Certain myths, within comparative mythology, offer examples of various aspects of the bond between humans and dogs. These myths illustrate how the human/dog bond evolves throughout history and the underlying themes associated with these bonds. While the emphasis and perceptions of human/dog relationships change within different mythologies, underneath these changes are several continuous themes including guide, guard, and healer.

Throughout history these themes are expressed within mythological stories about humans and dogs. The value of discussing these myths offers one avenue for increased awareness of the beginnings and evolution of the *human*/dog and *dog*/human bonds. Awareness of recurring patterns and themes illustrates aspects of the significance of these bonds. The continuity of these bonds is evident within cultures and societies throughout time.

Joseph Campbell offers one lens in which to consider this bond within the spheres of mind, culture, and nature through "the mythological dimension" of the four functions of a mythology. He notes the first function of a mythology involves the mystical, the ability "to awaken and maintain in the individual a sense of wonder and participation" (*Vol. 1: The Way* 8). The key words "awaken and maintain" reside within an expansion of early human perspectives concerning nature, leading to an increased awareness and appreciation of the surrounding natural world and the individual's place within the world. This new awareness involves a connection both with the immediate terrestrial environment and also with the immensity of the surrounding heavens. Both the immediate and universal perspectives are framed by the omnipresent forces of nature. Campbell describes this awareness and awakening "as the continuously created dynamic display of an absolutely transcendent, yet universally immanent, *mysterium tremendum et fascinas*" (8).

This description reflects the emerging reactions and responses of humans during prehistoric periods and continues up to the contemporary present. Responses reside within a sense of wonder at the immensity of the universe and within the center of each individual. As noted by Campbell, these perspectives provide a framework for interpreting human existence, utilizing whatever system, whether philosophical, scientific, religious or a combination of systems and provide a frame of reference for each individual as well as for societies as a whole (*Vol. 1: The Way* 8).

The mystical function of mythology is universal, while the second cosmological function is specific to time and place, with the cosmological function residing within the spheres of both nature and culture. As noted by Campbell: "The second function of a mythology, then is to fill every particle and quarter of the current cosmological image with its measure of this mystical import; and in this regard, mythologies differ as the horizons, landscapes, sciences, and technologies of their civilizations differ" (*Vol. 1: The Way* 8).

The third function serves a sociological purpose, "validating and maintaining, whatever moral system and manner of life-customs may be peculiar to the local culture" (Campbell, *Vol. 1: The Way* 9). Dogs serve as guards and guides in many rituals within cultures throughout history. For instance, they exist as active participants in hunting activities and as passive participants in sacrificial burial rituals. In both situations, dogs provide a physical and spiritual link to help "maintain and validate" life customs of humans. From a mythopoetic perspective, these activities create complex, interconnective spheres between humans and dogs. In addition, as sacrificial offerings, dogs help provide a transition from the temporal realm to access into the spiritual realm.

Transition from one phase of human existence to the next is central to the fourth, and most significant, function of a mythology. Campbell notes: "A fourth, and final, essential function of mythologies, then, is the pedagogical one of conducting individuals in harmony through the passages of human life, from the stage of dependency in childhood, to the responsibility of maturity, and onto old age, and the ultimate passage of the dark gate" (*Vol. 1: The Way* 9). According to Campbell, "Within service to this function, the most 'universal themes and motifs are to be recognized'" (9). Scientific research continues to reveal the importance of relationships with dogs as people traverse though the stages of life. Dogs offer companionship for this journey, and to many people, within contemporary societies,

1. Links Between Dog Domestication and Comparative Mythology

companionship presents the most valuable and powerful aspect of the human/dog bond.

From prehistoric up to present time, the second, third, and fourth functions of mythology, as described by Campbell, affect human/dog interactions and the perceptions by humans of dogs. Dog archetypal themes of guide, guard, and healer weave throughout these interactions and perceptions. The impacts of these themes and functions between humans and dogs grow exponentially throughout history, most often with positive impacts but sometimes with negative. The impacts and perceptions vary with different mythologies, reflecting the historical and cultural views of each time period and civilization. Specific examples of these themes and similarities within different cultures and time periods are discussed in Chapters 5 and 6.

Major catalysts for the evolution of both themes and functions appear in mythological stories. Comparative mythology offers avenues for exploring the development of the human/dog relationship within the spheres of mind, culture, and nature. In many myths, place encompasses the realms of heavens, earthly landscapes, and the underworld. From earliest times, humans gaze up into the heavens, explore, and study their physical environments, looking within themselves, seeking answers concerning human existence. Often, humans and dogs and/or gods and dogs inhabit these realms.

People create mythological stories, in part, to provide meaning and a framework for their existence. Based on archeological and pictorial evidence, these stories emerge thousands of years before the advent of structured cultures. Ancient storytellers reach even further into the past, providing theories about creation, explanations about the natural world, and the emergence of human life. The interactions of humans and dogs, or humans and canine gods, reside at the center of many of these stories.

In addition, based on archaeological evidence, humans and dogs shared an existence long before humans strove to create pictorial and written mythological stories. Research by "generations of archeologists have investigated not only how and why dogs were domesticated, but also when, where and how many times it occurred." Significantly, "Unique among all domesticated animals, the first unambiguous domestic dogs precede the appearance of settled agriculture in the archeological record by several thousand years" (Larson et al. 2). As such, domestic dogs and people began their journey together framed by the cultural and natural environments of prehistoric hunters and gatherers. The bond between dogs and people began in these early periods of human development. The longevity of these interactions and resultant mutual dependency have significantly contributed to the evolution of the bond between humans and dogs. These interactions, formed in a nexus of mind, culture, and nature, occur between humans and dogs, in part, because these two species choose to be together.

Written and pictorial stories, combined with archeological discoveries and research, offer strong evidence concerning the longevity and endurance of the human/dog bond. This bond has existed within the intertwined spheres of mind, culture, and nature for thousands of years. For example, archaeological discoveries at the Egyptian Saqqara catacombs (Ikam, 2013) and at Ashkelon in present-day Israel (Edrey, 2008) provide insight into the importance of dogs in ancient cultures. Recently discovered rock art panels in Saudi Arabia, dated to approximately 7,000–8,000 years ago, depict early hunting dogs (Grimm, "Images" 2017). Significantly, the earliest framework of the interactive bond between people and dogs resides in both burial and hunting practices.

The domestication of the dog serves as the initial catalyst for these interactions. Scholars such as Clutton-Brock (2017), Germonpré et al. (2009), and Grimm ("Dawn" 2015) explore the origins and paths of dog domestication. In order to consider the present and potential future evolution of this bond, it is useful to consider how human/dog interactions unfold within these spheres through time.

Each sphere of mind and culture, framed within historical context, helps create the psychological and social context for the bond between human and dogs. Early domestication of dogs evolves into interspecies relationships, framed by cultural and historical parameters within these spheres. These interactions are not expressed in linear patterns of development through time, but rather as interconnected themes, driven by cultural and historical parameters.

Shared Themes and Different Perspectives

Numerous themes, found in comparative mythology between humans and dogs, are applicable to scientific research concerning the human/dog bond. Dog ethology and comparative mythology often explore some of the same themes. From an initial review, the perspectives of comparative mythology and objectives of dog ethological research may appear widely divergent. Comparative mythology explores the stories of universal themes throughout history as is evident in cultures from prehistory up to the present time. These stories do not provide scientifically verifiable

1. Links Between Dog Domestication and Comparative Mythology

data, but they weave through the entire history of human existence. In contrast, scientific research strives to provide verifiable data, hypotheses, and conclusions.

Campbell reflects on the fields of science and mythology, and notes that the disciplines do not conflict with each other (*Power* 162). He observes that "science is breaking through now into the mystery dimensions. It's pushed itself into the sphere that myth is talking about. It's come to the edge" (162). Campbell describes the edge as "the interface between what can be known and what is never to be discovered because it is a mystery that transcends all human research" (162). Upon closer analysis, many similar themes exist between the two disciplines of comparative mythology and dog ethology as expressed in human/dog relationships. The mythopoetic themes of trust, guidance, and healing, and the resultant interspecies bond, also appear within scientific data, grounded in temporal research.

Why are domestication and the evolutionary path shared by people and dogs important to this discussion of the *human*/dog and *dog*/human bond? The answer lies in that domestication sits at the intersections of the spheres of mind, culture, and nature in the relationship between people and dogs. All three of these spheres are essential to the path of dog domestication and development of the human/dog relationship. According to Stahl, "Some suggest that the human-dog relationship developed perhaps 32,000 years ago or earlier" (Stahl 52).

Scientific research continues to explore and expand on aspects of the human/dog relationship, framed in time and space and scientifically confirmed by methods such as carbon dating. Based on present knowledge, the dog "is generally considered" the first animal domesticated by humans (Stahl 52). In addition, as noted by Stahl, "The reemergence of cognitive studies in comparative psychology and ethology, coupled with ongoing archeological discoveries and recent advances in genomics, have contributed to the current explosion of scientific interest in dogs (*Canis lupus familiaris*)" (51).

During the last twenty years increasing knowledge gained from "molecular and genetic data" offers expanding insights into the natural history of the dog (vonHoldt and Driscoll 23). These authors observe that while the research trend towards molecular inference will continue, "morphology and archaeology will remain vitally important in completing our understanding of the cultural context of the changes wrought by domestication" (23).

In addition, the contrasts between taming and domestication are central to the development of the human/dog bond. Researchers note that "domestication is fundamentally different from taming, which is the habituation of an individual animal to human presence. Domestication alters the genetic (and morphological) characteristics of a breeding population and, unlike taming, these changes are heritable" (vonHoldt and Driscoll 25). This ability to alter both appearance and temperament represents a very important catalyst in the evolution of dog breeding. The path and priorities for breeding dogs reflect changing cultural priorities concerning the roles of dogs in different cultures and time periods. Subsequently, these changes impact the development of the human/dog bond.

Significantly, the transition from hunting and gathering cultures to agricultural based societies influenced the mythologies of ancient cultures and shifted the focus of dog breeding. This shift led to a critical juncture in the journey of people and dogs. Distinct working types of dogs existed in antiquity including sighthounds and mastiff type dogs (vonHoldt and Driscoll 32). These dogs were bred to perform specific hunting functions for different types of game and as animals used in war. The literature of ancient cultures as well as sculptures and other forms of art depict these various types of working dogs. Dogs provided physical attributes in hunting and guarding activities as well as archetypal imagery in the mythologies of ancient cultures. See Chapter 3.

Over time, the emphasis on breeding dogs as working dogs to preform specific functions such as guarding, hunting, herding, and hauling became less important. For instance, "In Europe, dog breeds have existed since at least the 1300's" (vonHoldt and Driscoll 32). Priorities shifted and by the middle of the eighteenth-century priorities shifted to include more emphasis on form in dog breeding (vonHoldt and Driscoll 32). This shift in emphasis marks the beginning of the modern dog period, evident by the establishment of international breed organizations including the American Kennel Club, Fédération Cynologique Internationale, and The Royal Kennel Club.

The 2012 publication "Rethinking dog domestication by integrating genetics, archeology, and biogeography" discusses both the timelines of domestication and origins of dog breeds (Larson et al.). According to this work, "The dog was the first domesticated animal, but it remains uncertain when the domestication process began and whether it occurred just once or multiple times across the Northern Hemisphere" (Larson et al. 2). The authors seek "to ascertain the value of modern genetic data to elucidate the origins of dog domestication," utilizing data "in 1375 dogs (representing 35 breeds) and 19 wolves" (2). Significantly, the Larson et al. study utilizes the interactive disciplines of science and archaeology together to study

1. Links Between Dog Domestication and Comparative Mythology

dog domestication origins. In this process, the study also evaluates the geographic locations of 14 so-called "so-called 'ancient' breeds" (2) The findings help to illuminate the origins and timelines of the first domestications of dogs and when and where wolves evolved into the earliest prehistoric dogs.

According to the authors, "These results demonstrate that the unifying characteristic among all genetically distinct so-called ancient breeds is a lack of recent admixture with other breeds likely facilitated by geographic and cultural isolation" (Larson et al. 2). These findings provide perspective when considering the types of working class dogs in ancient societies versus specific breeds of modern dogs today.

In his book *Dog Behavior, Evolution, and Cognition*, Ádám Miklósi observes that "providing an evolutionary realistic framework for dog domestication is difficult" (124). He summarizes five "non-exclusive theories of domestication" and notes "Each theory is important in explaining a particular aspect of the process, so all five together probably give the most plausible account of the sequence of events" (125). Different aspects of these theories, discussing the evolutionary mechanisms, appear in both literature and scientific research. Consideration of four of the theories offers examples of intertwined aspects of dog domestication and development of the human/dog bond. In addition, these theories illustrate the complexity of research concerning dog domestication.

Miklósi notes that the first theory, individual-based selection, likely "occurred not at the start, but only at the end of domestication," for instance, as the breeding of dogs developed (125). Karen Lange discusses some of the aspects associated with crossbreeding dogs in "Wolf to Woof" (2–11). Aspects of the second "population-based selection" appear in theories concerning how wolves adapted to humans through interactions associated with human camps and food sources (Miklósi 125). Grimm and Lange look at impacts concerning these theories, as well as the possibility that wolves domesticated themselves.

Kay Frydenborg addresses the third theory of human-dog co-evolution in her book "*A Dog in the Cave: The Wolves Who Made Us Human.*" In this premise, changes in one species trigger related changes in the other species over time (Frydenborg 3). She writes: "If these mutual changes provide a survival and reproductive advantage, genetic mutations pass down through succeeding generations, and become permanent features" (3). Frydenborg also considers the fourth theory of human group selection. According to Miklósi, "little factual support is available for this theory," which involves the possibilities that "some traits emerging at the group level can be favored in specific conditions" (125).

Miklósi's fifth theory, concerning the cultural-technological evolution, provides the most significance for the interactions of comparative mythology and dog domestication research. As noted by Miklósi, "Diversification of dog roles runs in parallel with cultural-technological evolution" (125). This theory provides insight into the development of specific dog roles and their impact within the human/dog bond. Significantly, these roles expand from hunting activities to additional roles as working dogs, and ultimately numerous roles in contemporary societies. "Such diversification has taken place repeatedly during human history" (Miklósi 125).

The development of the hunter-gatherer societies and the mythological importance of dogs in ancient cultures is central to the development of the bond between people and dogs. For instance, in *The Historical Atlas of World Mythology*, Campbell discusses the "folkways and mythologies" of two groups, "hunting and gathering tribes" and "the earliest planting cultures" (*Vol. 1, The Way* 49). Mythologies, associated with transitory hunting and gathering cultures versus more structured and settled planting cultures, provide different frameworks and perspectives for reviewing dog domestication theories. Tracking the appearance and evolution of hunting and gathering tribes impacts the questions of *where and how*, concerning development of the earliest human/dog interactions. In addition, reviewing approximate timetables for appearance of these two groups impacts the probability of some dog domestication theories.

Campbell's view of "folkways and mythologies" is reinforced by scientific research today. For instance, research with dogs provides the opportunity "to understand the process of domestication and reveals how two species evolved together, especially at a time when early global colonization took place within the context of changing environments" (Stahl 52).

People and Prehistoric Dogs: Theories on Interactions

Dogs, as the first animal species domesticated, developed a mutually beneficial relationship with humans. Archaeologists and scientists have disagreed on the locations and dates of these first encounters, and subsequent domestication, when the first wolves began to evolve into the first prehistoric dogs. Yet, for the most part, scholars agree that over a period of a few thousand years this evolution and subsequent relationship with wolves did develop. Alexandra Horowitz writes: "Thus, early in the

1. Links Between Dog Domestication and Comparative Mythology

European Wolf, Black Wolf of North America, St. Bernard's Mastiff, Highland Greyhound, and Great Dog of Nepal. Digitally enhanced from edition of *A History of the Earth and Animated Nature* (1820) by Oliver Goldsmith (1730–1774) (CC0 1.0 Universal).

development of ancient civilizations, thousands of years before domesticating any other animal, humans took this one animal with them inside the walls of their fledgling villages" (40).

It is almost impossible to grasp the immense period of time which is being investigated, with ongoing scientific research, concerning the earliest interactions between humans and prehistoric dogs. Evidence, from this research, provides credence to the longevity and significance of the earliest human/prehistoric dog interactions and ultimately the interspecies relationship between humans and domestic dogs.

In the perspective of evolutionary time, these encounters and domestication occur briskly over a short period. As noted by Horowitz, "The change from wolf to dog was striking in its speed. Humans took nearly two million years to morph from *Homo habilis* to *Homo sapiens*" (40–41). The wolf evolved into the prehistoric dog "in a fraction of that time" (41). Based on this evolutionary time frame, development of the human/dog relationship has been on a fast track from the beginning. These prehistoric dogs are not the same subspecies as the *Canis lupus familiaris*, or the domestic dog of today. Yet, the close proximity of prehistoric dogs and humans opens opportunities for both evolution of the relationship and domestication of the dog.

Researchers have discovered new evidence concerning the earliest ancestor of the prehistoric dog and subsequent emergence of the domestic dog. This evidence suggests that the appearance and evolution of *Canis lupus familiaris*, the domestic dog, occurs much earlier than previously assumed.

According to Lange, "At the molecular level not much changed at all: The DNA makeup of wolves and dogs is almost identical" (4). Although the DNA make up is close to identical, at some point, the prehistoric path of human/dog interactions versus human/wolf interactions diverges significantly (4). The *point* in time, *cause* of this divergence and *path* of domestication continue to spark scientific debate. Emphasis is placed on the point in time, the cause, and path of domestication because the convergence of all three of these elements sets the context for development of the human/dog bond.

Three of the most asked questions in human history are *when, why,* and *how*? Significantly, it took several decades of research and analysis to agree that the domestic dog evolved from the grey wolf. Juliet Clutton-Brock observes: "After more than a century of argument and discussion, it is now generally agreed that the single progenitor of all domestic dogs, ancient and modern, was the grey wolf, *Canis lupus*" (8). This evolution starts with the premise that the humans and the earliest wolf ancestors of prehistoric dogs chose to share proximity to each other for some reason or combination of reasons. Why and how did these two species, in some cases, embark on this path? Researchers, within the multi-discipline fields of anthrozoology, among others, seek answers to these questions through scientific research including dog ethology, psychology, and neuroscience. New knowledge and perspectives, framed by these disciplines, illuminate and highlight aspects of the human/dog bond. The bond between people and dogs is not static; it continues to evolve and unfold as it has done since ancient times. This bond offers a story of continuity from the past to the present and promise for the future.

For instance, Clutton-Brock notes: "The dog is no longer a tamed wolf, as a result of selective breeding under human control, it has evolved into a new species, named by Linnaeus, *Canis familiaris*" (8). She adds that *Canis familiaris* "by further reproductive isolation and under the influence of both natural and artificial selections produces new breeds" (8). In ancient times, these characteristics allowed people to breed dogs to perform specific tasks as the earliest working dogs. In this process, people and

1. Links Between Dog Domestication and Comparative Mythology

dogs shared a close proximity to each other and a developing mutual reliance, as the dogs became both co-hunters and guards. These interactions helped create the environment for the earliest developmental phase of the human/dog bond.

Frydenborg also discusses the origins and shared history of humans and dogs. She writes: "The relationship of human and dogs may have begun as one of cooperation, rather than dominance and submission" between humans and "certain unusual wolves" (2). From this perspective, the early human/dog relationship was based in some part on forming a mutually beneficial partnership.

The contrast between two other theories on the evolution of dog domestication also offers insight into the path of domestication. The earlier theory reflects the "hypothesis that domestication originated from the practice of capturing and taming young wild individual animals" (Clutton-Brock 9). Subsequently, this concept "was generally replaced in the second half of the twentieth century by the theory that wild animals became associated with human groups and were thereby habituated and tamed from their own volition" (9). This second theory is significant since it illustrates that wolves, the earliest ancestors of dogs, chose to interact with humans. The taming of wild animals versus the choice of wild animals to share their existence with humans presents very different motivations for interactions. Ultimately, this point of departure creates the environment for the earliest development of the bond between people and prehistoric dogs.

Frydenborg discusses the possibility that the close proximity and development of this relationship laid the framework for a coevolution of both species, humans and dogs. As discussed previously, Miklósi describes human-dog coevolution as one of five "non-exclusive theories of domestication." According to Miklósi, "So far, there is no evidence of this theory despite widespread reference to 'coevolution' between humans and dogs" (125).

Biologist John Bradshaw offers this hypothesis: "It is entirely possible that some accident of genetics—some sort of mutation—gave a few wolves the ability to socialize to two species simultaneously, to direct their social behavior to mankind *and* other wolves" (52). He suggests, "that this ability to socialize to humans is not, as it is usually assumed, a consequence of domestication" (52). Rather, he conceives "it as crucial, if accidental, pre-adaptation that opened the door to domestication in the first place" (52–53).

Whether an accident or a result of domestication, prehistoric dogs embark on an interspecies relationship with humans. In this process, prehistoric dogs exhibit a trait which continues to the present—the ability to exist within two worlds, human and canine. In addition, Frydenborg suggests, "The capacity for the dog to adopt a dual identity—part human and part wolf—is essential in accounting for the transition from primitive pet to truly domesticated animal" (138).

David Grimm discusses another theory concerning how wolves increased their interactions with humans, leading to stages of domestication ("Dawn" 277). According to this theory, prehistoric humans left piles of carcasses outside their campsites edges and wolves were drawn to this easily attainable food source (277). Subsequent generations of wolf pups, born on the fringes of these human environments, became bolder and drew closer (277). This proximity of humans and wolves led to increased interactions and the earliest nucleus of the human/canine relationship. While guarding their food sources provided by humans, wolves and eventually prehistoric dogs also served as guards for the camps.

As humans realized the versatility and adaptability of prehistoric dogs they begin breeding these dogs for more specialized roles in hunting, herding, and guarding (Grimm, "Dawn" 277). The second phase of dog domestication unfolds, and the interactions between humans and prehistoric dogs increase. A team of researchers comparing thousands of ancient dog and wolf skeletons, for example, has revealed flattening of ancient dog vertebrae, suggesting the animals hauled heavy packs on their backs. "The team has also spotted missing pairs of molars near the rear of the jaw in ancient dogs, which may indicate that the animals wore some sort of bridle to pull carts" (277).

From the initial desires for increased mutual survival, domestication and evolution continued. From early times, humans strove to maximize the characteristics and traits they felt would be beneficial for the human/dog relationship. Humans, of course, pursued this goal from the human's perspective not the dog's perspective. People began to breed dogs to enhance certain characteristics for herding livestock, improving specialized hunting abilities, and guarding property and individuals. Emphasis on performing tasks expanded to include adaptability for human companionship, and later aesthetic appearance.

Lange offers a brief summary of the dog's progression from prehistoric camp dweller to contemporary companion. She notes: "No other species displays such diversity as the dog. Raymond Coppinger calls the dog a shape-shifter" (Lange 5). Yet, despite the huge variations in size and temperament, domestic dogs share more characteristics than just a single ancestor,

1. Links Between Dog Domestication and Comparative Mythology

the wolf. In prehistoric periods, the ranges of early dogs expand across widening global areas with varying environments, shaped by climate, topography, vegetation, and animal life. The path of dog evolution combines both the influences of nature or ethology and the impact of increasing human interactions. According to Lange, during this process, early dogs "developed tame dispositions and a host of genetically linked qualities, including trainability, tail-wagging, and multi-colored coats" (5).

Exposed to human settlements and human garbage, dogs no longer need to exclusively and aggressively hunt large prey as their main food sources and protein necessary for survival (Lange 5). From aggressive hunters, over time, dogs transition into scavengers of human garbage. The cultural changes initiated by exposure to humans and changing food sources allowed prehistoric dogs to develop smaller teeth and skulls than wolves (5). These changes result in the appearance of a type of dog which is recognizable today, a "mutt similar to the medium size, often golden-colored dogs that scavenge on the edges of towns worldwide" (5).

The Evolutionary Path of Dog Domestication

Evolutionary changes, while impacting the size and appearance of early dogs, also provide clues in contemporary times to *when* and *how* wolves began to evolve into early dogs. Ancient dog and wolf fossils provide archaeological clues for contemporary research concerning scientific theories about dog domestication. Some of this research, notably the work of Mietje Germonpré, is discussed herein. This research serves as another example of the interconnected spheres of both nature and culture in the development of human/dog interactions.

It is possible that prehistoric dogs adapted to early functions of hunting and herding without extensive interactions by humans (Lange 5). As noted, hunting and herding, as well as guarding, were the earliest functions of the working dog. Lange observes, over time, people began crossbreeding individual dogs for new dog roles, with emphasis on appearance as well as form (6). Significantly, while the new breeds fulfilled the needs and desires of humans, many of these breeds lost their abilities to survive in nature, thus increasing both the interactions and interdependency of dogs with humans (6).

Throughout crossbreeding, "the skeleton of the wolf has been manipulated without losing a single bone" (Lange 6). Crossbreeding has led to dog breeds with sizes, appearances, and temperaments ranging from the

The Dog as Guide, Guard and Healer

Ashurbanipal's servant with a dog, amid lion-hunts. From Room C, North Palace at Nineveh, Iraq, 645–635 BCE (British Museum, London).

Great Dane to the Chihuahua. This process provides another example of the intertwined spheres of nature, or ethology, and culture as evident in the desires of humans. Domestic dogs continue to exist with dual identities, shape-shifters in both appearance and temperament, while linked with the skeletal structure of their ancestor, the wolf.

How is the domestic dog, while so closely genetically linked to the wolf, an entirely different creature? The relationship between people and dogs, framed by aspects of domestication and psychological perceptions, offers insight. Domestication occurs "as an evolutionary process by which animal populations" … in this case domestic dogs, adapt to humans with resultant genetic changes due to environmental conditions (Miklósi 124). In addition, "it can be assumed that the human-created (*anthropogenic*) niche, differs in many respects from natural ones, and that is most obvious in the case of the dog" (Miklósi 124). The human/dog relationship and subsequent bond exists in this unique niche.

Two scientists, Charles Darwin and Mietje Germonpré, separated by over 200 years, provide critical hypotheses for unraveling the mystery of *how* and *when* prehistoric wolves evolve into prehistoric dogs. Darwin

1. Links Between Dog Domestication and Comparative Mythology

studies the origins of the multitude of contemporary dogs looking for a common ancestral link. Germonpré relooks at ancient wolf and dog fossils to reconsider the point in time when the paths of wolves and prehistoric dogs diverged. Evaluating this process helps denote the point when the domestication of dogs began.

During his life, "Darwin was, in addition to a geologist and naturalist, a life-long dog lover" (Frydenborg 29). Dogs offered not only companionship, but scientific inspiration. For twenty years, before publishing *On the Origin of Species* in 1895, he studied the "astonishing variety of canines," grouped under one category, the dog (30).

In addition, Larson et al. observe, "Darwin speculated about the origins of several domestic animals and suggested that, given the vast morphological variations across numerous breeds, dogs must have had more than one wild ancestor" (2). They add, however, that according to recent genetic studies "dogs are descended exclusively from the grey wolf (*Canis lupus*)" (Larson et al. 2).

From that point forward, two decades of research offer competing hypotheses on *when* and *how* wolves transitioned into prehistoric dogs. During this period, research studies confirm that domestication of dogs occurred much earlier than previously assumed. Evidence supports that the domestication of dogs began within the transitory hunter-gatherer cultures and well before cultures based on farming within settled communities. Some of this research focuses on ancient canine fossils previously discovered in the Altai Mountains of Siberia, Goyet Cave in Belgium, and Předmostí in the Czech Republic (Frydenborg 63).

Clutton-Brock provides observations concerning how these fossils exhibit "the characteristics of incipient domestication" (9). She notes, "These characteristics include a reduction in size, a shortening of the jaws and widening of the snout, often without reduction in size of the teeth, so that the cheek teeth are compacted" (8). These canid remains date to the Paleolithic epoch, approximately "26,000 to 20,000 years ago" (9).

In 2008, Mietje Germonpré, a paleontologist associated with the Royal Belgian Institute of Natural Sciences in Brussels, together with other researchers, decided to re-evaluate "some prehistoric canine skulls fossils" from a new perspective (473). Germonpré et al. examined "several skulls of fossil large canids from sites in Belgium, Ukraine, and Russia to look for possible evidence of the presences of Paleolithic dogs" (473). The researchers presented the following hypothesis: "Changes in dog morphology compared to wolf morphology appeared rather abruptly, that they

The Dog as Guide, Guard and Healer

Domestic dogs today (Free Range Stock).

were linked to the effects of domestication and that these characteristics became fixed in the dog population" (473).

Feydenborg observes, "Germonpré and her team demonstrated that modern wolves can be accurately distinguished from modern dogs by combining measurements of the proportions of their snouts and the sizes of their teeth. Almost all modern dogs, they found, have smaller teeth and broader, shorter snouts than do modern wolves" (55). Utilizing these findings, Germonpré et al. reviewed existing prehistoric fossils, including the Goyet Cave fossils, to re-evaluate when wolves began to evolve into prehistoric dogs.

The Belgian Goyet Cave fossils, which include "a large number of Middle and Upper Paleolithic artifacts," were originally discovered during the 1860s excavations by Édouard Dupont (Germonpré et al. 474). In addition to cave bear and lion fossils, discoveries also included a bone harpoon, shell necklaces, and needles. Germonpré et al. conducted genetic analysis on the Belgian fossil large canids "with the goal to compare the analyzed Belgium specimens with the recent dog and wolf DNA haplotypes described to date" (474). According to their findings, "The fossil large canid from Goyet Belgium, dated at c. 31,700 BP is clearly different from recent wolves, resembling most closely the prehistoric dogs" (473).

1. Links Between Dog Domestication and Comparative Mythology

These research discoveries join other archeological findings which first illustrate the intertwined evolution of humans and prehistoric dogs. The discovery of these skulls and the archeological fossil evidence gleaned through further analysis of these fossils provides strong evidence of the *longevity* of the human/dog relationship.

2

Contemporary Research
New Methods and Old Discoveries

Scientific research offers various theories on the origin, development, and migration of the early wolves, which ultimately evolve into *Canis lupus familiaris*. The scientific theories on *when* and *how* this evolution occurs have been numerous, and often contentious. Grimm, in his article "Dawn of the Dog," summarizes some of the challenges and conflicting theories concerning dog domestication.

For instance, Germonpré's 2009 research reveals the Goyet Cave fossil, most likely, is the skull of an ancient dog rather than a wolf. According to Grimm, however, critics questioned Germonpré's findings and conclusions ("Dawn" 277). Comments concerning these findings and other works reflect some of the contrasting research methods and theories expressed by various scholars. Grimm discusses aspects of these contrasting research methods and theories concerning the path of dog domestication. In general, researchers argued that some studies were too influenced by geographic locations and others argued ancient DNA from ancient fossils should be used, not an analysis of DNA from modern dogs ("Dawn" 276). Based on different studies and theories, the projected dates for the appearance and transition of ancient wolves to prehistoric dogs ranged from 12,000 years to 16,000 to possibly as early as 135,000 years ago ("Dawn" 275). Through years of research, the answers to *when*, *where*, and *how* concerning dog domestication continued to be elusive. Recently, it appears a major breakthrough concerning this mystery has unfolded.

Faced with divergent theories and methods, researchers Greger Larson and Keith Dobney realize a global collaboration, fueled with significant research funds, might unlock the mystery. Previously, they had been working together combining computer analysis of ancient fossil DNA with geometric morphometrics to investigate aspects of the pig's domestication. They then turned to researching the domestication of the dog, utilizing their previous experience to analyze wolf and other ancient fossils (Grimm, "Dawn" 277).

In 2012, Larson and Dobney secured significant funding from European agencies to analyze as many samples as possible, from as many places as possible. Samples were collected from around the world from universities, museums, and private collections (Grimm, "Dawn" 279). For instance, locations included Serbia, Sweden, Istanbul, and the Smithsonian Institution archives located in Washington, D.C. (279). In seeking this funding, they presented the following arguments, "that the domestication of dogs set the stage for taming an entire host of plants and animals" (qtd. in Grimm: "Dawn" 278).

Using the funding as a catalyst, Larson and Dobney brought together competing scientists who began sharing research and data with a common goal of finally unlocking the mystery of dog domestication. Their collaboration now includes over "50 scientists from around the world—experts on dogs, domestication, zooarchaeology and genetics. Larson estimates that the team has analyzed more than 3000 wolf, dog, and mystery specimens..." (Grimm, "Dawn" 279).

Using new perspectives and new technology, researchers are discovering more evidence of *when* and *how* dog domestication occurred. For instance, utilizing computers, researchers can now "perform geometric morphometric analysis of the skull. The thousands of measurements it will take will go far beyond mere length and width to determine actual shapes: the precise circlets of eye sockets, the jut and jag of every tooth" (Grimm, "Dawn" 279). As noted by Hulme-Beaman, ancient DNA can reveal "where an animal came from, but only such morphometric data can show you domestication in progress—the sharper angling of the snout, for example, that took place as wolves morphed into dogs" (Grimm: "Dawn" 279).

Additional discoveries and analysis of prehistoric existing fossils continue to yield further evidence from other sites. Research concerning fossils, from Paleolithic sites, places the first human and prehistoric dog interactions much earlier than previous evidence. These findings are both astonishing and enormously significant, potentially pushing back the first human/prehistoric dog interactions from approximately 14,000 years ago to over 30,000 years ago (Stahl 52). This research provides scientific evidence concerning the longevity of human and prehistoric dog interactions. The human/dog bond rests significantly on both the longevity of these interactions and the subsequent domestication which occurred, ultimately leading to the appearance of the domestic dog, *Canis lupus familiaris*.

The above examples highlight various theories on the beginnings of human/dog interactions, viewed through the lens of domestication. These examples highlight the different perspectives and conclusions of scholars concerning the earliest interactions of humans and prehistoric dogs. Scholars approach the questions of *when, why* and *how* through different perspectives and offer varying conclusions and theories concerning dog domestication.

The three spheres of mind, culture, and nature, as evident in psychology, cultural development, and science, impact these theories. Scientific research continues to reveal the intertwined characteristics of these three spheres. As so often is the case in human history, the development of the human/dog bond rests on the summation of interactions within the spheres of psychology, cultural development, and science.

Countless scholars continue to explore the complexities, both beneficial and in some cases detrimental, of the multifaceted reality inhabited by humans and dogs. The temporal spheres of place and time provide a framework for the continued evolution of this bond. According to Lange, "The dog evolved in company of humans and cannot exist without them" (10).

This situation illustrates an example of vivid contrasts in perceptions of the human and dog relationship. On one hand, dogs struggle for existence, and on the other hand, they are perceived by many people, anthropomorphically as a unique animal specie, more human than animal. According to Serpell, "In symbolic terms, the domestic dog exists precariously in the no-man's-land between the human and non-human worlds. It is an interstitial creature, neither person nor beast, forever oscillating uncomfortably between the roles of high-status animal and low-status person" (254). The domestic dog transcends both these worlds, adjusting and adapting to human perceptions and the realities of their canine existence, based on varying cultural and historical perspectives.

Ancient Cultures and Mythologies: Roles of Dogs in Life and Death

Obviously, vivid contrasts exist between contemporary scientific perceptions of human/dog interactions and perceptions within the ancient world. In many ancient cultures, dogs and canine gods exist both in the worlds of the living and the dead. Dogs exist not within a no-man's land, but as beings which transcend the greatest of distances beyond time and

2. Contemporary Research

Saqqara, Pyramid of Djoser, December 2008 (Huber Gerhard, CC BY-SA 4.0).

physical space. Dogs move between the temporal realm of earthly existence and the spiritual realm of the dead, often crossing these thresholds as guides and guards between both realms. Mythological dogs and canine gods transcend these worlds, just as contemporary domestic dogs transcend the worlds in which they exist. These contrasts offer stark examples of how perceptions evolve, framed within the context of different cultures from ancient times up to the present day.

Throughout history, human perceptions concerning dogs are influenced by cultural and historical parameters. Human/dog interactions often exhibit similar characteristics present in human to human interactions. According to Horowitz, "The dog is a member of a human social group; its natural environment, among people and other dogs" (43). She adds, "Dogs show what is called with human infants 'attachment': preference for the primary caregiver over others" (42). These attachments provide significant impact on the human/dog bond. The attachments between people and dogs are analyzed utilizing both humanistic psychology and scientific research later in this book. See Chapter 11.

The interactions between people and dogs have not always been positive throughout the cultures of history. At different times, within some cultures, human/dog interactions are marked by human neglect, cruelty, and even loathing. The perceptions and importance of dogs, from the

The Dog as Guide, Guard and Healer

human viewpoint, vary in the mythologies of different cultures. Many of these conflicting perceptions involve aspects about death, rituals associated with death, and perspectives concerning transitions from life to death, and death to life.

In ancient cultures, it is not only the ability to transition boundaries from life to death that leads to the dog's associations with burial rituals and death. In some cultures, negative aspects of both the dog's interactions with humans and their instincts increase their association with death or uncleanliness. According to David White, "the dog's gluttony," combined with "its indiscriminate eating habits allow it to consume carrion, excrements, and other impure substances, including the bodies of humans slain in battle" (2392). Mythologies throughout the ancient world note the ferociousness of dogs employed in battle and the terror of dogs scavenging unburied corpses on the battlefield and corpses buried in shallow graves.

Death and guarding the realms of the dead are intertwined in the mythologies of many civilizations. The dog is a multitasker, a shapeshifter, a guide and guard, transitioning the realms of the living and dead. In numerous myths, dogs serve as guides or guards in human explorations and journeys, both physical and spiritual. Dogs in comparative mythology provide significant roles in preparation for the journey and the journey itself. In many cases, dogs figure prominently in these rituals for the journey to the underworld and through the underworld. These journeys are often framed within the intertwined, universal questions concerning the meaning of human existence. Is there life after death? Can human existence, or life after death in some form, be assured or encouraged through rituals on earth? Are there temporal situations on earth which require intervention to assure a smooth transition to the spiritual world? Mythologies throughout history, ancient to contemporary, seek to answers these questions.

Exploring canine hunting and burial rituals offers one lens to consider these questions. Humans create and participate in these rituals, in part, to seek spiritual access through temporal actions. In many cultures, this access exists not only for the humans, but also for the animals. Campbell writes: "For hunters, the two orders of ritual, burial and animal worship, were complementary, the metaphysical reasons for the first directly implying a need for the second" (*Vol. 1, The Way* 56). According to many mythologies, the path of life is not linear, proceeding from birth, through earthly life, to death. Instead, the path is fluid and circular, and represents a continuous progression from life to death and death to life. Significantly, in many mythologies, both humans and animals share access to

2. Contemporary Research

this continuous circle. As noted by Campbell, in numerous societies and cultures, the interaction and mutual respect of the hunter and the hunted includes the "interpretation of death as, but a passing applied to both humans and the hunted" (*Vol. 1: The Way* 56).

Campbell discuses both the transformation of human consciousness and expression of the interdependence of humans and animals in this continuous circle. Approximately 40,000 years ago, "A fundamental transformation of human consciousness occurs," which coincides "with the sudden appearance in Europe of the two symbolic visual arts of rock painting and stone sculpture" (Campbell, *Vol. 1: The Way* 129). Campbell highlights both the importance of human expression through this early art and the covenant between humans and animals. He observes, "The animals were willing victims and the paintings an essential constituent of the system of rites of gratitude" (129). He notes that "this mythology of the covenant was not only realized, but also maintained and taught through generations" for some 20,000 years (129).

From the earliest recorded history to the contemporary present, dogs show a remarkable ability to perform different roles and beneficial functions for humans. This ability becomes a chief characteristic within the interdependent relationships between humans and dogs. Through domestication and close proximity to humans, dogs evolve into herders, haulers, watch dogs, and specialized hunters. All of these functions are aspects of the working dog. In the context of ancient literature, this multitasking ability precedes the actual physical domestication of the dog. Mythological stories often express the dog's ability to balance different functions and move within interconnected spheres, inhabited by both gods and humans. In ancient cultures, hunting stories of canines associated with gods provide numerous examples of these fluid skills and functions. Specific examples of these stories are discussed in Chapter 5.

In addition, the first pictorial descriptions of humans and dogs involve the hunt, as evident in European cave art. Later, hunting dogs appear on both pottery and sculpture. Campbell discusses European rock art found in two areas which span over 30,000 years and occur in very different physical and spiritual landscapes. These areas include the "Franco-Cantabrian province: c. 35,000 to 8,000 BC, region of the temple caves and the Spanish-Levantine province: c. 10,000–3,000 BC" located in "the eastern hills of Spanish Valencia, Catalonia and Aragon" (*Vol. 1 The Way* 80).

The Paleolithic *Lascaux* art portrays the great beasts, probably once native to that region of southwestern France (Campbell, *Vol. 1 The Way* 80). Viewed through Campbell's four functions of mythology, these cave paintings instill the mystical function within individuals. This art "awakens and maintains in the individual a sense of wonder and participation" on a grand, archetypal scale (80). The Spanish ledge art also instills participation, but on a more personal and approachable level, evoking both the mystical, but also the sociological functions of a mythology.

Campbell contrasts the two styles of art in this manner: "So instead of a subterranean, timeless world of archetypal herds," the Spanish art, located in shallow caves, or on rock ledges, illustrates "in broad daylight fascinating village, hunting and battle scenes" (*Vol. 1 The Way* 80). In the Spanish rock engravings and paintings, human figures dominate the art rather than animal forms. According to Campbell, the Spanish figures are small, with the animals no more than two feet in height, yet this art also reveals a great deal concerning the cultures of these people. For instance, he notes, "The bow and arrow and domesticated dog had arrived" (80). In these Spanish paintings, dogs participate in both the mystical and sociological functions of mythology.

The act of hunting is essential to survival, and also to the framework of many cultures. European cave paintings visually express a cosmological, spiritual, and sociological covenant, in the form of art, between the hunter and the hunted. Later, additional cave paintings, rock carvings, and sculptures confirm the participation of dogs in the hunt and the rituals involved in the hunt. The presence of dogs, as spiritual guides and physical participants in the hunt, creates a collaboration and participation in this basic convent necessary for human survival and development.

Since prehistory, humans and dogs have participated and interacted together in physical actions associated with hunting and burial rituals. These physical actions, within the temporal realm of nature, help provide access to the mythopoeic realm. Humans create specific rituals associated with the physical process of hunting, as well as many burial rituals, to help open this mutual interactive pathway for both humans and animals, the hunter and the hunted. These rituals are prevalent in mythologies throughout the world including Europe, Asia, and North America. Campbell notes: "For it has been observed that in hunting societies, generally the principal food animal is the normal pivotal figure of the religious cult" (*Vol. 1 The Way* 54).

Concerning burial rituals, what is the spiritual significance of animals, specifically dogs, within the temporal world and their potential impact on the underworld journey? An analysis of dog burial rituals within two ancient Egyptian and Asian cultures illustrates the multi-layered facets of mythology and archaeology. Through archaeological research, the mythopoetic importance of rituals associated with dog burials can be explored.

In ancient civilizations of the Mediterranean and Near East, dogs perform various utilitarian tasks for people, including hunting, hauling, and guarding. In addition, numerous cultures, including the Egyptians, Persians, and Greeks value dogs for both utilitarian purposes and also their companionship (Miller 488). Literature, especially mythological stories, attests to the presence and importance of human/dog interactions as well as the spiritual significance of dogs to the gods. Dog burial sites, especially in Egypt and the Levant region of the Mediterranean, provide evidence of the physical importance of dogs in daily life and in burial rituals associated with the afterlife.

Scholarly interpretations backed by archaeological research reveal the significance of domestic dogs in these ancient cultures. These findings also illuminate the convergence of what Campbell terms the cosmological and sociological functions of a mythology. Archaeological discoveries are specific to the landscapes, history, and cultures of individual societies and linked with more universal concerns regarding death and the afterlife. Dogs provide a link between the temporal and spiritual aspects of the rituals performed by these ancient groups. In addition, burial rituals reveal a sociological function of mythology, "reinforcing both the moral system and customs particular to each society" (Campbell *Vol. 1 The Way* 8).

Dog Burial Practices: Insights from Archaeological Discoveries

A further discussion of dog burial practices provides additional insight into the importance of dogs in ancient cultures. A recent discovery in the Saqqara catacombs next to the Temple of Anubis offers physical evidence of the importance of dogs in association with the Egyptian canine god. The 2500-year-old catacomb south of Cairo was originally discovered in the nineteenth century. Recently, Salima Ikram and other researchers made a startling new discovery that the tomb contains "around eight million mummified dogs and puppies" ("As it Happens" 4). From a contemporary perspective, it is difficult to grasp why living creatures, specifically dogs, would be sacrificed in such a manner and magnitude. According to Ikram, an offering of a living creature, rather than an inanimate object, provides greater impact to the gods associated with the animal, in this case Anubis ("Man's best friend" 300). She

The Dog as Guide, Guard and Healer

A scene from a wooden Egyptian sarcophagus depicting Anubis, the god of mummification and the afterlife, c. 400 BCE (André, CC BY-SA 2.0).

observes, "A living creature has more potency and is of course a greater sacrifice" ("As it Happens" 5).

As noted by Ikram, "There is a long history of animal burials, both ritual and pet, in Egypt" ("Man's best friend" 299). Dogs (*Canis lupus familiaris*) figure predominantly in these burials, including both ritual (votive) deposits as well as groups of dogs buried "far from any human remains" (Ikram 299). These discoveries include catacombs with mummified dogs, pet cemeteries, and more recently, since 2005, discoveries of humans and dogs buried together.

According to Ikram, "major canine cemeteries" number over 20 and extend from south of Cairo to north of Luxor ("Man's best friend" 302). She notes that "the most commonly found type of dog burials consists of votive mummies," from approximately sixth century BCE until the fourth century CE (Ikram 301). During this period, "Millions of dogs of all ages, have been interred in these cemeteries, all with varying qualities of mummification" (301). Many of these catacombs are located close to temples dedicated to gods, especially Anubis, the canine god. The votive mummies "are thought to have been offered by pilgrims and kept in the temples until

2. Contemporary Research

specific festivals when they were interred in the associated catacombs or tombs" (Ikram 301). Dogs, as votive offerings, provide spiritual sacrifices to the gods while reinforcing the cultural practices associated with travel and festivals. In these rituals, dogs create a conduit to the spiritual and sociological functions of a mythology as discussed by Campbell.

Recently, excavations reveal a previously unknown burial type, containing both human and dog remains, dating from the Graeco-Roman period in Egypt ("Man's best friend" 299). Two examples of human/dog burials provide evidence of the growing importance of dogs in relationship to their interactions with humans. Eight graves, discovered at Saqqara, Gaza, and Baharia Oasis, dating from the 26th Dynasty, contain dogs "identified as 'amuletic' animal mummies found in conjunction with human burials" (Ikram 303). In these locations, the dogs are placed either at the north side of the coffins, or several dogs surround the burial pits. The dogs, as offerings to Anubis, help guide the deceased in "a transitional zone between this world and the next" (303). Significantly, "as Egyptian culture evolved, the physical dog was considered to be either an adequate replacement for, or a valuable complement" to the Anubis amulet, which was placed on the deceased, "to insure the continuing and unbroken assistance of Anubis" (Hartley qtd. in Ikram: 303).

Ikram observes that a second example, located at Baharia Oasis, involves dogs buried with children ("Man's best friend" 305). In these burials, the majority of the children are infants, some with dogs carefully placed by the children. The burials reveal the children sometimes were moved to accommodate dogs in niches, and at other times, based on the fossils remain locations, the children appear to be carefully moved over to accommodate the dogs (305–306). Again, these examples of joint human/dog burial appear to confirm the growing importance of dogs as companions, rather than only as sacrificial animals.

Two sites, the Egyptian Saqqara catacombs and ancient Ashkelon, located along the Mediterranean coast in present day Israel, confirm the importance of dogs in ancient cultures. A closer look at both sites provides information revealing similarities, but also differences, concerning ancient dog burial rituals. There are more questions concerning the purposes of the burials at Ashkelon versus those in the Saqqara catacombs. Some of the questions revolve around the lack of a temple or deity directly linked to the Ashkelon site (Miller 493).

According to Meir Edrey, "In 1985, the Leon Levi Expedition, under the direction of L.E. Stager, unearthed numerous canine skeletons and skeletal remains, mostly puppies" at Ashkelon (267). Stager originally estimated the "number of dog-burials to be much higher than 1400, but due

The Dog as Guide, Guard and Healer

to erosion of the site by the sea the original dog-burial number cannot be established" (Edrey 267). The Saqqara catacombs and Ashkelon sites contain the largest number of dog burials, from the ancient Mediterranean world and Near East, discovered to date. Edrey observes, "Nowhere in the ancient Near East, with the exception of Egypt, had so many dog burials been found at a single site—and with no apparent reason for the burials" (267–268). At Ashkelon, both the number of burials and the "care with which the dogs have been buried" intrigued scholars (Miller 492). Also noted by Miller, "Normally dead animal were left in the place where they died or thrown on a refuse heap outside the city walls, but a number of cultures preferred to inter their dead canines" (490–491).

Edrey also reviews some of the burial practices for dogs at Ashkelon. He notes, "The dogs were buried in shallow and apparently unmarked pits. They were laid on their sides, tails tucked between the hind limbs" (267). In some areas of the city, "the dogs were buried under streets and in narrow alleys and were thus cramped in smaller pits" (267). Potential doubts arise concerning theories that the dogs had been sacrificial offerings since "No butcher marks were noticeable on the skeletal remains and there were almost no signs of violence" (267). This evidence points to burials associated with some other purposes than only sacrificial offerings.

Why did many ancient cultures choose to engage in burial practices for dogs? Archaeological findings suggest various reasons which illustrate the intertwined relationships between humans and dogs. While the motives for the Ashkelon burials are not apparent, there are several clues when viewed from a comparative mythology perspective. Some of the theories offered by scholars center on sacrifices associated with different cults. In addition, a good case can be made that the Phoenicians valued dogs in their personal lives for both utilitarian purposes and companionship (Miller 493). In these situations, the burials may have resulted from individual interactions between Phoenicians and dogs, serving to fulfill a personal bond of some sort, versus an offering to a larger spiritual identity of a god or goddess.

The Saqqara and Ashkelon burials reflect aspects of both the second and third functions of mythology as described by Campbell (*Vol 1: The Way* 8). The burials suggest an individual connection between humans and dogs, and a more universal connection where the dogs serve as a vehicle for spiritual access between humans and gods. The specific motives of the Ashkelton burial rituals are speculative, but the physical evidence supports rituals reflecting respect and purpose.

2. Contemporary Research

Ancient Clues Lead to New Perspectives

The Bonn-Oberkassel dog remains, discovered in 1914, represent the oldest known example of humans and dogs buried together. This grave discovery dates to the Upper Pleistocene, approximately 14,000 years ago (Janssens et al. 126). The grave was originally thought to contain the remains of one dog, a man, and a woman. Recent re-examination reveals a tooth of a smaller and older dog which makes this the oldest known burial containing remains of two dogs with humans (126). Dental pathology, conducted on the younger dog, also provides new perspectives concerning the interactions of hunter-gatherers with Paleolithic dogs in western Europe.

In the article, "A new look at an old dog: Bonn-Oberkassel reconsidered," researchers present evidence that the motivations for domestication of dogs may not have been driven solely for utilization purposes, such as hunting and hauling. Rather, these early hunter-gatherers may have had an emotional connection with dogs. Based on the dental pathology, it appears that the younger dog, buried between 27 and 28 weeks old, experienced three episodes of canine distemper (Janssens et al. 126). Why is this significant? Researchers note, "canine distemper has a three-week disease period with a very high mortality rate" (126).

The authors hypothesize the young, sick dog would have had no utilitarian purposes, and that "this puppy could have survived only with intensive human care over several weeks" (Janssens et al. 135). Significantly, the researchers "hypothesize further that the inferred care probably was due to compassion or empathy, without any expectation of reciprocal utilitarian benefits" (135). Compassion and empathy form two cornerstones of the human/dog bond. These over-14,000-year-old remains of two dogs provide evidence of this bond. Furthermore, in the conclusion of the article, the researchers "suggest that the Bonn–Oberkassel dog provides the earliest known evidence for a purely emotion-driven human-dog interaction" (135).

The new perspectives, gained from these ancient fossils, offer collaboration on two major points of this book. First, these fossils reinforce the longevity of dogs associated with humans in early upper Pleistocene Period human/dog burials. More significantly, this research provides, perhaps, the earliest evidence of an emotional bond between humans and dogs. The Bonn–Oberkassel dog helps illustrate that dog domestication has been driven not only by utilitarian motives, but also involves an emotional connection framed by both cultural and psychological parameters.

One of the most famous discoveries of a human/dog burial involves an elderly human and young pup discovered underneath a home at the

Natufian site in Ain Mallaha, Israel. In this grave, approximately 12,000 years old, a human and a pup were buried together, the pup curled above the human, with the person's hand touching the pup (Grimm "Dawn" 279). Although it is impossible to determine whether this fossil is a dog or wolf pup, this discovery represents some of the earliest fossil evidence of the dog's domestication (Lange 4). Here, the canine is buried, joined with its human counterpart in one of the most intimate rituals, the ritual associated with death.

Recent discoveries of cave art highlight both the longevity of human/dog interactions and offer new insights on the timetable of dog domestication. In northwestern Saudi Arabia, at Shuwaymis and Jubbah, discoveries reveal intriguing information concerning the nature of prehistoric hunting with dogs. For three years, a team of researchers from the Max Planck Institute, working in partnership with the Saudi Commission for Tourism & National Heritage, "catalogued more than 1400 rock art images" (Collins). This "study revealed nearly 7,000 images of animals and humans" including 349 which "depict dogs—156 at Shuwaymis and 193 at Jubbah" (Collins).

The oldest carvings, dated to approximately 10,000 years ago, depict images associated with hunter-gatherers (Grimm "Images" 2). The more recent images, dated to approximately 7,000–8,000 years old, depict cattle, sheep, and goats, associated with herding activities (2). In the middle, between the oldest and earliest carvings, researchers found over 250 images of early hunting dogs ("Images" 2). According to Grimm, "All are medium-sized, with pricked up ears, short snouts, and curled tails—hallmarks of domestic canines" ("Images" 1). In addition, experts notes these images "closely resemble the modern species of Canaan dog, found running wild in the deserts of the middle east today" (Collins).

These discoveries offer visual evidence concerning early hunting practices involving dogs. The carvings provide visual images of actual domestic dogs, rather than symbolic graphic images. In addition, these dogs are engaged in specific hunting activities adapted to the actual terrain and needs of hunter-gatherers in the Arabian desert area (Grimm "Images" 1).

The carvings, dated to the Neolithic Period, reinforce both the presence and importance of early domestic dogs in the physical activities associated with hunting and subsequently, the mythology of the hunt. As noted by Grimm, these images suggest domestic dogs were both trained and controlled much earlier in human history than previously documented (Grimm "Images" 1). Many of these dogs "are tethered to a human

2. Contemporary Research

armed with a bow and arrow" ("Images" 2). These restraints, extending from the hunters waist to around the dogs necks, represent the first known examples of hunters possibly using leashes to control and/or protect dogs during hunting ("Images" 5).

Angela Perri, a zoo archaeologist, notes the importance of these images of actual hunting activity, as compared to archaeological research utilizing ancient fossils (Grimm, "Images" 2). The visual images provide a story of the hunt as compared to analysis of ancient fossils, concerning place and time. Although critical to the study of domestication, fossils do not provide actual pictorial examples of hunting with dogs.

Maria Guagnin, an archaeologist, dates the images to more than 8,000 years ago, which would make them the oldest depictions of domestic dogs, older than previously found pottery paintings dating to almost 8,000 years ago (Grimm, "Images" 5). Even if additional research finds these images date to a later period, "The leashes are by far the oldest on record, with earliest previous evidence being restraints on a wall painting in Egypt, dated to about 5,500 years ago" (5).

Utilizing a different perspective, Paul Tacon, an archaeologist, notes "that the lines in the engravings could be symbolic," representing depictions of a bond between the hunters and the dogs (Grimm, "Images" 5). Significantly, he adds these pictures appear to portray actual dogs, "with particular coat patterns, stances and genders" (5). In these images, the artists perhaps reveal more than the importance of dogs in the physical acts of hunting. In addition, these lines or leashes may represent a psychological or spiritual connection between the hunters and the dogs, revealing one of the earliest prehistoric examples of the intertwined spheres of mind and culture between humans and prehistoric dogs.

In the mutual pursuit of hunting, dogs also serve as guides, both in the temporal and spiritual realms. Many of the physical and mental aspects which make dogs superb hunters provide opportunities for their later development into superb companions. Both psychology and ethology, or mind and nature, play prominent roles in the companionship between people and dogs. These characteristics began to emerge with the earliest bond of humans and dogs in hunting. This bond resulted not only from increased opportunities for mutual survival through enhanced collaborative hunting skills, but also from the mutual benefits of shared companionship.

Time and time again, archaeological findings reveal a bond and a relationship that rests not only on the benefits of mutual survival. Rather, these discoveries reveal interconnected mythological, psychological, and ethological aspects of the human/dog bond. During prehistory, humans moved from the struggle for individual survival to the creation of cooperative social groups. In this process, ancient people began to gather together within groups, to collaborate towards mutually beneficial objectives, and to celebrate the living and the dead through rituals. All of these developments speak to something more than just striving for mere survival. Dogs were involved in these transitions and played significant roles as guards for the camps and as partners in hunting.

Archaeological findings highlight the importance of dogs in these transitions and developments, including hunting, as sacrifices in ancient cultures, and in human/dog burial rituals. The relationships, between humans and dogs in these activities, are intertwined with nature and the mythologies of the human participants. Dogs have been part of this journey with people since prehistory. The human/dog relationship continues to advance along an intertwined path, defined to a great degree by interactions within various evolving cultures, framed by the ethology of both people and dogs within shared environments. In this process, the *human/*dog and *dog*/human bonds continue to unfold, to evolve, and to expand. Early humans and prehistoric dogs began their relationship long before the first settlements appear in ancient cultures, and later, among others, in western European and Native American cultures. This story now turns to the shared journey of dogs and people as they travel from prehistoric times up to the Victorian era.

3

Journey from Antiquity to Victorian Parlors

Research within the fields of archaeology and ethology provides insight into the evolutionary paths and diversification of prehistoric dogs. These findings help illustrate the interconnected spheres of culture and nature in the journey of people and dogs in prehistory and across the globe—a journey shared by the world's oldest companions and collaborators for survival. Interactions between early humans and wolves serve as the catalyst for the beginning of the human/dog bond. According to Miklósi, approximately 300,000–400,000 years ago, older members of the *Homo genus* left Africa "and probably encountered wolves along their journey" (124). Based on these dates, these early humans lived "for over 400,000 years alongside wolf populations over a vast area ranging from the Atlantic Ocean to eastern China" (125–126).

According to "archaeological and evolutionary genetic research..." it appears "that humans colonized East Asia in several waves between 45,000 and 120,000 years ago" (Miklósi 126). "Approximately 20,000 years ago, when the continental ice sheets of the last ice age began to recede, humans began to push into new regions and continents" (Miklósi 127). During this timeframe, the earliest prehistoric dogs began to interact with the hunter/gatherers groups in hunting activities and by guarding the perimeters of camps.

Expansion proceeded rapidly "in several waves into East Central Asia, Siberia, and from there north-westwards to Europe and eastwards over the Bering Strait into North America" (Miklósi 127). During this period, "the basis of human societies began to transition from hunting and gathering to agriculture" (127). The abilities to balance the methods of food gathering and agriculture created more flexibility and stability in societies allowing for expansion into new facets of human progress (Miklósi 128). Dogs figured significantly in both these endeavors. In addition, dogs shared a unique interactive social bond with humans.

The Dog as Guide, Guard and Healer

The combination of their adaptability to new roles and companionship with humans created significant impacts on the history of their migrations with people. These abilities offer one possible explanation of "why dogs appear relatively rapidly at western and northern European sites around 12,000 years ago, and accompany humans crossing to North America probably with a second or later waves around 15,000 years ago" (Miklósi 128). According to Miklósi, "It is likely that the diversification of dogs is associated with rapid technical changes during the Neolithic revolution when, around 5,000–7,000 years ago, humans started to select dogs for various working roles" (128). During this period, humans began to breed different types of dogs for specialized activities such as coursing hounds, shepherd dogs, and guard dogs for dwellings and property. Archaeological findings, literature, and art including carvings, sculptures, and mosaics provide examples of these types of hunting and guarding activities.

Dogs travel quite a varied, wide-ranging journey from the earliest camps of hunters and gatherers to stuffed pillows in Victorian parlors. Along the way, dogs expand their roles as working dogs and companions. From ancient societies to contemporary times, humans continue to breed different types of working dogs for specific purposes and temperaments and other breeds for appearance, personalities, and companionship.

The following topics illustrate links between migration paths of people and dogs, development of hunting and agricultural practices in ancient cultures, and the emergence of early dog breeds. These links include: (1) Connections of migration paths of people as they move from hunter/gatherer or nomadic societies to more settled agricultural societies; (2) Interactive aspects of early dog breeds in mythologies of ancient cultures and as actual working dogs in ancient societies; and (3) Shifts in breeding goals which emphasize more form and appearance with less focus on hunting and guarding.

These developments significantly impact the course of human history and evolutionary path of the human/dog bond. The interconnected journey of people and dogs tracks the migration paths of humans and the development of ancient civilizations. These migrations begin with the earliest interactions of humans and wolves leading to the evolution of prehistoric dogs, followed by the appearances of domestic dogs in ancient cultures. Wolves provide a continuous genetic link through the development of dog breeds from the earliest breeds in antiquity (Parker et al. 1162). Later shifts in breeding emphasis result in the emergence of the modern dog in the 1800s.

3. Journey from Antiquity to Victorian Parlors

What attributes or goals did ancient societies strive for in their dog breeding practices? The cultural frameworks of their societies and the desires for specific characteristics in working, hunting, and guarding dogs drove this process. The selection of dogs for mating with the desired characteristics resulted in the earliest dog breeds (Brewer et al. 26); "repetition through several generations created a physical—behavioral type or breed" (Brewer et al. 26).

Brewer et al. consider two perspectives concerning the origins and criteria for developing dog breeds (Brewer et al. 25). The earliest evidence of dog breeds, based on achieving specific goals, began in cultures such as ancient Egypt and Mesopotamia (25). A central goal of early breeding involved mating two dogs with desirable characteristics in order to produce a similar next generation (25). This objective "is the fundamental basis of establishing a breed and was likely practiced very early in the dog's history" (25).

In ancient Egypt and Mesopotamia, the goals of creating dog breeds for specific tasks were framed by the cultures including religious and hunting practices. Brewer et al. observe: "As geneticists have pointed out, diversification of form ensures a population is divided into limited contact permits only occasional genetic exchanges between them" (26). This type of diversification occurred as groups of people moved from one geographical area to another, expanding their presence, and ultimately the roles of their dog companions.

As breeding practices became more focused and sophisticated, several new ancient breeds, or early types of dogs appear. People discovered that with improved breeding techniques dogs could perform new roles, and improve their abilities in earlier roles, notably hunting. Inherent in those endeavors were the abilities of dogs to adjust to new environments. The transitions from hunter/gatherer or nomad group to settled villages based on agriculture, created many of these new niches in the interconnections of people and dogs. Settled homes, with livestock such as cattle, goats, and sheep required guard dogs and herding dogs. More stationary cultures and villages opened up new opportunities for companion dogs, including the early lap dogs depicted in these ancient cultures.

The earliest goals of breeding in the ancient world are significantly different from the goals of contemporary breeding in the modern world. The development of modern dog breeds rapidly increases in the 1800s (von Holdt and Driscoll 32). During this period, some scholars develop a different perspective concerning the requirements for establishing new dog breeds. According to Brewer et al., this perspective includes adherence to

The Dog as Guide, Guard and Healer

the following requirements: ... "certain animals intentionally crossed, pedigree records maintained, and maintenance of the breed guided by established standards..." (25). Brewer et al. write: "Adhering to such a definition implies that breeds are intentionally derived cultural phenomena and have existed only in the literate and very recent past" (25). The pictorial representations and literature of ancient cultures tell quite a different story.

Connections: Migration Paths Through History

The following discussion illustrates intertwined links between the development of ancient cultures, dog breeding practices, and the evolving human/dog bond. These three elements help frame the journey of people and dogs from ancient times until the present, and reside in the advancement of human cultures and interactions between the world's oldest companions—people and dogs.

Rock carvings, burial sites, and literature illustrate the importance of dogs in ancient cultures including daily life and burial rituals, hunting,

Egyptian Sight Hound (Karen Green, CC BY-SA 2.0).

3. Journey from Antiquity to Victorian Parlors

and companionship. For instance, burial sites at the Egyptian Saqqara catacombs and ancient Ashkelon provide insight. Archaeological findings at these sites reveal the importance of dogs in daily life and burial rituals associated with the afterlife. Cave art in northwestern Saudi Arabia, at Shuwagmis and Julbah, provide information concerning prehistoric hunting with dogs. See Chapter 2. Literature from Egypt, and Greece and other cultures illustrates the importance of dogs in ancient societies.

For example, "Pictorially; the earliest representations of the dog came from Neolithic rock art of the Western and Eastern Deserts in which dogs are shown accompanied by human figures, cattle, giraffes, and antelope..." (Brewer et al. 28). The earliest style by western hunters ... "depicted dogs that look much like the dogs found today living among Berber peoples: they have long bodies, long legs, pointed erect ears, and tails carried high over their back. The later two characteristics are indicative of the earliest dogs: erect ears are typical of the wolf and other wild canids, and the cocked tail develops in tame young wolves raised in captivity" (28). These earliest pictorial representations by western hunters "are followed by pastoral scenes that depict large dogs similar to those shown in the western desert hunter's scenes as well as slender, erect-eared dogs" (28).

This pictorial art reveals the expanding journey of people and dogs, and the development of hunting and agricultural practices. These representations also reveal links between migration paths and the development of early breeds. What are these links? How are agricultural and hunting practices linked to the development of new breeds? And how do these breeds impact the interactions with people in these practices? A study of working type dogs in ancient Egypt, Mesopotamia, and Greece provides examples of these interconnections and insights into the progress of human development in ancient cultures. These dog types include Tesem and Saluki sight hounds, Molosser/Mastiff guard dogs, and early Shepherd herding dogs. Their working dog roles encompasses hunting, herding, and guarding people, homes, and settlements. And, these dogs provide companionship to their human counterparts.

Three main early breed types of dogs existed in ancient Egypt: the pariah dog, greyhound-like sight hounds, and a mastiff-type dog (Brewer et al. 32–39). Brewer et al. note that: "...in reality, most Egyptian dogs were mongrels, whose genetic background was the product of indiscriminate breeding between any number of domestic and feral forms" (39). They add: "The term many Egyptologists use to refer to mongrels is pariah, although technically any stray dog, even a pure breed, is a pariah" (39).

During this period, there are two types of sight hounds, the Tesem and the Saluki/Sloughi (Brewer et al. 32). Egyptian art extensively depicts both of these types of sight hounds. According to Brewer et al., "Tesems first appear on printed pottery and rock art dated to Naqada I and II times (3750–3400 BC) and are frequently portrayed in Old Kingdom and Middle Kingdom desert hunting scenes where sight-hound would have a distinctive advantage over a scent hound" (32–33). In Egyptian tombs, images depict Tesems sitting under their master's chairs and on leashes (33). Rock art examples in the Atlas Mountain areas reveal that Tesems roamed with their human companions throughout North Africa (33).

The Saluki type of sight hound "pictured in Egyptian art has a shorter, heavier muzzle than the Tesem, is lop-eared and has a curved or sabre tail" (Brewer et al. 33). Tesems and Saluki appear together in several hunting scenes and Saluki are also depicted on artifacts from Tutankhamen's tomb (Brewer et al. 34). Ancient art illustrations of these dogs are sometimes compared to the modern Saluki breed. These similarities include "feathered hair in their ears, thighs, and tails characteristics of the modern Saluki breed" (Brewer et al. 34). This ancient breed in Egyptian art provides one familiar face in the modern dog world, but these ancient dogs are not the exact same breed as the modern Saluki dogs.

The origins of another modern sight hound, the greyhound, also extend back into the ancient world. Greyhounds appeared on the walls of tombs and were mummified along with their owners (Jeffers). Pharaohs including Tutankhamen, Amenhotep II, Thutmose III, Queen Hatshepsut, and Cleopatra VII ... "were known to own greyhounds..." (Jeffers). Jeffers notes that "the modern greyhound is strikingly similar in appearance to an ancient breed of sight hound that goes back to the Egyptians and Celts." He adds that the greyhound's origins and migration story are linked to the Gauls in western Europe, ancient Greece, and the Middle East (Jeffers). The Romans believed that the earliest greyhounds arrived with the Celts from Gaul in western Europe while the Celts "believed that greyhounds came from Greece" (Jeffers). As evident in the ancient art of Egypt and Mesopotamia, in all likelihood, the earliest greyhound breeds originated in the Middle East.

Early Civilizations and New Roles

Dog breeds with specific skills and appearances appear not only throughout the ancient physical world but also within the mythologies of

3. Journey from Antiquity to Victorian Parlors

various cultures. For instance, dogs traverse ancient mythologies in Babylonia, Egyptian, Greek, and Roman cultures. Mythological stories reveal their roles as guides, guards, hunters, and companions. Several famous hunting and guard dogs in mythology are discussed in Chapter 5. For example, origin stories concerning Laelaps combine hunting, breed characteristics, and allegories. In one story, the goddess Artemis gives Procris a dog named Laelaps, perhaps the ancestor of Laconian and Vertragus hounds. This story connects the exploits of the mythical Laelaps to origin stories of actual early hunting hounds. Greek and Italian authors Xenophon and Arrian discuss the attributes of Laconian and Vertragus hounds in their works on hunting (Grout). Another origin story involves Zeus, who gives Laelaps to Europa. Her husband, Cephelus, decides to take Laelaps to hunt the Teumessian fox terrorizing the Athenian countryside. See Chapter 5 for the paradox of the hound who always catches its prey and the fox destined never to be caught.

Dogs often accompany Greek and Roman gods and goddesses as hunters and companions. These mythological dogs possess many similar characteristics and skills as earthly dogs including hunting, and guarding boundaries, thresholds, and crossings, both physical and metaphysical. Hecate, the goddess of such crossings, also possesses a pack of hounds which herds souls to the Underworld. See Chapter 5 for comparisons between Hecate, the goddess of death, and Artemis, goddess of the hunt, the wild, nature, and chastity.

The story of Actaeon and Artemis centers on her own modesty, and the impropriety of Actaeon who watches her bathing. Furious, Artemis turns Actaeon into a stag and sends her hounds to hunt him down. Jeffers notes that "depictions of this scene occur many times in Greek and Roman art." In the first century CE, Ovid, the Roman author, also retells this story in *Metamorphoses* (Jeffers).

Perhaps the most famous sighthound in mythology, named Argos, appears in *The Odyssey*. "Speed was an essential quality of a hunting dog for which the most common epitaph in Homer is Argos ('swift footed'), the name of Odysseus' own hound" (Grout). Odysseus trained Argos "as a puppy to chase after wild goats, deer and hares, no quarry ever escaped him" (Grout). For twenty years, Argos waits for his master Odysseus to return from the Trojan War. Odysseus returns home dressed in rags and disguised to avoid detection. No one recognizes him except Argos, who although too weak to stand, wags his tail with joy to see his master.

Dog sculptures and figurines, while artistic representations of ancient working dogs, do not depict actual dog breeds present in the modern world. These ancient figurines and sculptures often evoke not only the magical protective powers of dogs, but also some realistic and relatable characteristics of actual physical dogs. Dog sculptures guard doorways to homes, to temples, and provide markers for boundaries of property and at road intersections, serving both as guards and guides.

For instance, mastiff or other guard type dogs figure predominantly into the interactions between mythological beliefs and temporal practices. Artistic representations on sculptures, clay tablets, and in literature testify to the mastiff's working roles of war dog, hunting dog for larger prey, and guard dog in the ancient cultures of Egypt, Mesopotamia, and later the classical world (Brewer 58–60). Descriptions of the mastiff conjure up the idea of a fierce adversary and relentless hunter that could fight lions, and evoke terror in enemies on war fields (Brewer et al. 58). For instance, "Assyrian reliefs from Ashurbanipal's Palace at Nineveh" circa 650 BCE … "show mastiff-type hounds involved in hunting lions, onager, and gazelle" (58).

Archaeological findings, discovered under doorways, include clay or bronze guard dog figurines attributed to the late second and early first millennium BCE (Brewer et al. 65). For example, "Assyrian cuneiform tablets" prescribe that ten clay dogs should be buried, five on each side of the doorway, each inscribed with their name (65). The purpose of these dogs was to keep "away evil demons and ghosts that brought misfortune, sickness and death" (65).

In the North Palace of Ashurbanipal (668–631 BCE) Laynard found "a half-set of five such terracotta dogs" at the doorway entrance (Brewer et al. 65). These figurines represent mythological and physical functions concerning protection against enemies. Their inscribed names evoke magical properties to protect against evil and also describe physical characteristics of real dogs which illustrate their guard dog functions. For instance, one of the Nineveh sculptures has "Banisher of Evil written on his shoulders in cuneiform" (65). In this grouping, "others had names such as 'Enemy catcher,' 'Enemy biter,' 'Don't, think bite!,' 'Consume his life' and 'Loud barker'" (Lagunard quoted in Brewer et al. 65). These inscriptions provide a quite clear picture of the desired results should intruders seek to enter the home or property.

In pictorial representations two other types of hunting dogs, coursing dogs and terrier-like dogs, offer some similarities in appearances as well as characteristics notable in modern breeds. These dogs excel at hunting utilizing either speed or scent and tenacity. Two different types of hounds, sight and scent hounds, play predominant working dog roles in ancient Egypt, Mesopotamia, and Greece. These dogs excel in the

3. Journey from Antiquity to Victorian Parlors

temporal world of hunting and provide hunting and guiding roles in the mythological world.

Coursing involves pursuing game, especially hares with grey hounds and other sight hounds "using sight rather than scent" (*Oxford* 285). Coursing dogs "were generally smooth, short-haired animals with slender bodies set on long legs, pointed heads, either small pointed on flapping ears, and a long thin tail" (Brewer et al. 62). According to Brewer et al., this type of dog "is one of the most frequently represented of all the breeds and clearly held a position of some esteem both as a valuable hunting hound and as a companion of the gods" (67–68). For instance, seals and seal impressions in Assyrian sites at Ninevah and Kuyunjik provide examples of Saluki type dogs. Excavations at nearby Tepe Gawra revealed over 300 seals and impressions including numerous hunting dog scenes (68). According to Tobar, "The animals depicted are rarely of any domesticated variety, except for the commonly represented Saluki…'" (quoted in Brewer et al. 68).

The Arabian "Bedouin so admired the physical attributes and speed of the Saluki that it was the only dog permitted to share their tents and ride atop their camels. In early Arabiac culture, the birth of the Saluki ranked in importance just behind the birth of a son" (Jeffers). Coursing dogs, notably Salukis, are still used in Morocco for modern hunts (Brewer et al. 63).

Terrier type dogs also appear on seals and as glazed figurines including "crude clay figurines" found at excavation sites from various periods (Brewer et al. 71). According to Brewer et al., "Terrier and kindred types are small dogs with a curly tail, either short-haired or feathered" and often appear in hunting roles (71). These figurines are described as terriers "because of their pointed muzzle and ears and a tail sticking straight up" (71). Again, these figurines do not represent actual terrier breeds known today but rather exhibit characteristics associated with modern terriers.

Mesopotamian cylinder seals also reveal information about cultural activities within the ancient world. These seals depict religious and mythological activities and illustrate important functions including marks of ownership (Anatasia). For instance, "Seals were either impressed on lumps of clay that were used to close jars, doors, and baskets, or they were rolled onto clay tablets that recorded information about commercial or legal transitions" (Anatasia).

The earliest sculptures and carvings do not represent exact breeds of modern dogs but illustrate the general forms and characteristics of different dog types often as illustrations in hunting scenes. The miliary viewed hunting "...as an important recreation that taught many of the skills which would be needed in warfare; something emphasized by Xenophon" (Brewer et al. 84). In his treatise *Cynegeticus: On Hunting with Dogs*, Xenophon offers a detailed discussion of hunting. This type of game hunting involves using scent hounds to track mostly hares that are ultimately driven into nets. He writes: "...my advice to the young is, do not despise hunting or the other training of your boyhood, if you desire to grow up to be good men, good not only in war but in all else where the issue is perfection of thought, word, and deed" (3).

Classical Breeds: Roles and Attributes

With the advent of the Classical period, the number of breeds expand and classical literature adds extensive knowledge to the roles of dogs as hunter, guards, and companions. Brewer et al. observe that "classical dog literature mentions some fifty breeds which is a remarkably large number..." compared to the four or five breeds identifiable "from ancient Egypt or Mesopotamia" (85). These works describe various types

The Emperor Trajan with hunters and a Celtic Greyhound. From *Arrian on Coursing: The Cynegeticus of the Younger Xenophon*, trans. William Dansey (London: J. Bohn, 1831).

3. Journey from Antiquity to Victorian Parlors

of dogs, opinions on desired attributes, and documentation on breeding practices.

The increasing number of dog breeds "described in the literature clearly reflects the geographical expansion of the classical world from the time of Xenophon to its maximum extent under imperial Rome" (Brewer et al. 85). The geographical migrations of people and dogs spread to "Britain in the West..." and into the Far East to India "...and from the Ukraine in the north to Egypt in the south" (85).

Classical philosophers, historians, and other scholars highlight the social skills and abilities of dogs in their shared cultural niche with people. These works also reveal the mythological importance of dogs as guides, guards, and healers in the classical world. Characteristics of the following breeds illustrate the intertwined spheres of physical roles and mythological roles in hunting and religious activities. Examples from literature highlight these roles. For instance, in the first paragraph of *Cynegeticus*, Xenophon praises the gods concerning the importance of hunting with dogs. He opens his treatise with "To the gods themselves is due the discovery, to Appollo and Artemis, patrons of the chase and protectors of the hound" (I). Later, he adds "Thanks to the careful heed they paid to the dogs and things pertaining to the chase...," (I) Xenophon's thoughts highlight the interconnected spheres of mythology and the temporal importance of hunting dogs in the classical world.

While the classical world expanded throughout these areas, the majority of new dog breeds were developed in Italy and Greece (Brewer et al. 85). Leach comments on the number of breeds: "The Greeks had the huge Molossian dogs from Molossis in Epirus, the white Laconians from the Peloponnesus, used especially as shepherd dogs, and the fierce Arcadian hounds who were said to be descended from lions" (80). The Molossers "group of dog breeds is associated with the Molossi tribe that lived in Epirus in the northwest region of Ancient Greece" (Barrientos). "Mastiffs are considered to be their descendants" (Barrertos). These dogs served as guardians and herding dogs, but also hunters of large game. According to Virgil, " Never, with them on guard ... need you fear for your stalls a midnight thief, or onslaught of wolves, or Iberian brigands at your back" (*Georgics*, III. 404ff; qtd. in Grout).

The famous swift Laconian hounds from Sparta appear in mythology, prized for their hunting skills and perseverance as well as in the physical world. These hounds "relied greatly on their sense of smell while hunting hare and deer" (Barrientos). Several other breeds of hounds were used in hunting and herding such as the Salentine hounds from southern Italy and

The Dog as Guide, Guard and Healer

"Umbrian hounds from the Apennines" (Leach 81). Both breeds excelled at hunting and sheep herding. For instance, Horace, the Roman poet in 30 BCE says: "It is the tawny Spartan and the Molossian ... who are 'the shepherd's dangerous friends' (*Epodes*, VI)" (qtd. in Grout).

And, then there was the lap dog, quite similar in some respects to the Maltese of today. Leach notes that "most numerous of all was the tiny, sharp-nosed, bushy-tailed Maltese dogs from the land of Malta: universal household pet among both Greeks and Romans" (81). In Greece, this early lap dog was "called the sleeve dog" because women carried this little dog around "in their long flowing sleeves" (81). Leach adds that the Phoenicians in Malta bred this dog as early as 1500 BCE (81). Although similar in some characteristics, this breed was a different type of dog from the modern Maltese of today.

Treasured dog companions were often buried in their own marked tombs. For instance, burial sculptures of dogs highlight the importance of hunting hounds and lap dog companions. Examples illustrate the interconnected spheres of actual hunting and burial rituals including "hounds on sarcophagi" and lap dogs figurines on grave stela with their mistresses (Brewer et al. 87).

Pictorial representations on vases, wall paintings, frescoes, and mosaics provide additional insight into the importance of dogs in ancient Greek and Roman cultures as guards and hunters. Early "depictions of dogs" on Greek vases appear around the seventh century BCE (Brewer et al. 86). More detailed vases "from the classical period" (fifth century BCE) appear to show "two main types of hound: the sleek smooth-haired hound used for hunting deer and hares and the stockier more rough-haired hound used for boar" (Brewer et al. 86).

Mosaics illustrating "mythological and hunting scenes became common by the second century AD" (Brewer et al. 86). These mosaics appear throughout the classical world including exceptional examples in North Africa and Sicily (Brewer et al. 86). Leach observes: "The Molossians were the watch dogs of the nation, although they seem to have been used for guarding sheep as well" (80). Depictions of belled dogs in entrance floor mosaics frequently guarded ancient Roman dwellings (Leach 82). The Latin description *Cave canem*, meaning beware the dog, is often included in the mosaics—a blunt warning that is also familiar today.

Examples in art and literature highlight the impacts of hunting and agriculture practices in the appearance of new breed types. Again, the importance of hunting is a driving force within the classical world leading to the development of new breeds and improving existing breeds. Classical

3. Journey from Antiquity to Victorian Parlors

literature concerning hunting begins with Xenophon who hunted with scent-hounds on foot, driving the hares into fixed nets (Brewer et al. 87). In addition to discussing methods and equipment for hunting in fields, he talks about the "many benefits which the enthusiastic sportsman may expect to derive from this pursuit" (Xenophon 57). These benefits include ... "the health, which will thereby accrue to the physical frame, the quickening of the eye and ear, the defiance of old age, and last, but not least, the warlike training which ensures" (57). About 400 years later, his Roman successor Grattius "describes approximately 22 breeds including the Celtic vertragus sight-hound" (Brewer et al. 88). Brewer et al. note: "Sight-hounds were fast enough to catch hares on their own and the huntsman is freed from the use of fixed nets. He could hunt on foot or from horseback" (89).

The literature of ancient Greece and Italy reveal different methods of hunting and desired characteristics of hunting dogs including opinions on which types of dogs are best for hunting, herding, and guarding situations. For example, "...the best known were the swift Laconian (Spartan) and the powerful Molossian, both of which were native to Greece and used by the Romans for hunting (*canis venatcus*) and to watch the house and livestock (*canis pastoralis*)" (Grout). *Cynegetica*, a Greek poem attributed to Oppian, discusses characteristics of the Laconian and the Molossian. Oppian recommends "the Laconian 'for the swift chase of gazelle and deer and swift-footed hare' (I412ff)" (qtd. in Grout). He describes the Molossians as "'Impetuous and of steadfast valour, who attack even bearded bulls and rush upon monstrous boars and destroy them.... They are not swift, but they have abundant spirit and genuine strength unspeakable and dauntless courage' (414ff)" (qtd. in Grout).

In the first century CE, Columella writes a comprehensive agricultural manual *De Re Rustica* which includes comments on the importance of farm-yard and sheep dogs. He notes: "Indeed, buying a dog should be 'among the first things which a farmer does, because it is the guardian of the farm, its produce, the household and the cattle' (VII.II.I)" (qtd. in Grout). These early shepherd dogs were trained not to herd flocks but to guard livestock from predators, especially wolves (Brewer et al. 91).

Ancient Breeds and Familiar Faces

The following examples provide a closer look at the hunting, herding, and guard dogs of ancient Egypt, Greece, and Rome and the interconnections between ancient breeds and modern dogs. Several modern breeds

The Dog as Guide, Guard and Healer

Guard at the gate (photo by Ollie Craig, pexel.com).

trace their working style roles and some aspects of their temperaments back to early roles as guardians of flocks, homes, people, and guides in the endeavors of hunting.

As noted previously, the earliest dog types began to appear in new areas as people migrated into different regions of the world. For example, one of the oldest breeds, the Basenji, came from Central Africa, a starting point in the migrations of people into other areas of the world (Barrientos 105). The modern Basenji looks remarkably similar to representations on rock carvings and other ancient Egyptian artifacts. The Basenji is "Perhaps the oldest breed of hunting dog in Egypt" (Barrientos). For instance, cave paintings found in Libya and dated to 6000 BCE depict hunters with dogs that have curved tails and were perhaps controlled with leashes. (See Chapter 2.) The Federation Cynologique places the breed in the spitz and primitive type (Barrientos).

Perhaps the most familiar coursing hound in ancient Egypt is the Saluki, companion to gods and pharaohs. Another ancient coursing hound, the greyhound has several characteristics similar to the Saluki. Modern greyhounds possess many of the physical characteristics such as long slender bodies and blazing speed as did the ancient coursing hounds used by the Greeks and Romans. Jeffers notes that "in coursing, the speed and agility of sight hounds are tested against their prey." In his work "One

3. Journey from Antiquity to Victorian Parlors

Hunting Hares," Roman Flavius Arrianus (Arrian) notes "that the purpose of coursing is not to catch the hare, but to enjoy the chase itself" (Jeffers). He notes that "the true sportsman does not take out his dogs to destroy the hares, but for the sake of the course and the contest between the dogs and the hares, and is glad if the hares escape" (Jeffers).

Jeffers adds the following observations which illustrate the connections between early greyhounds and greyhounds of today. He writes: "Art and coins from Greece depict short-haired hounds virtually identical to modern greyhounds making it fairly certain that the greyhound breed has changed very little since 500 BC."

Ancient breeds from Greece and the Greek Isles also provide hunting and herding skills in the early Mediterranean cultures. The Cretian Hound (Kritikos Ichnilatis) originated on the island of Crete and "is considered to be one of the oldest breeds of hunting dogs in the world" (Barrientos). Cretian hounds are quick and agile and possess exceptional scent. These attributes make them ... "extraordinary hare and wild rabbit hunters, but they have guarding instincts too" (Barrientos). Today, the Greek shepherd (Hellenikos Poimenkos), a "relatively large dog, with a solid body and massive head," also herds and guards their flocks and possesses many characteristics associated with livestock guardian dogs (Barrientos). In ancient times, Greek shepherd dogs were used to protect their flocks from wolves as described above.

Two ancient breeds of sledge dogs impacted the migration and establishment of people in Sibera and Alaska. Today they are highly prized sledge dogs in the Arctic. The Samoyed originated in Siberia approximately 1000 BCE and the Alaskan Malemute can be traced to Alaska's Northern Region dating approximately to 1000 BCE (Barrientos). In Arctic regions, sledge dogs such as the Alaskan Malamute and Siberian Husky breeds continue to assist Arctic people providing roles of hauling, herding, transportation, and companionship.

As previously noted, the concept of selective breeding for specific traits appears early within the ancient world. Over time, selective breeding goals expand to include temperament, adaptability to more specialized roles, and physical appearance. The focus of breeding continues to evolve with increased emphasis on appearance and changing priorities based on the interaction between people and dogs.

In the Victorian period, the perspectives changed further, shifting to "emphasize conformation and pedigree to a greater extent than functionality" (von Holdt and Driscoll 32). During this time, the modern dog period begins, marked by the establishment of different breed clubs. These breed clubs include the American Kennel Club (AKC), the Royal Kennel Club (RFC), and the Fédération Cynologique Internationale (FCI). Kennel clubs were created to set breed standards that "cover size, coat type, and temperament...," providing a point of reference for dog breeders "to help them maintain these unique qualities of each lineage" (White, Front). Differences exist between international clubs concerning which breeds are recognized and the purposes and goals of the individual organizations.

The American Kennel Club (AKC) established in 1884 "is a comprehensive registry for purebred dogs in the USA that maintains the records and pedigrees for various breeds" (White, Front). The AKC establishes standards that serve "as a benchmark for breeders, shaping the appearance, temperament, and health considerations for purebred dogs" in the United States (White, Front). The oldest kennel club, the Royal Kennel Club (RKC) established 1873 in England performs similar functions, setting a registry and standards for breeds, but it also functions as an international lobby group (White, Front). The influence of the RKC extends globally providing collaboration with other kennel clubs, establishing partnerships to exchange information and insights on breed standards, and helping coordinate canine events (White, Front).

The Fédération Cynologique Internationale (FCI) serves as the global authority for kennel clubs in different countries throughout the world. This organization known as the International Canine Federation in English is based in Belgium. The FCI includes "97 members and contact partners (one member per country) that each issue their own pedigrees and train their own judges" (FCI). The organization is divided into three sections, Europe (Fédération Cynologique Internationale European Section), the Americas and Caribbean (Sección de Las Americas y El Caribe) and Asia, Africa, and Oceanic (Asia, Africa & Oceannia FCI). While it is not a breed registry, "the FCI does set breed standards and ensures the alignment of the practices and standards of kennel clubs worldwide" (White, Front).

Each country establishes standards for the breeds in that county "in co-operation with the Standards and Scientific Commissions of the FCI" (FCI). According to the FCI, "These standards are THE reference for judges at shows held in FCI member countries" (FCI). Each member conducts international conformation shows as well as shows involving working type skills such as hunting trials and tests (CACIT), agility (CACIAG), coursing and racing (CACIL) and herding trials (CACITR) (FCI). These international competitions also illustrate links of continuity between the roles of working dogs in ancient cultures up to the present time.

4

Genetics, Breeds and Antiquity

Domestic dogs share an expansive history of collaboration and companionship with people. As the oldest companions of humans, they traverse a journey through prehistory and history, across the world's map and time. Parker et al. investigate their journey from a new perspective, researching and mapping the genetic structure of the purebred dog.

Parker et al. write: "The domestic dog is a genetic enterprise unique in human history" (1160). No mammal has shared such a close association with humans over so many centuries, nor been so substantially shaped as a result. "A variety of dog morphologies have existed for millennia, and reproductive isolation between them was formalized with the advent of breed clubs and breed standards in the mid—19th century" (Parker et al. 1160).

Parker et al. utilize "molecular markers" to identify and classify four genetic clusters of 85 domestic dog breeds, which often reveal similarities in morphology, shared original geographic locations or roles in human cultures (1161). These three factors, geographic origin, morphology, and role types directly impact the journey of people and dogs from the ancient past until the contemporary present. For instance, the migration paths and subsequent development of interactive human/dog communications impact the roles of dogs in cultures throughout history.

Developing increased understanding of genetic relationships between dog breeds provides new insights into influences that impact how various dog breeds evolved. Significantly, these influences framed by geographic origins and expanding roles of dogs impact the development of human progress as well. No other species has such a wide range of shapes, temperaments, and cognitive skills as the domestic dog. And no other two species possess such a winding, interconnected journey as humans and dogs. Parker et al. provide insights into questions concerning the migration of people and dogs in ancient cultures, as well as the development of early dog types. Their research, concerning genetic structures and evolutionary clusters, offers perspectives on *how* and *why* this shared journey unfolds.

For instance, what similarities and differences existed between hunter/gatherer and agricultural based cultures concerning the desired characteristics for various types of dogs? How did early types of working dogs, including hunters, guards, and shepherds, impact the developments of ancient cultures? The research of Parker et al. provides significant insights into these questions and the evolutionary history of dog breeds from new perspectives. And, why is this research significant to the study of dog archetypal characteristics of guide, guard, and healer? How did the presence of different types of dogs in the temporal world impact the metaphysical aspects of different cultures and the shared niche of people and dogs?

Often physical characteristics of different types of dog breeds influence human perspectives concerning dog archetypal characteristics of guide, guard and healer. Over and over, the spheres of the physical and metaphysical worlds interact and impact the development of human cultures and subsequently the human/dog bond. Ancient dog breeds reveal much to consider in these interconnected spheres. Dog breeds with origins in antiquity significantly impact in the development of early societies including Egypt, the Near East, and the classical world. Archaeological findings, literature, and art illustrate the importance of dogs and their roles in antiquity. In this process, dog archetypal characteristics of guide, guard, and healer impact the human/dog bond in the earthly physical and spiritual worlds, creating continuing links from ancient to contemporary times.

Genetic Clusters and Breed Groups

Research by Parker et al. allows them to separate 14 distinct breeds with origins in antiquity from the rest of the breeds with later European origins (1162). They "used standard neighbor-joining methods to build a majority-rule consensus tree of breeds..." including 85 breeds anchored by the grey wolf (1161). The population of the tree roots included eight grey wolf samples, with one from the United States and Canada, one from Mexico, three from Asia (China, Oman, Iran), and two from Europe (Sweden and Italy) (Parker et al. 1162).

Their research reveals four separate genetic clusters in the tree, based

4. Genetics, Breeds and Antiquity

Breeds of dog from *The Yuzhakov's Bolshaya Enc.* (1904, Wikimedia Commons).

on the genetic analysis of the 85 breeds. The first two genetic clusters included 14 breeds described below which trace their ancestry to antiquity (Parker et al. 1162). In the first genetic cluster, four major branches split from the central trunk (1162). Parker et al. note: "The deepest split in the tree separated four Asian spitz-type breeds and within this branch the Shar-Pei split first, followed by the Shiba Inu with the Akita and Chow Chow grouping together. The second split separated the Basenji, an ancient African breed. The third split separated two Arctic spitz-type breeds, the Alaskan Malamute and Siberian Huskey, and the fourth split separated two Middle Eastern sight hounds, the Afghan and Saluki, from the remaining breeds" (1161). The other breeds with ancient ancestry included the Tibetan Terrier and Lhasa Apso from Tibet, the Pekingese and Shih Tzu from China, and the Samoyed from the Arctic (Parker et al. 1163).

The first genetic cluster "includes Nordic breeds that phenotypically resemble the wolf, such as the Alaskan Malamute and Siberian Husky, and shows the closest genetic relationship to the wolf, which is the direct ancestor of domestic dogs. Thus, dogs from these breeds may be the best living representatives of the ancestral dog gene pool" (Parker et al. 1163–1164).

The genetic cluster of ancient breeds includes breeds from Africa, Asia, and the Arctic with varying appearances, originating from wide ranging geographic areas (Parker et al. 1163). How did these breeds develop in one genetic cluster? The migration routes of people and dogs provide possible insights. As noted by Miklósi, human expansion moved from East Africa into areas of Asia and Siberia, then into Europe, and ultimately North America (127). Some researchers theorize that pariah dogs from Asia accompanied these migrations which provides links between diverse locations and breeds (Parker et al. 1163).

Additional research revealed two other breed clusters with breeds that provide significant impact on the development of human cultures. Breeds in the third clusters relate primarily in appearance and heritage to Mastiff type breeds (Parker et al. 1163). Studying connections of breeds in this group provide additional links from early to contemporary roles of dogs, typically in working style roles. The same is true for the fourth cluster which includes several herding breed dogs (1163). The majority of the 85 dog breeds appear to originate from later European stock at approximately the same time (Parker et al. 1164).

These genetic clusters illuminate the interconnected spheres of dog ethology and breed groups, based not on similar appearances, but on the genetic makeup of the breeds. Studying these four genetic clusters, including the physical abilities and temperaments of individual breeds within the clusters, provides expanded perspectives into the evolutionary history of dogs and people. This information offers new links back to the world's earliest hunting dogs, such as the Saluki, guard dogs such as the Mastiff, Shepherds for herding flocks, and dogs as companions. These early dog types, as well as the rapidly expanding number of breeds in the classical world, reveal insights into the cultural lives of ancient and later societies and the importance of dogs in the journey of human progress.

Mutual Gaze and Facial Features

Prehistoric and subsequently domestic dogs have interacted with people throughout history in various cultures and individual societies. Over time, these interactions have led to domestic dog breeding decisions impacting dogs' appearances, temperaments, and social skills. For

4. Genetics, Breeds and Antiquity

Stare of a Grey Wolf (Maxima, GoodFon).

instance, the following research study provides insight into how domestication and artificial selection impacted the development of communication skills between people and dogs.

Kaminski et al. explore how the domestication of wolves into dogs and subsequent artificial selection in breeding practices impact the behavior, anatomy, and communication skill of dogs. In this process, they review the impact of anatomical facial changes between grey wolves and domestic dogs as a result of domestication and consider the behavioral impacts of these changes. Their findings illustrate the importance of facial changes in how dogs communicate with people and the subsequent responses from people. Their work provides an example of the interrelated spheres of culture and ethology in the course of dog domestication and the subsequent development of the human/dog bond.

Significantly, Kaminski et al. provide the following observations concerning dogs. During the course of domestication, "selection processes have shaped both their anatomy and behavior and turned them into human's best friend" ("Evolution" 1). They find that the most remarkable behavioral adaptation of dogs is their "ability to read and use human communication in ways that other animals do not" (1). In addition, they write: "The dog—human bond is unique and diagnostic of the evolution of human cultures" (1).

Research has also determined that "dogs are more skillful in using human communication cues" like pointing gestures or gaze direction even than both "the human's closest living relative" chimpanzees and wolves, the dog's closest living relative (Kaminski et al., "Evolution" 1). These observations address one of the major tenets of this book: People and dogs exist within a unique cultural niche, framed by shared communicative skills including physical gestures and eye contact.

As previously noted, "Recent research suggests that eye contact between humans and dogs is crucial for dog-human social interactions" (Kaminski et al., "Evolution" 1). While wolves avoid direct eye contact with humans, dogs "establish eye contact when they cannot solve a problem on their own" (1). In addition, eye contact between people and dogs helps dogs understand when "communication is relevant and directed to them" (1).

Eye contact between dogs and humans provides a major component for both referential and social communication between the two species. In addition, "the dogs' motivation to establish eye contact with humans seems to be an indicator of the level of attachment between humans and dogs" (Kaminski et al., "Evolution" 1). These observations illustrate both the behavioral aspects of dogs and the motivation of dogs in establishing communication with people. Behavior, motivation, and attachment meet at the nexus of communication through eye contact.

As Kaminski et al. note: "Thus, mutual gaze between dogs and humans seems to be a hallmark of the unique relationship between both species during human cultural evolution" ("Evolution" 1). In addition, Kaminski et al. find that during domestication changes in the evolution of facial muscles in dogs have enhanced this communication (1). Their research study below illustrates these observations.

In this research, specimens for "comparative facial dissections" were obtained from the taxidermy industry as well as the Michigan Department of Research for four wild grey wolves and domestic dog specimens "were obtained from the National Museum of Health and Medicine" (Kaminski et al., "Evolution" 4). For the behavioral component, "data was collected from nine wolves from two different animal parks" and "27 dogs from multiple shelters across the United Kingdom" (4). The research focuses on whether "Selection for traits that facilitate eye contact between dogs and humans might have" resulted in "anatomical differences in the facial musculature around the eyes between dogs and wolves" (Kaminski et al., "Evolution" 1). In addition, the authors evaluate "behavioral differences between the species in terms of how they use these muscles to promote eye contact" (1).

Significantly, their research found "that facial musculature between domestic dogs and grey wolves was relatively uniform and differed only around the eye" (Kaminski et al., "Evolution" 2). The differences involve the LOAM (levator anguli oculi medialis) and the RAOL (retractor anguli oculi lateraris) muscles ("Evolution" 2). The LAOM eyebrow muscle raises the inner eye corner and the RAOL muscle "pulls the lateral corner of the eyelids toward the ears" (2). Differences in conjunctive tissues result in wolves having "less ability to raise the inner corner of their brows independent of eye squinting relaxation" as compared to dogs (2). Kaminski et al. also analyze both the level of intensity of this eyebrow movement and frequency of the movement between the dogs and wolves (2). They find that anatomical differences between dogs and wolves correspond "with the behavioral analysis of the facial movements oriented toward a human in 27 dogs (C. familiaris) and nine wolves (C. lupus)" (2).

Why are these anatomical differences important in how dogs interact with people? According to the authors, this research shows that not only "dog body shape and skeletal anatomy" have changed, as previously known, but also soft tissues have changed due to "artificial selection pressures" which is a "striking difference for species separated only about 33,000 years ago" (Kaminski et al., "Evolution" 2). They observe that "these remarkable fast muscular changes can be directly linked to enhanced social interactions with humans" ("Evolution" 3).

Kaminski et al. also find that "dogs produce more common and exaggerated AU101 eyebrow facial movements than wolves" ("Evolution" 3). In addition, they write: "The AU101 movement causes the eyes of dogs to appear larger, giving the face a more paedomorphic, infant-like appearance, and also resembles a movement that humans produce when they are sad" (3). The authors add that these high intensity movements are exclusively produced by dogs and hypothesize "that dogs' expressive eyebrows are the result of selection based on human preference" ("Evolution" 1).

The responses of people to dogs' eyebrow movements reflect similar communicative cues used by people (Kaminski et al., "Evolution" 3). They write: "In humans, eyebrow movements seem particularly relevant to boost the perceived prominence of words and act as focus markers in speech" (3). In addition, eyebrow movements, considered ostensive cues, are particularly relevant interactions "when infants are learning something from others" (3). This research provides an excellent example of the interactive spheres of culture and ethology between people and dogs as evident in a shared communicative cue, the raised eyebrow.

The Dog as Guide, Guard and Healer

Breed Groups and Working Styles

This book explores how the domestic dog (*Canis familiaris*) responds in various tests where dogs must make choices based on their perceptions of human cues. For instance, choice tests consider how dogs pay attention to humans, seek direction, and make decisions in different situations. Huber and Lonardo discuss several of these studies concerning the cognitive processes of behavior reading and perspective-taking skills. Some of these studies consider "dogs' sensitivity to other's gaze and directions" (278). See Chapter 9.

Additional questions revolve around how *specific breeds* of domestic dogs react to communications with people. For instance, do differences between breeds and life experiences impact how dogs view attention to humans and react in choice test situations? How do different breed groups respond to signals and situations involving cooperation with humans? The following study explores these questions. Heberlein et al. investigate "…whether dogs of different breed groups differ in their ability to pay attention to human's perceptions, first according to the genetic relatedness between dog breeds, and second according to working style differences" (19).

Gaze of a Domestic Dog (PickPik).

4. Genetics, Breeds and Antiquity

What links exist between the characteristics and responses of modern breeds and ancient breeds concerning cooperation and working styles as hunters, guards, and shepherds? Do breed types impact how dogs pay attention, seek direction and cooperate with people? Heberlein et al. write: "It is conceivable that breeds that have been extensively bred for cooperating and working closely together with humans, such as working and herding dogs, might pay more attention on the human's perception than more independent working breeds, for example, some hunters, or ancient dogs" (20). Studies concerning canine perspective-taking show that paying attention to human cues, such as gaze direction and pointing, assist dogs in evaluating human perceptions.

The four genetic clusters identified by Parker et al. provide perspectives concerning links between different breed groups and modern working dog styles. These four groups are classified by Parker et al. as ancient, Shepherd, hunting, and Mastiff types (Heberlein et al. 21). For instance, sight and scent hounds, guard dogs, and herding dogs figure predominantly in working type roles within ancient and later cultures.

The main experiment included 56 breeds with 84 male and 103 female dogs (Heberlein et al. 21). The dogs lived with private owners either alone or with other dogs and their ages varied from five to 14. The study included two main analyses based on the dog's breed group and their working style. In the first analysis, Heberlein et al. assigned the dog's breed based on one of the four breed groups defined by Parker et al. In the second analysis, the tested dogs were grouped based on their following working styles: independent working style which includes scent and sight hounds, hunting dogs, and hauling dogs, the cooperative working style which includes breeds used for herding and police work, and the family style which included companion breeds (21).

According to Heberlein et al., "Several dogs sport activities, such as agility or obedience training, favor that dogs pay more attention to their owner's body language and signals" (20). To investigate the impacts of their life experiences, the 187 dogs were also tested to determine how different breeds responded due to these activities (20).

The experiment setup involved a training phase and testing phase. In addition, three control tests were conducted in order to evaluate alternative explanations for the dogs' choice behavior (Heberlein et al. 20). The first control test investigated whether the dogs' responses were influenced by cues from the owners. The second control test evaluated how dogs reacted to eating behind a barrier screen. The third condition addressed the actual training of the dogs, concerning whether the owner's presence impacted their choices (20).

The Dog as Guide, Guard and Healer

The experiment was conducted in a quiet outdoor enclosure at the University of Zürich as described below. The space contained two separate entrance and exit doors, opposite each other at the ends of the enclosure. Two T-shaped barriers were placed in the middle of the space. An elevated observation cabin for the owner was placed on the side of the enclosure parallel to the T-shaped barriers (Heberlein et al. 21).

The dogs were first trained not to approach the food until the food choice tests started (Heberlein et al. 20). The experiments involved two conditions, the hidden-pseudohidden and the hidden-hidden condition. The first experiment involved the hidden—pseudohidden condition. This experiment included an opaque barrier and a transparent barrier, each with a box containing a dog biscuit behind the barrier. During testing the dogs always had visual access to the food items. The tests alternated whether the owners had visual access to the food items from the observation platform (20). According to Heberlein et al., group level results showed that the ancient and hunting types first chose the biscuit behind the opaque barrier not visible to the owner (23). The dogs from the Shepherd and Mastiff type groups did not take that biscuit.

Heberlein et al. write: "...there was variation in the performance between breed groups depending on their genetics and selection for specific working styles, as well as on the experience in dog activity" (26). Dogs in the ancient and hunting genetic groups as well as the dogs assigned to the independently working and the family style groups first chose the hidden food items behind the opaque screen (26). The results indicate that the dogs used their perspective-taking abilities to ascertain what their owners could see or not see (26).

Observations in the hidden-hidden condition experiment also illustrated how dogs pay attention to the perceptions of their owners (Heberlein et al. 21). In this experiment, the barriers were both opaque and the biscuits invisible to the owner. In this condition, the dogs always took the biscuits and preferred the side farthest away from the owner on the observation platform (Heberlein et al. 26).

Concerning the dogs' activity and training, Shepard and Mastiff type dogs were involved at higher percentages than dogs in the hunting and ancient groups... (Heberlein et al. 26). Over 60 percent of the Shepherd type and 42 percent of the Mastiff type dogs participated in dog sports (26). In comparison, only 14.7 percent hunting type and 14.8 percent ancient type dogs participated in dog sports (26). Significantly, when the dog types and working style breeds that were active in dog sports were excluded from the experiment results, similar results were still found (26).

4. Genetics, Breeds and Antiquity

Heberlein et al. conclude "…that dogs pay attention to the perception of humans and that they use this information when choosing between two forbidden food items. We found differences among four genetically distinct breed groups, as well as between three groups based on their working style. Dogs categorized as ancient type and hunting dog type, as well as independently working style and family style groups, performed similarly and seemed to be more attentive to their owners' perceptions than the dogs from the other groups" (27).

The research of Parker et al. and Heberlein et al. illustrate several connections that impact the human/dog bond. These connections include the following: (1) the genetic clusters research of Parker et al. which groups dogs based on similarities of genetic material; (2) the roles of dogs as hunters, guards, shepherds, and companions based on breed groups and communication skills with people; and (3) connections between breeds' working styles and modern breeds, framed by environmental and life experiences between dogs and their owners. Several of these connections reveal links back to breeds in antiquity and connections with working style roles of dogs in ancient cultures.

The Heberlein et al. food choice research provides perspectives framed by visual access of dogs to their owners, motivation, and perspective-taking. The results of these tests hinge on eye contact, an essential element in interactions between dogs and people. The ability to establish eye contact plays a central role in referential and social communications between dogs and people. As noted by Kaminski et al. motivation and eye contact impact perspective-taking in dogs ("Evolution" 1).

How do these skills impact working dog roles in antiquity and contemporary dog roles? Heberlein et al. note that ancient breeds, especially hunting types that work independently, might react differently from herding dogs, which maintain closer visual contact with their human counterparts (20). Guard dogs might also work more independently because they are focused on protecting flocks or properties, often working alone in solitary situations or during night hours.

The Parker et al. research concerning genetic breed clusters provides additional insight. For example, the first seven breeds that split in Parker's research include ancient breeds with similar skills and characteristics found in contemporary breeds. All of these breeds perform at least two types of working dog roles in ancient cultures. Significantly, in their interactions with people they also offer companionship, a foundational characteristic in the human/dog bond.

The first split includes the Shar-pei, Shiba Inu, Akita, and Chow

The Dog as Guide, Guard and Healer

Chow, breeds that originated in China and Tibet. Ancestry of the Shar-pei extends back to the Han Dynasty in China (Hausman and Hausman 246). Artifacts depicting these dogs date to circa 220 CE (246). Once considered as "the rarest breed in the world," these dogs were bred for herding, guarding, and hunting (246).

The Chow Chow also appears in the Han Dynasty. Archaeological discoveries include one recognizable Chow Chow illustration on a Han Dynasty bas-relief circa 150 BCE (Hausman and Hausman 75). The origins of the Chow Chow are unknown for certain but their ancestral home "was either the Far North (Mongolia and Siberia or northern China)" (76). In the Tang Dynasty seventh century CE, their popularity "was unquestionable, housing for five thousand dogs and ten thousand huntsmen" was common (Hausman and Hausman 75). Originally bred for hunting deer and bear by scent, Chow Chows are known for their endurance. They were also bred to guard junks in China and are still considered excellent watch dogs today (Hausman and Hausman 78).

The Alaskan Malamute and Siberian Husky in the third split worked as sledge dogs with people in the Pleistocene-Holocene transition period 9500 years ago, and still do so today in Arctic areas (Sinding et al.) Parker et al. note that these Arctic type dogs exhibit the closest genetic relationship to the domestic dog's original ancestor, the wolf (1163–1164). Arctic type dogs reveal examples of ancient genetics and the evolutionary past linking Pleistocene wolves, the earliest sled dogs and the intertwined journey of early Arctic people and dogs.

Hunting attributes of the Basenji from central Africa which split second and the Afghan and Saluki sight hounds which split fourth have been discussed previously. The Basenji scent hound and the Afghan and Saluki sight hounds work out front of their human counterparts, tracking their quarry versus looking at their companions for direction. In contrast, the Alaskan Malamute, Siberian Husky, and Samoyed sled dogs work more closely with signals conveyed by their human counterparts.

Yet, what about the smaller breeds who guarded tombs, lived with royalty, and still work very hard as diminutive guardians and companions? The ancient Pekingese and Shih-Tzu had jobs too in the ancient world. Pekingese-type dogs trace their ancestry and working roles to guardians of ancient tombs, companions in royal courts, and Tibetan monasteries. These miniature dogs are associated with lions as mythological figures and companions in the Buddhism religion. For instance, "The Lion Dog of Tibet resembles the Pekingese, but in Asian legend the Lion Dog is a combination of the eagle and the lion, an heraldic creature of

Chinese myth" (Hausman and Hausman 204). The Pekingese was known as a shapeshifter with the ability "to change back and forth from a dog to a lion…" (204).

Old Chinese writings described these lion dogs as "Hand Dogs" saying when a human hand touched a new eaglet, the eaglet "would turn into a Chinese Lion Dog" (Hausman and Hausman 202). Later, Pekingese-like dogs, in Japanese myth, became the Dog of Fo. For instance, a Japanese painting in the eleventh century shows "the entry of the Buddha into Nirvana. Beside his praying disciples, there is a sacred Lion Dog" (202).

Shih Tzu also claim connections to ancient royalty and mythological lion lineage. According to the AKC, "The Mandarin phase 'Shih Tzu' translates to 'little lion'" (Ripley AKC). This ancient breed "was likely given this name because of its association with the Tibetan Buddhist God of Learning" (AKC). Legend says that "they traveled with a small lion dog that could transform into a full-sized lion" (AKC). These little dogs were companions with royalty during the Ming Dynasty and today treat their human companions as royalty (AKC).

These examples illustrate some of the ancestral links between the earliest breed groups, as defined by Parker et al. and the characteristics of modern dog breeds today.

Links Between Breeds and Roles

A review of the American Kennel Club breed groups offers insight into how modern dog breeds are grouped based on physical traits, personality traits, and the work that the breeds were originally developed to do (AKC). Several of these categories provide additional links back to the roles of dogs in ancient cultures and aspects of their shared niche with people throughout history. The physical and personality traits of the 195 breeds recognized by the AKC mostly fall under one of seven major dog groups. These seven groups are hound, working, herding, sporting, non-sporting, terrier, and toy (AKC). The AKC registered breeds are assigned "to one of the seven groups representing characteristics and functions the breeds were originally bred for" (AKC).

The hound, working, and herding groups offer special significance in connections between ancient breeds, modern breeds, and similarities in characteristics. Brief descriptions of these groups follow. In many cases, the descriptions include characteristics of appearance and abilities present in ancient breeds.

The Dog as Guide, Guard and Healer

The Hound Group includes sight hounds and scent hounds, which chase their prey in different ways. These types of hounds and their hunting abilities illustrate characteristics of ancient Tsem, Saluki, and greyhound breeds in Egypt and Mesopotamia. According to AKC, "The sleek, long-legged sighthounds use explosive speed and wide vision to chase swift prey." In contrast, "...tough, durable scent hounds rely on their powerful noses to trail" their quarry (AKC).

The Working Dog Group "includes some of the world's most ancient breeds" (AKC). These breeds "were developed to assist humans in some capacity," including hauling carts, pulling sleds, guarding properties and protecting families (AKC). These breeds "...tend to be known for imposing stature, strength, and intelligence" (AKC). Breeds in the Herding Group protect and move livestock including cattle, sheep, and even reindeer in far northern climates (AKC). The earliest shepherd dogs herded livestock in ancient cultures and also guarded their flocks.

In the eighteenth century, "The feisty short-legged breeds in the Terrier Group" pursued vermin and rodents in underground sewers (AKC). Early dogs with terrier characteristics were also used as hunters in Egypt and Mesopotamia. Their distinctive size, pricked ears, and curved tail show terrier attitude and determination in ancient tomb pictures, carvings, and seals. The contemporary AKC description concerning toy dogs also illustrates characteristics of lap dogs in ancient Greece and Rome. Diminutive breeds of the Toy Group often sit in the laps of their owners and excel "at being attentive companions" (AKC). Companionship and love are concepts of the human/dog bond that exist from ancient times until now.

Modern breeds, developed mostly since the 1800s, also include sporting and non-sporting dog breeds developed as companions and partners for people in all facets of contemporary cultures. The AKC major dog group descriptions highlight one of the most important aspects of the human/dog bond—the interactions between individuals and companion dogs. The interactions and resultant companionship between people and dogs create a core aspect of the human/dog bond.

The above descriptions are also applicable to dog types and working styles in the ancient and classical worlds. Key words often describe both characteristics found in ancient dog types as well as modern breeds. While modern breeds have different genetic makeups, similarities in some characteristics highlight aspects of continuity in the development of different dog breed types.

Significantly, the physical and mental abilities of these breed groups provide insights into archetypal characteristics of guide, guard, and

4. Genetics, Breeds and Antiquity

healer. For instance, the physical attributes of working group guard dogs often translate into the mythological roles of guard dogs in different cultures. Shepherd dogs both physically guard and guide their flocks and provide support to their human counterparts. Dogs bred to be companions since antiquity excel at providing attention and companionship in their relationships with people. Such connections provide avenues to explore the shared journey of dogs and people from the archetypal perspectives of guide, guard, and healer. This book now turns to explore these connections weaving through mythologies and cultures from ancient times until now.

5

The Nature of Dog Archetypal Images

In comparative mythology, realms within the natural world often provide a porous framework, serving as pathways for interspecies interactions between humans and dogs. The natural world, both physical and allegorical, creates settings for stories concerning people and dogs, and dogs and gods. Within the realms of the sky, the earth, and the underworld, humans, gods, and dogs traverse through comparative mythology. These realms are porous, meaning that often the stories transpire in more than one space, for instance, unfolding within the sky and earth or earth and underworld. These porous transitions are significant to the development of the archetypal images of guide, guard, and healer in the evolving relationship between people and dogs. Over time, the human/dog bond unfolds and expands, framed within the influences of various mythologies.

In many cases, stories within different cultures and time periods reveal similar patterns illustrating these archetypal images. The repetition and similarities of these patterns reinforce the influences of comparative mythology and nature in the development of the human/dog bond. For instance: review of mythologies associated with the celestial stars and planets, liminal crossroads within earthly landscapes, and the underworld illustrate these points.

Each night the sky provides a captivating display, serving as a reminder of the interactions of mythological stories and the psychological perceptions of humans in ancient cultures. Gazing at the night sky offers a celestial display of stars, galaxies, and planets which extends into the dawn hours. Comparative mythology and nature meet in the heavens providing a continuous thread from ancient times up to the present day.

Originally, this is not the nature of modern astronomy, but the creative nature of past cultures. Humans study the night sky, creating a celestial map framed in stories, long before the advent of scientific research. Ian Ridpath reinforces this point: "Constellations are the inventions of human

5. The Nature of Dog Archetypal Images

imagination, not of nature" (1). Rather, the constellations "are symbolic, a celestial allegory" (1). He describes the night sky as a canvas, where human imagination projects "the deeds and personifications of deities, sacred animals and moral tales" (1). The surrounding natural environment provides the framework for the mythopoetic celestial creations of ancient people, including the Greeks, Romans, and Native Americans.

Several mythologies provide examples of these projections, as seen in the activities of gods with other gods, with people, and with animals including dogs. As noted by David White, "archaic astronomical systems from Europe, Asia, Africa, and North America identify star clusters or planets with supernatural dogs" (2392).

Eventually, early astronomers join Greek and Roman mythologists in studying the constellations. Ridpath observes, "Greek astronomy reached its pinnacle with Ptolemy," which occurs during the period CE 100–CE 178 (7). In his work *Almagest*, Ptolemy provides a "catalogue of 1022 stars, arrayed into forty-eight constellations" (Ridpath 7). The stars are arranged "with estimates of their brightness," largely based on the work of the Greek astronomer Hipparchus from three centuries earlier (7).

The descriptions and stories of the present day constellations occur, for the most part, in Greek and Roman literature. According to Ridpath, "the constellations recognized by twentieth century science are primarily those of the ancient Greeks, interspersed with modern additions" (vii). The two constellations *Canis major* (the great dog) and *Canis minor* (the little dog) are located within the original 48 constellations.

Both in the time of Hipparchus and today, what is the most brilliant fixed star in the night sky? It is Sirius which marks the snout of *Canis major*, the great dog. According to Ridpath, "almost certainly the constellation originated with this star alone" (40). Only the planet Venus, the sun, and the moon outshine Sirius, known as the Dog Star (Leach 58).

In Greek and Roman mythology, Sirius plays a significant role in the summer season. The hottest, most sultry, and uncomfortable days of summer are named for the Dog Star, and are still called the dog days of summer. Ridpath explains, "The name of the star Sirius comes from the Greek word *seirius* meaning 'searing or scorching' an appropriate name for such a brilliant star" (40). He further comments, "In Greek times its rising at dawn just before the Sun marked the start of the hottest part of the summer, a time that hence became known as the Dog Days" (40–41). People, animals, vegetation, and crops suffer the effects of Sirius during the time when Sirius travels closest to the sun. According to Leach, the Greeks and Romans thought "these were the terrible days," a time when "drought lengthened week by week, and summer crops were scorched and destroyed" (59). During this period, people suffered fevers and sunstrokes and "dogs went mad from the heat" (59).

Stories concerning Sirius illustrate two aspects of the intertwined spheres of comparative mythology and nature surrounding the most brilliant star in the sky. This star, associated with the dog, represents both the evening celestial display couched in mythology, and the description of the summer period still known as the dog days of summer.

Furthermore, the present discipline of astronomy shares connections with early celestial mythologies. In 1922, the International Astronomical Union (IAU) officially adapted the 88 constellations which are used today. Subsequently, at the IAU's request, the Belgian astronomer Eugene Delporte (1862–1955) created "a definitive list of boundaries for these eighty-eight constellations" (Ridpath 12). The perceptions of constellations as celestial allegories has evolved, framed by contemporary astronomical study. Ridpath writes: "Constellations are now regarded not as star patterns but as precisely defined areas of sky, rather like countries on Earth" (12). The history of constellations, as seen through comparative mythology, has transitioned into what Ridpath describes as "an international treaty on the demarcation of the sky, which astronomers throughout the world" continue to utilize up to the present day (12).

Celestial Dogs in the Starry Sky

Mythological stories offer explanations on why and how the gods create celestial canines, often mimicking some of the dogs' earthly habits such as chasing prey and serving as guards. As would be expected, Zeus figures prominently as both a catalyst and mediator in many of these narratives. In some cases, the reasons for association of dogs with star clusters, the moon, and planets lies with motivations for punishment, concealment, and reward. Ironically, the desire for punishment by the ancient gods transitions into immorality in the contemporary night sky. Closer review of various myths illustrates these points.

Sirius and the Milky Way appear in several mythologies, notably Greek, Roman, and Native American cultures. Sirius illustrates a perfect example of the multi-tasking celestial dog, providing the functions of hunter, companion, and guard. In Greek mythology, the Dog Star guards Orion, and chases game, the fox, and the hare. According to the Greek poet Aratus, *Canis major* serves "as the guard-dog of Orion, following on

5. The Nature of Dog Archetypal Images

the heels of its master, and standing on its hind legs with Sirius in its jaws" (Ridpath 40).

Orion, the hunter, is "one of the most ancient constellations, being among the few star groups known to the earliest Greek writers, such as Homer and Hesiod" (Ridpath 96). In *The Odyssey*, Homer describes "Orion as a giant hunter, armed with an unbreakable club of solid bronze" (96). In the night sky, Orion's dogs, the constellations *Canis major* and *Canis minor*, "follow at his heels, in pursuit of the hare" known as the constellation Lepus (96).

The story of Laelaps, the dog who chases the fox, offers an allegory which goes far beyond an expertise in hunting. How often through history do people pursue a goal, a dream, or individual which can be never caught? This was the fate of Laelaps. According to mythologists Eratosthenes and Hyginus, the constellation *Canis major* represents Laelaps, "a dog so swift that no prey could escape it" (Ridpath 40). Obviously, a dog with such expertise would be very valuable to the Greek pantheon and rulers of Greece. A brief review of Laelaps' owners include possibly Artemis, Zeus, the king of Crete, and ultimately Procris and Cephalus. Stories vary on who gave Laelaps to Procris, "daughter of King Erechteus of Athens and wife of Cephalus" (Ridpath 40). Most likely the dog was originally a gift from Zeus to Europa, "whose son Minos, King of Crete, passed it on to Procris" (Ridpath 40).

Ultimately, her husband Cephalus inherits the dog and takes it to the town of Thebes, north of Athens, "where a vicious fox was ravaging the countryside" (Ridpath 40). Off goes Laelaps chasing the fox too swift to ever be caught—yet Laelaps was destined to catch whatever it pursued (40). Leach summarizes this paradox noting, "Zeus, seeing the predicament between the infallible catcher and the forever uncatchable, turned

The Death of Procris by Piero di Cosimo (©The National Gallery, London).

the two into stone" (54–55). While Zeus initially turns both the fox and Laelaps into stone, he places the dog "in the sky as *Canis major*, without the fox" (Ridpath 40). As punishment, the fox remains a boulder while Laelaps guards Orion and races through the heavens each evening chasing his prey.

The origination of the constellation *Canis minor*, the little dog, also brings together "the deeds and personifications" of deities, human nature, and moral lessons. Procyon, the brightest star in this small constellation, is called *Canis minor*. The "name in Greek means 'before the dog,' from the fact it rises earlier than the other celestial dog, *Canis major*" (Ridpath 42).

Although *Canis minor* is most often identified as one of Orion's dogs, another legend, recounted by Hyinus, offers a more complex and illuminating story. In this legend, the star represents Maera, the dog of Icarius, placed in the sky by Zeus as a reminder of a tragic tale involving the people of Attica, Dionysus, Icarius, and Erigone. In this story, Icarius offers his hospitality to the god Dionysus, and "as a reward was given the gift of wine" (Morford et al. 326). Icarius, in turn, offers the wine to people of Attica, who after first feeling "the effects of the blessing," thought they had been poisoned (326). Jumping to conclusions in haste and anger, they turn on the giver of the blessing and kill Icarius.

Maera, who witnessed the killing, "ran howling" to Erigone, Icarius' daughter and led her to the location of her dead father (Ridpath 42). Overcome with grief, "Both Erigone and Maera, took their own lives where Icarius lay." Zeus placed their images among the stars as a reminder of the tragedy (42). Subsequently, "To atone for their tragic mistake, the people of Athens instituted a yearly celebration in honor of Icarius and Erigone" (42). This story reveals a moral lesson concerning the potential consequences of not accepting a blessing as such, and the ramifications of responding out of haste and ignorance, with anger and violence. Zeus does not let the lesson go in vain, but creates these star patterns as visual remainders of an allegory concerning human nature. This story combines the human responses of anger, regret, and atonement by the people of Attica. These responses are contrasted by the loyalty of the dog Maera, who follows her owners unfailingly through this tragedy.

In Native American cultures, several mythological stories discuss dogs and the Milky Way. According to Leach, "The Milky Way is 'where the god ran' in Cherokee Indian mythology" (62). The story involves a hungry dog from the north sky, irresistible white corn meal, and a getaway which literally leaves tracks. One morning, the people realize that some of the corn meal they ground each day disappears during the night.

5. The Nature of Dog Archetypal Images

Looking around, they discover the tracks of a dog and the next evening they keep watch. Down from the north sky comes the dog who begins enjoying his corn meal dinner. According to Leach, "The people jumped out and whipped him away," and he ran back to the north (62). She adds, "But he had walked in the meal, and the meal from his running feet left a great white trail across the sky: the Milky Way, where the dog ran" (62).

Other myths describe the dog as a guide traversing the sky and helping lead souls to the spirit world. For instance, the Seminole Native Americans of Florida describe a "different dog path in the sky" (Leach 62). They call this path "*ifi heni*, the dog way, by which dogs travel to their heavenly home" (62). This path leads up to the Milky Way which represents "the spirit road (*solopi heni*) by which the souls of the good travel to the land of the dead in the west" (62). In early times, the Seminole would kill a dog "as soon as its owner died," so that the dog might accompany the deceased on the journey to the spirit world (62). The dog, traveling along the dog way, catches up with the soul of its owner and the two continue together to the spirit world. In this mythology, the dog serves both as a *psychopomp* and a companion illustrating the interactive relationship between people and dogs.

Natchez Native Americans also describe the Milky Way as "the dog trail" (Leach 62). As noted by Leach, "The dog road, *ifi beni*, is sharply visible on clear nights" (62). These myths combine both the aspects of the *psychopomp* and visual liminal images representing travel from life on earth to the spirit realm. Significantly, the Milky Way also provides the path for not only people but dogs to follow to the spirit world.

Mythical Messages Framed Within Nature

In the roles of guide and guard, both earthly and mythical dogs communicate with howling and barking, as well as with other forms of communication. Pertinent to ancient mythological stories and more recent folklore, the barking and howling of dogs provide several functions and often imply different meanings. For instance, barking dogs guard their immediate territory and sound the alarm to others, both animal and human, of impending danger and intruders. Their barking serves as rallying cries to members of their packs during hunts and at other times warnings of potential intruders or personal dangers to people. Dogs provide these tasks not only for people, but in other cases, for the gods. In addition to barking and howling, the baying of hounds, in these cases supernatural

The Dog as Guide, Guard and Healer

hounds, figure predominately in many stories. The following contemporary description by Adrienne Farricelli is useful in reviewing responses of dogs in these stories: "Howling is the noise produced by wild canines and in certain circumstances by domesticated dogs; whereas baying is the sound exclusively emitted by hounds" (3).

Legends and folklore abound with stories, known as the Wild Hunt, concerning the meanings and functions of howling dogs often associated with death and the gathering of souls. Leach notes that the Wild Hunt begins with "the baying of the hounds," as they "stream across the sky in the night, heralding winter and cold and storm, presaging death, and causing earthly dogs to howl" (64). While interpretations of the Wild Hunt vary, with different cultures and periods, everywhere the stories involve "some ghostly hunter with his pack of hounds forever continuing the chase" (64–65).

According to Dale-Green, "The original Wild Hunt was led by Woden, the Teutonic storm-god," who nightly rushed across the sky with hounds and hunters, "in pursuit of a phantom boar, horse or woman" (58). Leach also notes that in many tales, "a king, or local lord or god" leads the hunt (65). In thirteenth-century literature, King Arthur "was seen by moonlight over the forests of Brittany and Savory, Scotland, and Somerset" (65). The Wild Hunt was called "Arthur's Chase well into the nineteenth century" (65).

According to Leach, "the phenomenon of the furious huntsman with his spectral hosts and yelling hounds" occurs in Scandinavia, northern Germany, and France, as well as in the northern United States and Canada (66). These folklore stories often provide interconnections between the supernatural hunters and hounds riding through the sky to collect souls, and the howling and barking reactions of dogs in the physical world. Dogs, in the physical world, sit at the liminal crossroads between earthly life and the supernatural realm. They warn people on earth of impending death, sensing both danger and hearing the howls of the supernatural dogs and charging hunters.

According to Dale-Green, the folklore of Wales provides one example of the complexity of these interconnections (61–62). For instance, "The Welsh *Cwn Annwn* (Dogs of Hell) or *Cwn y Wybr* (Dogs of the Sky) are a pack of spectral hounds belonging to Annwn, King of Hell" (Dale-Green 61–62). Some people believe that the hounds "hunt the souls of the wicked as soon as they leave the body; others that they lead a cavalcade of doomed souls to hell" (62). Significantly, earthly dogs alert people to the supernatural appearance of the hounds. Langley Cornwell describes this belief:

5. The Nature of Dog Archetypal Images

"God gave the king of Annwn control over demons so he could protect the world. As such, he would ride on supernatural rounds on a hunt for mortal souls. Only dogs could see the death-bringing 'Hounds of Annwn,' and howled their acknowledgement."

The following tales provide examples of some of the other beliefs concerning the Wild Hunt. Motivations include punishment for perceived transgressions ranging from hunting on Sunday, to confrontations with the Devil, to repercussions from religious traditions. For instance, in the English Wild Hunt, also called Gabriel's hounds, the howling of the supernatural dogs foretell death for the listener "or someone nearby" (Leach 65). As Leach explains, "The hounds are interpreted as the souls of the unbaptized, who, unadmitted either to heaven or hell, must wander thus forever; or the dogs are pursuing the souls of the unbaptized" (65).

Some stories are associated with specific times of year. For example, "The Norwegian *gandreid* (literally, spirits' ride)" and the Northern Germanic myth involving Odin or Frigga both occur during the Yuel season (Leach 65). Odin or Fregga lead "the homeless dead, followed by the baying pack on dark, stormy nights," and the Norwegian *gandreid* occurs especially during "Epiphany—the twelve days between Christmas and the Twelfth night" (65).

Dogs reside at a liminal crossroads, aware of impending death for individuals in some stories and groups of souls in other stories. Many of the stories evoke terror and apprehension associated with unknown aspects of death. In addition, visual images of the stories are framed by familiar landscapes often associated with specific natural occurrences such as night and storms. For instance, "In the lore of West England, the Devils Dandy Dogs passed over the moors during storms, breathing fire and tearing hapless strangers to pieces" (Sax 178).

The responses of some people to the eerie and plaintive howling of dogs, especially at night, still resonate framed within this folklore up to the present day. Leach notes that many of these beliefs "have been recorded as recently as the late nineteenth century" (66). For example, says Cornwell, "A dog howl means the wind god has summoned death and the spirits of the dead are being released. A howling dog, in an otherwise silent night, is the first warning of supernatural events."

Dogs serve multi-tasking functions, both positive and negative, as seen through the perspectives of people within cultures from the ancient past up to the contemporary present. For instance, in the Native American stories discussed above, dogs serve as companions and guides in celestial journeys through the night sky. Even though associated with death, dogs provide positive aspects of guiding and guarding the way toward the spirit world. In contrast, the howling of dogs and subsequent chasing of souls during stories of the Wild Hunt strike a very different perspective.

The mystical aspects of death can include the emotions of wonder, awakening, tranquility, but also terror. Dogs, associated with the Wild Hunt, evoke the emotions of apprehension, panic, and terror, framed within different cultures and time periods. For instance, the folklore of the Wild Hunt provides one example where negative perceptions of dogs are influenced by cultural legends. These tales combine the supernatural framed within physical realities, usually associated with darkness, storms, wind, and the howling of actual dogs. In these situations, the supernatural world interacts with the natural world. The impact of these interactions helps explain the longevity of these tales throughout several centuries up to and including the twentieth century. In mythological and folklore stories, perceived reality of human experiences often translates into longevity of the stories.

Avenging Hounds and Guides at the Crossroads

The motif of avenging hounds also occurs in stories concerning the gods, such as Hecate and Artemis. Dale-Green observes, "In Greek mythology, Hecate, Queen of Hell" is also known as "Our Lady of the Hounds" (87). Every night, accompanied by her pack of dogs she leads "a swarm of ghosts through the Underworld" (87). These dogs function both as relentless herders of ghosts and avengers for Hecate. In addition, her companions, the Furies or Erinyes, appear "dog-headed and serpent-maned" and their barking announces their approach (87).

In a different story, Actaeon, the hunter, suffers the wrath of Artemis, the goddess of the hunt. This story illustrates "the hallowed purity of the goddess Artemis," and the vehemence of retribution, demanded by Artemis and delivered by Actaeon's hounds (Morford et al. 229). While hunting with his dogs, Actaeon accidently stumbles upon Artemis and has "the misfortune" to see Artemis naked while bathing (229). Artemis, in fury and embarrassment, transforms Actaeon into a stag, sending her own hounds in pursuit. Although his outward form changes into the stag, his mind remains unaltered but he cannot speak As a result, Actaeon, the hunting dogs' master becomes their prey, torn to pieces as he is unable to utter any words (230–231).

The associations of Hecate and Artemis with dogs reflect completely different motivations and functions. Dogs, in general, serve as Artemis'

5. The Nature of Dog Archetypal Images

companions and hunting partners. In contrast, dogs serve as herders and guards of the dead for Hecate. According to Morford et al., "The dominant conception of Artemis is that of the virginal huntress" (235). For instance, a frieze of dogs' heads in Artemis' temple at Epidaurus documents her as "huntress and lady of the hounds," worshipped as both the guardian of hunters and of the hunted (Leach 24). During her festival, the ritual of crowning hunting dogs "was a rite performed to protect the dogs from the avenging spirits of wild animals they had killed" (24). This ritual provides another example of Campbell's sociological function of mythology, as seen in the interconnected relationships between the hunters, the wild animals pursued, and the hunting dogs.

The mythology associated with Artemis illustrates the interconnections between people, wild animals within nature, and dogs. According to one description, "An animal often appears by her side, and crescent moon-like horns rest upon her head; the torch she holds burns bright with the light of birth, life, and fertility" (Morford et al. 234–235). In this context, Artemis is worshipped as the goddess of three realms, the spiritual, the natural, and the cultural worlds within Greek society.

Actaeon in Caserta (Reggia de Caserta, MiC Italian Ministry of Culture).

The Dog as Guide, Guard and Healer

In contrast, Hecate resides in the underworld, moving back and forth between crossroads on earth and the underworld. Hecate's realms, as "a goddess of roads in general and crossroads in particular," include the night, death, and especially "ghostly activities" at crossroads (Morford et al. 234). According to Leach, "Hecate (Greek death-moon goddess) was considered to be manifest in the dogs which ate corpses and howled at the moon" (18). In addition, Hecate was "often called the *dog-headed death* (or *moon*) *goddess* in reference to her frequent depiction with three heads: lion, dog, and horse" (Leach 18).

Throughout history the relationship between humans and dogs evolves, shaped by associations within expanding contexts of culture and social parameters. For instance, in the ancient civilizations of Egypt, Persia, India, and Greece, dogs are often associated with death and the transition from life to death. Dogs transition from scavengers of burial grounds to guards at the entry to the underworld, and in some cases to guides through the underworld.

According to White, an "intimate association" exists between dogs and death in the world's religions (2392). He notes that "gods of death, such as the Greek Hekate, the Indian Yama and Bhairava, and the Teutonic Garmr, are often identified with or accompanied by dogs that guard the gates to their realms" (2392). He adds: "Alternately, the dog serves as a *psychopomp*, a guide who leads or herds the recently deceased over the dangerous paths leading to the world of the dead—hence the sacrifice of dogs or the burial of dog effigies with the dead" (2392). Several examples of archeological evidence illustrating the importance of dogs in burial rituals are explored in Chapter 2.

Numerous cultures associate death with a journey from the earthly realm to the spiritual realm. Mythological dogs figure predominately in many of these journeys, with both positive and negative impacts. In general, perceptions of hell dogs, or dogs associated with the underworld, evoke fear, dread, and prayers by the living to avoid these dogs in death. The actual nuances of several myths reveal much more complex situations. In these cases, dogs serve predominately as guards, but also as guides. The presence of guard dogs in the underworld, or at the gates to the underworld, is an anticipated danger associated with this journey. The complexity for people on earth arises in contemplation on how to pass by these guards, or to enlist their assistance for the underworld journey.

Avoidance and assistance represent two very different goals. As noted, mythological dogs move through the land of the dead as both guard and *psychopomp*. The multi-tasking and liminal nature of dogs in these capacities exist at crossroads and in transitions, moving from the earthly realm to the spiritual realm. Mythological dogs both guard the crossroads between earthly life and the underworld, and also lead and herd souls of the dead into and through the underworld. For instance, Shunsuke Okunishí describes the "hellhound (or the watch dog from hell)" as a mythical dog "perceived as dual and thus endowed with special powers that allow it to guard the border between the realm of the living and that of the dead, at the same time acting as a guide for the souls" (1).

The connotations of the two words "lead" and "herd" illustrate the complexity of these multi-tasking roles. These actions often evoke positive outcomes such as safely leading the way through uncharted territories to the spirit world, or protectively herding the souls of the dead through challenges and obstacles in the underworld. In contrast, the hounds of hell herd souls doomed to wander forever, or drive the dead toward dreaded fates in the underworld.

In these capacities as guard and guide, mythological dogs and canine/dog gods serve as central characters, especially in stories associated with movement and transformation from life to death. Interactions with these dogs help create the movement of the myths, offering challenges and creating action and ramifications within the stories. In this context, the interrelated archetypal images of guard and guide run through numerous stories associated with death in religious traditions.

Mythological dogs serve as both beneficial guides and relentless guards obstructing escape, dragging and driving souls or spirits of the dead to destruction. The dogs participate in securing these fates, whether positive or negative, as seen through the mythological and religious cultures of different groups. In this process, the functions and interactions between dogs and people are not perceived as all beneficial or negative. Sometimes these relationships unfold in the liminal state of the unknown. This transitional realm allows the dogs to perform several purposes in mythologies associated with death.

Guards at the Gates

Dale-Green writes: "The most famous and the most terrifying of all mythical dogs is undoubtedly the Hell-hound" or "Hound of Hell" (85). The Hound of Hell guards the gate to the Underworld by keeping the dead from escaping and often devouring those souls doomed to enter. In some cases, the dog literally tears the dead apart, while in other myths,

The Dog as Guide, Guard and Healer

Statue of Hades and Cerberus, his dog (Ministry of Culture, Archaeological Museum of Heraklion, Hellenic Ministry of Culture, Archaeological Heraklion Museum, H.O.C.R.D.; Aviad Bublil, CC BY-SA 3.0).

5. The Nature of Dog Archetypal Images

the dog drags the dead into more allegorical jaws of death. According to Dale-Green, "Hell-hound myths probably spring from the dog's lupine ancestry. In Norse mythology, the 'jaws of death' are those of Fenris—a cosmic wolf, son of Loki, the Devil" (85).

In some literature, Fenrir and Garm, the bloodstained guard dog of Hel, appear identical. The wolf and the dog blend into one terrifying creature, guardian of Hel, and attack dog for evil at the end of the world. According to John Lindow, Garm appears only a few times in Norse poetry, including three stanzas concerning the battle at the end of the world (134). As this time approaches, with the battle of the gods versus evil, Garm will break his chains joining the "forces of evil and destruction against the gods" (Dale-Green 85). This defining moment is described "in *Vóluspá*," stanzas 44, 49, and 58: "Gram howls loudly before Gnipahellir. / The bond will burst, and the wolf run free" (134).

A significant contrast exists between Fenrir, in Norse mythology, and Cerberus, guardian of Hades in Greek mythology. Fenrir "has two roles in the mythology: one as the maimer of Týr early in the mythic present, the other as the killer of Odin at Ragnarók. In between, he lies bound" (Lindow 111). According to Dale-Green, "The gods chained and fettered Fenris" to a high rocky cliff, "where they left him to the end of the world" (85). When Fenris breaks free, he rushes toward battle seeking revenge, "his upper fangs scraping heaven and his lower raking the earth" (85). He seeks to destroy both the realm of the gods in the heavens and the realm of mortals on earth. After a fierce battle between Odin, "the king of the gods," and Fenris, the king is "killed and devoured by the avenging wolf" (85).

The relationships between people and dogs or gods and dogs offer both positive and sometimes negative repercussions in mythology. This duality exists in mythological stories, framed in the past and within the physical world in the present. Both Garm and Cerberus are not associated with positive aspects of protection after death or as guides through the underworld. Far from that, they represent destruction, doom, and terror.

Three-headed Cerberus stalks through the underworld guarding the gates to Hades and rarely suffers humiliation, except in one notable exception discussed below. Even though chained, Cerberus moves though his realm sitting next to his master, the king of Hades, patrolling the underworld and guarding shades, spirits, and ghosts of the dead from trying to escape. Cerberus suffers few challenges to his supremacy throughout literature. As noted, Fenrir appears in only a few works of Norse literature. Cerberus parades though numerous works of Greek and Roman literature from the time of the Homeric poems, in eighth century BCE, through Ovid's *Metamorphoses* and Virgil's epic *Aeneid* in the first century CE. A selection of four different works highlights Cerberus' fame, ferociousness, and deviousness.

Descriptions in literature and representations in art depict Cerberus "as a three-headed dog with a serpent's tail, mane of snakes, and a lion's claws" (Atsma 1). Other works describes a gigantic dog with fifty heads with some of the heads appearing as snakes along his back. Leach writes: "Possibly the monstrous form developed from the most ancient of all concepts of the hell gate: the gaping jaws of death, or hell itself, personified" (137).

Leach presents another perspective concerning the earliest incarnations of Cerberus. She notes that prior to classical writings and later myths, Cerberus is not completely ferocious. Rather, he has the reputation of being "a gentle creature with the rightful residents of Hades," never attacking the newcomers with the exception of those trying to escape (Leach 135). Instead, he reserves his wrath and terror "for the *living* trying to get in" (135-136). Orpheus, Aeneas, and Hercules, among others, attest to this fact. In some stories, Cerberus keeps watch "at the mouth of the Acheron, and according to others at the gates of Hades" (Atsma 1). In addition, he guards the halls of the king and queen of the underworld, Hades and Persephone. In such situations, Cerberus guards his territory and master from *living* intruders, a natural inclination of both earthly as well as mythological dogs.

Whatever his earlier redeeming characteristics may be, his later incarnations evoke dread and terror. Cerberus exists both as a terrifying visual form in art and as a personification of pitiless and devious wrath in literary descriptions. In some later works, the positive aspects of physical dogs, such as enthusiastic greetings, are actually contorted into his devious reactions toward people. For instance, a passage in the Greek poem *Theogony* summarizes his deviousness. Cerberus, "has no pity, but a vile stratagem: / as people go in / he fawns on all, with actions of his tail / and both ears, / but he will not let them go back out, but lies in wait for them / and eats them up, when he catches / any going back through the gates" (Hesiod 770-774).

Four stories illustrate different methods and enticements to disarm Cerberus. In these stories, the living employ activities familiar to earthly beings—the enticements of food, the soothing tranquility of beautiful music, and the coercion of physical strength. Aeneas and Psyche enlist food and Orpheus soothing music to pass by Cerberus into and back out of the underworld. In his twelfth labor, Hercules utilizes a combination

5. The Nature of Dog Archetypal Images

Stories From Virgil, with Twenty Illustrations from Pinelli's Designs-Cerberus (GetArchive).

of food and physical strength to drag a chained Cerberus up from the underworld.

Both Psyche and Hercules face impossible tasks that involve trips to Hades and passage by Cerberus. In the myth of Cupid and Psyche, Psyche faces the anger of Venus who imposes "the ultimate task—descent into the realms of Hades" (Morford et al. 221). Venus orders Psyche "to take a box to Persephone and ask her to send back in it a fragment of her own beauty" (221). In *The Golden Ass*, Apuleius stresses the importance of barley cakes to disarm Cerberus. After crossing the river Acteron, Psyche "must disarm him by offering him a cake as his spoils and proceed to Persephone" (qtd. in Atsma 7). On her return trip, Psyche must give Cerberus "the remaining cake to neutralize the dog's savagery" (qtd. in Atsma 7). The enticement of food offered as a bribe works well with both mythological dogs in the ancient past and domestic dogs in the contemporary present.

Hercules and Orpheus also seek to descend as the living into the underworld, to the temple of Hades and Persephone, to achieve their goals and return back to the earth. In order to attain immortality among the gods on Olympus, Hercules faces 12 dangerous and impossible tasks, as imposed by the Mycenaen King Eurystheus. The final labor, and most

The Dog as Guide, Guard and Healer

difficult according the Hercules, involves bringing Cerberus up from the underworld alive to King Eurystheus (Morford et al. 575). When he stands before the king of Hades and demands Cerberus, he receives this reply: "He is yours if you can master him without using your club or your arrows" (Dale-Green 92). Hercules finds Cerberus chained at the gates to the underworld. With Athena's help, and in several versions a narcotic cake, Hercules half drags and carries him across the River Styx, bound in chains "up to the earth" and delivers him to King Eurystheus (Dale-Green 92). Hercules later returns Cerberus to Hades, uninjured, expect perhaps for his pride.

While Hercules wields superhuman strength, Orpheus charms Cerberus with mesmerizing music from his lyre. Orpheus, a legendary musician and poet, must pass by Cerebus in order to rescue his wife Eurydice, who accidentally died from a snake bite on earth. As Orpheus plays his lyre, Virgil describes the moment: "Still more: the very house of Death and deepest abysses of Tartarus were spellbound, and the Eumenides (Erinyes) with livid snakes entwined in their hair; Cerberus stood agape and his triple jaws forgot to bark" (qtd. in Atsma 4).

Aeneas, in Virgil's *Aeneid* faces his own challenges with Cerberus. Accompanied by Sibyl, "priestess of Apollo," Aeneas is ferried by Charon across the River Styx where they encounter Cerberus (Morford et al. 379). Day-Lewis describes this encounter in his translation of the *Aeneid*, Book 6, 417: "Huge Cerberus, monstrously couched in a cave confronting them, made the whole region echo with his three-throated barking" (qtd. in Atsma 4). In response, Sibyl tossed him a cake "infused with sedative drugs. The creature, crazy with hunger, opened its three mouths, gobbled the bait" and fell asleep, "sprawled out on the ground, the whole length of its cave kennel" (qtd. in Atsma 4). With the watch dog neutralized, Aeneas and Sibyl "strode rapidly from the bank of the river (Styx) of no return" (qtd. in Atsma 4).

In other situations, mythical dogs, while relentless, can also be tempted by food just like earthly dogs. As the dogs track their prey, in some cases, they can be diverted by tasty treats. White notes that the dog as hell hound tracks down and "even devours the errant dead" (2392). In order to possibly avoid this fate, often the dead are buried with a cake to distract the dogs "as in the case of the Sárameya—the twin dogs of the Indian death god Yama" (2392). Ancient Greek funeral practices also included burying a cake or other food "with the dead to sustain them en route to the underworld" (Leach 381). Later this cake became associated with the "honeyed soporific cake" Hercules gave to Cerberus in order to

5. The Nature of Dog Archetypal Images

enter the underworld (381). Leach notes: "By extension a *sop to Cerberus* is any conciliatory bribe" (381).

The responses of human, gods, and dogs in mythological stories often illustrate similar aspects within relationships between people and dogs in the physical world. Archetypal characteristics of guide, guard, and healer weave throughout these interactions. For instance, characteristics of guide and healer influence psychological practices and healing rituals in the evolving human/dog bond. These characteristics influence the journey of people and dogs from the ancient past to more contemporary times. Links with healing rituals and surprising progressions continue to unfold along this journey framed by physical and spiritual spaces.

6

Ancient Roles

Spiritual and Physical Spaces

Stories concerning dogs often express dualism in both physical roles and archetypal images. Within this context, stories illustrate the liminal nature of dogs as guards at thresholds and guides through spiritual journeys. These interactions influence the cultural developments of relationships between people and dogs, reflecting both positive and sometimes negative aspects in these mythologies. According to the *Oxford American Dictionary and Thesaurus*, dualism is the "division into two opposed or contrasted aspects, such as good and evil or mind and matter" (392). In addition, dualism is described as "the quality or state of having two parts, elements, or aspects" (392). Numerous myths and legends explore the roles of dogs concerning good versus evil, life versus death, hope versus fear, and light versus dark.

For instance, numerous "hell hounds" associated with the Wild Hunt, Greek Cerberus, and Norse Garm depict negative aspects of these roles. In contrast, Anubis provides positive and negative influences as guard and guide in Egyptian society. Dogs associated with Hinduism and ancient Near East traditions also exist in dual roles of guard and guide. In these capacities, dogs provide essential roles within the spiritual and earthly realms. These roles are framed within the perceptions of people concerning the functions of dogs in the spiritual world and the realities of their interactions with physical dogs on earth. These perceptions are expressed in rituals within cultures and literature throughout the development of human history.

An in-depth look at Anubis, the Egyptian canine god, illustrates the convergence of both the temporal and spiritual importance of dogs in many ancient cultures. The domestic dog and Anubis, the jackal-headed god of afterlife, play a central role in Egyptian cultural life and mythology. As in many cultures, domestic dogs serve the functions of guard, and also provide companionship. Dogs also hold "a key position in Egyptian

6. Ancient Roles

religion, being closely associated with the gods Anubis and Wepwawet, deities related to travel" (Ikram "Man's best friend" 300). This travel exists in the temporal world, as travel through the desert, and in the spiritual world, as travel from the earthly life to the next life.

The complex temporal and spiritual relationship with Anubis includes the desire for protection in travel and as a guide in the afterlife, but also includes concerns about the physical burial of the dead in earthly life. Jackals and wild dogs living on the edges of settlements "were carrion eaters, who might dig up shallowly buried corpses" (Pinch 104). Egyptians strove to placate Anubis, deemed "the lord of the Sacred Land," the desert cemeteries, in order to avert such a "horrible end for their dead" (104).

Pinch describes Anubis as "the terrifying canine god," usually "shown as a seated black jackal or as a man with the head of a jackal or wild dog" (104). According to Pinch, as "Master of Secrets" he possessed "gruesome secrets" of the embalming process, the physical preparation associated with mummification, especially the bandaging of mummies, and with the Opening of the Mouth Ritual (104). This ceremony was performed to return the senses, enjoyed in earthly life, to the dead in the afterlife (104).

During the Old Kingdom, images of Anubis, the most important funerary deity, could be carved at tomb entrances "to warn off grave robbers at a time when no other deities could be shown in non-royal tombs" (Pinch 104). Anubis, the multi-tasking canine god, serves the functions of guide into the afterlife and guard of the dead within earthly life. Most of the epitaphs associated with Anubis link him with burial rituals and death, including the description "the dog who swallows millions" (Pinch 104).

As Pinch observes, "One of the most famous of all Egyptian images" involves Anubis in the vignette for Spell 125 of the *Book of the Dead* (28). This collection of more than 190 spells "was not the central holy book of Egyptian religion" but rather a "series of manuals to assist the spirits of the elite dead to achieve and maintain a full afterlife" (26). In this vignette, Horus and Anubis weigh "the heart of the deceased person" against "the feather that represents Maat, the goddess of truth. If the heart was found to be heavy with sin, it would be devoured by a monster" (28). In all of his capacities, Anubis personifies a multifaceted canine god, both essential to Egyptian life and feared in Egyptian life.

In Hindu mythology, two mythical dogs also perform several functions associated with death. The two dogs of Yama, the Hindu god of death, "seem to serve the threefold function of messenger, *psychopomp*, and guardian. As messenger, they pick out those chosen to die and as *psychopomp*, they conduct souls to the City of Yama" (Leach 143). They also

The Dog as Guide, Guard and Healer

"serve as guardians only to prevent the wicked from entering" (143). In this mythology, "the sun- and moon-dogs of Yama," guard "the gates of the kingdom of the dead by day and by night" (Dale-Green 89). The dogs are the sons of Saramá, the "watch dog of Indra, king of the gods" (89).

The two watch dogs of Yama and the two watch dogs of the Zoroastrians share similar guard dog duties and some physical attributes. Souls of the dead must pass by the dogs on the path to the City of Yama and over the Chinvat Bridge to the spirit world of Zoroastrians. Literature describes both pairs of dogs as four-eyed. Okunishi notes: "The first record of a four-eyed dog appears in ancient Indo-Iranian culture; it is mentioned in *Rig-Veda*, the ancient Indian sacred text composed during the first millennium BCE" (1). According to White, the term four-eyed refers to "a dog with pronounced markings over its eyes" (2393). He adds: "This doubling of dogs' eyes is not limited to Indian or Indo-Iranian religions" and is associated "with a broader phenomenon of doubling in the symbolism of death" (2393).

Book 10 Hymn XIV, in the *Rig-Veda*, describes the two sons of Saramá: "Run and out speed the two dogs, Saramá's offspring, brindled, four-eyed, upon thy happy pathway. / Draw nigh then to the gracious-minded Fathers where they rejoice in company with Yama" (Okunishi 1-2). This text reveals one of the earliest interactions between the gods and dogs in Indian mythology. Bibek Debroy writes: "In the Hindu tradition, Saramá is the mother of all dogs. She is the dog of the gods. Thus, dogs are known as 'sarameyá's" (ix) .

Another story in the *Rig Veda* (10/108/1–2) provides additional insight into this mythology. In this text, Indra sends Samará, as a messenger, across a great distance including across a dangerous river to a hideout of the *panis*. The *panis* are robbers who have corralled some cattle in their mountain chambers. As previously discussed, sometimes dogs convey messages with no verbal sounds at all, but instead with a quiet presence that senses the imminent future. In other situations, dogs deliver messages by communicating with barks, howling, and other verbal "warnings" to intruders and robbers, both literal and mythical. The story of Saramá, the *panis*, and the cows illustrates the literal and metaphorical characteristics of the relationships of people and dogs, or dogs and gods. The earthly characteristics of dogs including loyalty, fearlessness, devotion to their master, and messenger are all present.

Saramá's dialogue with the *panis* reflect these attributes. The *panis* first inquire what has brought her to their hideout and how did she cross the dangerous Rasa River? Samará responds: "I come appointed messenger of Indra, seeking your ample stores of wealth, O Panis" (Griffin qtd. in Debroy 70). The *panis* respond asking who is Indra and why did he not come himself, rather than send an envoy (and perhaps thinking a dog envoy no less). Samará warns them that Indra, her master, "can never be destroyed. He is the one who destroys everything" (Debroy 72). She adds: "The deep waters of the river could not run counter to the wishes of my master" (72).

Samará warns the *panis* they must give up the cows and that they will be no match for the forces of Indra. The *panis* switch tactics, imploring Saramá to stay and offering her a share of their riches. "Turn thee not back, for thou shalt be our sister" (Griffin qtd. in Debroy 71). Loyal Saramá rejects the offer, warning them that when she tells Indra what has happened, "he will come and invade you. He will deliver the cows" (Debroy 73). She adds: "O *panis*! Flee far away. Free the cows and let them go up to heaven. Brihaspati will receive the cows that you have secreted so well" (73).

Samará faces a task she will achieve no matter how treacherous the journey or dangerous the river she must cross. Her loyalty to her master Indra is unshakable, whether challenged by verbal taunts from the *panis* or bribes of wealth. Samará's task represents both a literal and a metaphorical challenge to herd the cows, desired by Indra, to safety by warning the *panis* they must release the cows so they can go "up to the heaven" (Debroy 73).

According to Debroy, "The word Samará comes from the root *sri*, meaning to run. Therefore, Samará is something that is fleet of foot" (74) In a metaphorical interpretation, Samará represents "Usa, or dawn" and in contrast, the *panis* stand "for the forces of darkness" (74). Debroy adds: "Night, or the force of darkness, has stolen the rays of light (the Sun) in the form of cows and Saramá or Usa has been sent as a messenger to retrieve them" (73–74). From this perspective, the story of Saramá and the *panis* represents a metaphorical struggle between light and darkness, framed within visual images of nature.

While Saramá and her sons play an important role in several stories, generally the dog was not significant "to the people of the Rg Veda" (Debroy 67). In contrast, "the ancient Iranians made it a sacred animal" (67). Aspects of Zoroastrianism, an ancient religion of Iran, illustrate the importance of relationships between people and dogs in life, rituals associated with death, and the duality between good and evil in both life and death. Richard Foltz notes that Zoroastrianism, "one of the world's oldest surviving religions," emphasizes the importance of interactions between human and non-human animals framed within the duality of good and evil (367). Foltz explains, "All animal species are seen as being in one of two categories—either beneficent or malevolent, aligned either with the forces of good or with the forces of evil in an ongoing cosmic battle" (367).

The origin of this monotheistic tradition is uncertain, shrouded in both the ancient past and a language difficult to interpret (Foltz 367–368). Foltz notes, "There is no general consensus on when or where" Zarathustra, the founding prophetic figure lived, "or even if he existed at all" (Foltz 367–368). The *Gathas*, the earliest sacred text attributed to Zoroaster as he is known in the West, "likely date to sometime in the second millennium BCE" (368). According to Foltz, "The language and structure of the *Gathas*, as well as the pantheon of deities and the type of society they evoke, are very close to that found in the *Rig Veda*" (368).

In these 17 Zoroastrian hymns, the cow is "by far the most prominent and highly revered animal," which highlights the importance of cattle in this ancient Iranian culture (369). Significantly, in these texts "animals in general are described as having souls, and there is no clear hierarchy that places them on a level below that of humans" (Foltz 369). These texts offer one the earliest reflections on whether or not animals do have souls and what might be their place in the pantheon of earthly creatures within the spiritual world. The debate on these questions continues to the present day.

A significant gap exists "between the time, place, and social context of the earliest Zoroastrian texts" and the majority of a sacred text, the *Avesta* (Foltz 370). Classical Zoroastrianism, from the Sasanian period, 224–751 CE, "divides nonhuman animals into 'good' and 'evil' species" (370). Good species, which include the dog, "must be protected at all costs by humans, who are subject to extremely harsh penalties if they abuse them" (370). In later works, "the dog appears more prominently than the cow, ranking next to humans in the 'good' creation" (370). These beliefs help explain the reverence and concern for the welfare of dogs in Zoroastrian society. In addition, these beliefs provide a context for the significance of dogs in rituals and myths concerning death and the journey from death to the spiritual world.

Several traditions concerning dogs illustrate this point. For instance, traditionally "every Zoroastrian household should give food to a dog at least once a day, before feeding humans" (Foltz 371). This portion, "called *chom-e shwa* ('meal for the dog') in Zoroastrian Persian and *kutra`-no bu`k* ('share for the dog') in Gujarati" serves two purposes (371). First, the food provides sustenance for the dog, and secondly, "is seen as being destined for departed souls" (371).

6. Ancient Roles

In a later tradition, if a religious ritual requires two people and only one is present, "a dog may substitute for the second person" (Foltz 370). In other rituals, a dog must be present. For example, Foltz explains "when a Zoroastrian dies, a dog must be brought in to see the corpse before the death can be verified." This ritual called *sag-did*, literally means "dog-seeing" (370). In addition, dogs accompany priests in funeral processions and are also "given funerals like those of humans" (371).

Dogs, in this religious tradition, see into the other world after life and also guard the sacred bridge to the next world. This bridge, known as the Chinvat Bridge, separates the land of the living from the land of the dead. All souls upon death must cross the bridge guarded by two four-eyed dogs. According to a later text in the *Vide'v da'd*, "when the soul crosses the Chinvat to the afterlife it is met with an emanation of its own spiritual self (*dae'na*) in the company of two dogs" (Foltz 371). Boria Sax describes the guard dogs in this manner: "Dogs guarded the Chinvat Bridge that led to the next world, protecting the righteous, but leaving the unrighteous to demons" (179).

According to Sax, "The Zoroastrians believed that dogs were able to see spirits, and so they could protect families from evil powers beyond the awareness of human beings" (179). In appreciation, "families were expected to feed hungry dogs, using ritualistically prepared food. The members of the family then said prayers as the dog ate" (179). These beliefs illustrate another example of the development of the human/dog bond. Dogs serve as protectors of people on earth, seers into the future after life, and guards at the gateway to the next life. In this ancient religious tradition, the sharing of the food and the respect provided dogs in life and death illustrate the intertwined relationship of people and dogs in one of the earliest Near East cultures.

The human/dog bond continues to evolve since ancient times, weaving though cultures and history. Communication methods and behavioral patterns help frame the interactive bond between people and dogs. These interactions move back and forth along interspecies cords of attachment and are influenced by dog archetypal images of guide, guard, and healer.

Loyalty and Devotion: Links from Past to Present

Loyalty and devotion reside at the top of the list formed by attachment and interactive forms of communication between people and dogs. Exploring these bonds, from the perspectives of ancient mythologies and contemporary research, offers insight into the significance and continuity

The Dog as Guide, Guard and Healer

Yudhishthira with a dog as a chariot from heaven arrives (GetArchive).

of the human/dog bond throughout human history. Shared loyalty is one of the most significant aspects within the human/dog bond today as well as in mythologies of ancient cultures.

6. Ancient Roles

According to Lynette Hart and Mariko Yamamoto, "Certain traits make dogs ideally suited to be human companions" (251). These traits include loyalty and devotion. Hart and Yamamoto observe that "dogs develop specific attachments for individuals and remain near or in physical contact with their owners as if attached by an invisible cord" (251). They also note that "even adult dogs can form these attachments quickly to a new person" (251). These observations highlight two important behavioral aspects of the human/dog bond. First, they express the consistency of a dog's loyalty to an individual and secondly, that cords of attachment are not necessarily predicated on long term exposure to the individual. Rather, these attachments reside within a bond not created only by present circumstances and benefits nor familiarity from the past.

For instance, news coverage during natural disasters provides examples of personal stories illustrating this bond. Ancient stories and contemporary news coverage highlight situations where dogs will not abandon their human counterparts and where humans will not abandon their dogs. Loyalty, during times of crisis, is not a new theme in the history of relationships between people and dogs. In ancient mythologies, dogs serve as guides and guards during periods of physical and mental crisis. This theme is present throughout the history of human and dog interactions.

Numerous stories and legends exist in mythology concerning the loyalty between people and dogs. Leach observes that some legends concerning dogs occur "because of the fame of their masters" (231). She adds, however, that most dogs "have been immortalized because of their own exceptional cleverness or prowess or courage or faithfulness" (231). Many of the most famous stories involve the faithful dog waiting for their master or mistress to return from extended travels (231). According to Leach, "recognition of a long-absent master who returns in disguise and is unrecognized by all save the aged, loving dog" is one of the motifs discussed in Stith Thompson's *Motif-Index of Folk Literature* (231).

The three stories below illustrate dual facets of loyalty, both loyalty from dogs to humans and from humans to dogs. In the first story, the dog chooses to share his existence with humanity, represented by a Penobscot cultural hero. In the second story from *The Odyssey*, Argus chooses to wait throughout his life, bonded by an invisible cord of faithfulness to Odysseus. The third story from the *Mahabharata* illustrates the interactive bonds between Yudhishthira and a little dog where they both make choices framed by loyalty.

According to Leach, Long Hair, a hero in the Penobscot Indian culture, is credited with domestication of the dog (27). Leach writes: "When

The Dog as Guide, Guard and Healer

Long Hair asked the animals which ones would live with men, they all walked away in anger—all except the dog, who said he would share the lot of man, good and bad" (27). Long Hair rewards the dog's loyalty by saying "that all other animals would run when he barked" (27).

In *The Odyssey*, Argus waits for 19 years for the return of Odysseus. Upon his return, Odysseus, dressed in rags, is unrecognizable to his family but Argus recognizes him, bonded to him throughout those years (Leach 231). Neglected and covered in vermin, Argus could not stand, but "raised his head and wagged his tail" and "died in his weakness from joy at the sight of him" (231). This famous story reflects both the invisible bond that connects a dog to their companion as well as the foundation of love and loyalty within that bond.

The loyalty of waiting faithfully for a loved one and the loyalty of not leaving behind the one loved often reinforces the bond between people and dogs. Love and loyalty, associated with all types of journeys, exists throughout history between people and dogs. Not only heroes and wanderers share in the joy of returning from a journey, whether a day or much longer and being greeted by their dog or dogs.

In the *Mahabharata*, the journey of Yudhishthira and a little dog unfolds during a dream. The story begins as Yudhishthira, together with his four brothers and their wife Draupadi, are on a long journey walking toward heaven. They are "walking north over a great desert of salt and white sand beyond the Himalaya, where the sun's hollow rays had sucked up every drop of water" (Buck 363). First, Draupadi dies, falling "silently to the ground" (363). At that point, Yudhishthira looks down at his feet and sees a "small brown dog walking, panting beside him" (363). Their journey continues and one after another all of his brothers die. Only Yudhishthira and the little dog remain and they trudge onward, climbing toward heaven.

Suddenly, "The drums of heaven thundered" (Buck 365). Indra, the "Lord of the Gods" appears in his chariot and settles "down next to Yudhishthira" (365). Indra then says *"Namas*. We bow to you. Get in; I've come to take you from this death-desert" (365). Yudhishthira replies, "this little dog who is my last companion must also go" (365). Indra responds that no, Yudhishthira "cannot enter heaven with a dog" (365). Yudhishthira must leave the dog for "He is unholy and has no soul." (365). At this point, Yudhishthira replies, "He is devoted to me and looks to me for protection" (365). Yudhishthira will not abandon the dog who has been a loyal companion and in turn needs protection. Indra cannot comprehend this position exclaiming "Don't you understand? *You have won heaven!*

6. Ancient Roles

Immortality and prosperity and happiness in all direction are yours. Only leave that animal and come with me; that will not be cruel" (365).

Yudhishthira will not abandon his loyal companion even if this decision jeopardizes his chances for all the riches Indra offers. Instead, Yudhishthira confirms that the land where they are lies still within his kingdom. He replies to Indra, "I do not turn away my dog; I turn away from you. I will not surrender a faithful dog to you" (Buck 365). He adds "Whoever comes to me from fright or from disaster or from friendship—I will never give him up" (365). In his choice, Yudhishthira highlights the values of loyalty, compassion, and protection.

Yet, there is still more to this story. Suddenly, the little dog no longer lies at Yudhishthira's feet but has transformed into his father, Dharma, the God of Justice (Buck 366, 415). Dharma explains that he has followed Yudhishthira across the desert, taking the form of a dog. He says, "You have compassion for all creatures, and that is not weak but strong, and what you believe in you have defended to heaven's gate" (Buck 366). This story, written over 2000 years ago, offers a compelling message for today concerning loyalty and companionship. The desire to protect the weak, to reward loyalty, and to value companionship, through both adversity and happiness, are worthy attributes found not only in human interactions but also in interactions between people and dogs.

Sanctuaries and Rituals

Stories couched in comparative mythology often illustrate links between dog archetypal images and actual practices in ancient societies. Many of these interactions also resonate though contemporary relationships between dogs and people. For instance, dogs often serve as liminal guides at the crossroads of life decisions and provide encouragement and comfort in times of illness and stress. Dogs and people possess a bond framed by loyalty and companionship as they traverse their journeys together.

The association of dogs with spiritual and healing practices occurs in mythological stories and cultures from ancient to contemporary times. For instance, the ancient Egyptian city of Hardai became known as Cynopolis (City of Dogs) due to the number of temples associated with Anubis, the worship of dogs, and its dog cemetery (Leach 251). Significantly, the importance of dogs extended to living dogs as well as offerings to Anubis. Not only the canine god Anubis, but also living dogs were worshiped.

The Dog as Guide, Guard and Healer

A sculpture of Gula, Mesopotamian deity of healing (CC0 1.0 Universal).

In Cynopolis, dogs were considered sacred animals, "venerated, honored, specially fed, mummified, and given special burial" (Leach 173).

6. Ancient Roles

Several other cultures in the ancient Near East "associated dogs with healing deities such as Eshmun in Phoenicia and Gula in Mesopotamia" (Miller 492). One premise for this association involves the healing aspects of dogs licking wounds. Stager offers this hypothesis concerning the Phoenicians: "Presumably the dog became associated with healing because of the corrective powers evident from licking its own wounds or sores" (qtd. in Miller 492).

Tallay Ornan observes the dog's attribution "to a healing goddess is explained by the fact that the saliva of canines, like that of other mammals, has medicinal properties which work like antibiotics" (18). In addition to healing attributes, the dog serves as Gula's symbol, companion, and protector for homes and families. In Isin, located south of present-day Baghdad, "archaeologists have uncovered a temple complex dedicated to Gula," and called "the *e-ur-gi-ra* or 'dog house,' with plaques and figurines of dogs found in the vicinity" (Miller 492). In the area 33 dog burials were "found in a ramp leading to the temple" (491). These dogs were buried "in shallow pit graves just as Ashkelon" (492).

Ornan also notes: "The connections between Isin, the cult of Gula, and the dog are corroborated by the discovery of actual dog burials, dating to ca. 1000 BCE, at the goddess's shrine at Isin" (14). In addition, "dog figurines dedicated to the goddess" were found at other Babylonian sites, "such as Aqar-Quf (Dur-Kurigalzu), Nippur and Sippar" (14). These discoveries highlight the importance of dogs in rituals associated with the worship of Gula.

According to Leach, the dog functions as both a watch and guard for the goddess and also as a symbol of Gula. She notes the dog seems to represent a double symbol "possibly as vehicle and certainly as representing her guardian aspect, her protective role (as physician and healer) of families and homes" (20). For instance, a Babylonian magic ritual, performed by priests for protection against demons, illustrates these dual capacities. This ritual "assured the house-holder that 'the great dog sits at the gate,' and that Gula herself sat at the door" (20–21). This duality expresses both the archetypal image of healer and the physical image of guard.

Ornan also notes that "in addition to being a divine attribute and symbol in the imagery" of Gula, the dog appears "as a guardian image" during the periods 2000–1000 BCE (18). Not only does the dog appear in imagery such as figurines and tablets, but skeletons of dogs have been found under doorways (18). The duality of dogs as guards exists both in the mythical symbol of Gula and the physical presence of dogs at the actual thresholds to homes.

The Dog as Guide, Guard and Healer

In other capacities the dog also serves dual functions as her symbol and physical presence. For instance, "Ancient Babylonian boundary stones frequently show Gula seated on a throne with a dog beside her" (Leach 21). Sometimes the dog carries the throne and goddess on his back, and in other cases, the dog sits alone as a representation of the goddess (21). In addition, Gula's dog, with its prominent tongue, presents both a visual symbol in literature and physical presence in sculpture. Leach observes that on stone, monument and seal imagery, Gula's dog "even when he appears alone, is unmistakable" (21). One reason for this visual connection is that "the healing tongue of the dog, recognized from most ancient times, makes him the patent symbol of the great physician and healing mother" (Leach 21). These images transcend physical reality to represent the archetypal symbol of Gula as healer.

The Babylonian god Marduk also shares similarities with Gula concerning dogs as companions and as symbol. Dale-Green describes the dog "as the sacred symbol of Marduk, the Babylonian and Chaldean god of healing" (133). In addition, M.H. Farbridge "states that in pre–Babylonian Marduk myths, the solar Marduk was sometimes represented by the symbol of a dog" (qtd. in Leach 21). Leach also notes that four dogs accompany Marduk (21).

The sick evoked incantations to both Marduk and Gula, seeking "help against disease—demons whose grasp meant death; and they awoke individuals stricken with sickness to new life" (Dale-Green 134). Both deities were also known as "Restorer of the dead to life" (134). These descriptions highlight aspects of ancient healing practices associated with surrendering to sleep or death, and awakening to life or relief from sickness. In many ancient cultures, the ill sought cures in rituals involving healing practices associated with sleep notably in temples and other sanctuaries dedicated to healing deities. These practices known as incubations were "healing sleeps in which patient received visions of the god" (Dale-Green 135).

The two divine physicians, Gula, the Babylonian goddess, and Asclepius, the Greek god, also share many associations and connections in the ancient world. For instance, both deities are associated with healing and doctors, including physical and mythical practices involving dogs. In these contexts, dogs serve as both companions and symbols of healing. Tallay Ornan states that "indeed, it is possible that the allusion to dogs in the cult of Asklepios originated in the worship of the Mesopotamian goddess of healing" (18). Furthermore, B. Halpern suggests "that the cult of Gula was transmitted via the coastal city of Asheklon, where a huge

6. Ancient Roles

fifth-century BCE dog cemetery was uncovered, and that the very name of the Greek god derives from the name of the city" (qtd. in Ornan 18).

Asclepius, the god, undergoes a metamorphosis over time. At first, up until the times of Homer, he is considered a mortal physician, then a demi-god or demon, and later an Apollonian deity. Early on he obtains his animal attributes, the snake and dog, and later the cock. Meier notes that "probably Asclepius took over the dog from his father Apollo—Apollo-Maleatas—who was a mighty hunter and lover of dogs and whose sanctuary on the Cynortion at Epidaurus was called 'Cyon' (dog)" (19).

Healing Practices and Dog Residents

The physical healing practices and mythical rituals involving dogs in temples and other sanctuaries provide insight into the importance of dogs within ancient cultures. Dogs were used in healing practices since people believed that being licked by a dog, especially in areas containing sores or lesions, could promote healing. Later, these beliefs and practices associated with dogs occur in Greek temples dedicated to Asclepius. Dogs were kept in the temples located at Epidaurus, "Athens, Rome, Piraeus, and at Lebene in Crete" (Dale-Green 135). In both Greece and Rome, these special

Care and healing (Free Range Stock).

healing dogs were known as cynotherapists (Debory 12). The definition of cynosure is "a person or thing that is the center of attention or admiration" (*Oxford* 310). The word comes from the Greek word *kunosoura,* meaning dog tail (310). The dogs kept in temples "licked the wounds of the sick and dying, especially at the temple of Asklepios at Epidaurus. Evidently there were miraculous recoveries" (Debroy 12).

Discoveries of dog figurines and images of veneration of dogs highlight the interconnections of dogs and people in early healing and spiritual practices. In the ancient world, people address healing from both a mythical perspective as well as with physical practices. The importance of dogs is evident in their association with healing practices in ancient Near Eastern and Mediterranean cultures.

The Sanctuary of Asclepius at Epidaurus is one of the greatest sanctuaries of healing in the ancient Greek world. Since the early Mycenaean period, sixteenth century BCE, inhabitants and pilgrims worship deities associated with curative powers in the region of Epidaurus. Archaeologist Angeliki Charitonidou writes that early on the worship focuses on the deity Maleatas, and later the Olympian god Apollo (9). She notes that from the fifth century BCE extending until the fourth century CE "the god Asklepios held first place in the religious life of Epidaurus" (9).

According to Charitonidou, "A host of believers sought refuge in his Asklepieion (as all sanctuaries of Asclepios in ancient Greece were called) seeking their salvation" (7). In addition, the importance of Asklepion sanctuaries extended throughout the ancient world. While the influence of Asklepion sanctuaries was wide spread, Epidaurus possesses the most fame and longevity. As noted by Thrámer, "there were in the whole of the ancient world about 410 Asklepion sanctuaries, almost all of which were linked to Epidaurus" (qtd. in Meier 17).

In these sanctuaries, dogs, both their physical and their symbolic presences, play significant roles in healing practices. These practices represent an early example of treatments addressing the physical and psychological aspects of illnesses and injuries. Those who journey to these sanctuaries often seek both physical and mental healing, but also respite from the surrounding physical world.

The type of healing that occurs at Epidaurus is called dream incubation (Tick, *Practice* 4). According to the psychiatrist and psychotherapist C.A. Meier, "Incubation's effectiveness is very closely bound up with the importance accorded to dreams" (iii). Greeks in ancient times, especially during the earlier periods, felt dreams represented something that really happened; dreams were not considered an imaginary experience (iii). Due

6. Ancient Roles

to their perceptions of dreams as existing in reality, "people felt it necessary to create the conditions that cause dreams to happen" (iii). In pursuit of these goals, people selected sites conducive to both physical and mental preparation for healing rituals and subsequent cures from illness.

C.A. Meier observes that in classical times people viewed "sickness as the effect of a divine action, which could be cured only by a god or another divine action" (2). He adds: "The inner connections between the divine sickness and divine physician formed the core of the art of healing in the ancient world" (7).

People of the ancient Greek and Roman world selected dramatic settings, most surrounded by scenic woods with abundant supplies of water for healing sanctuaries. The woods became sacred groves associated with deities and the springs provided water for cleansing rituals and spiritual healings (Meier 68–69). The selections of such sites served physical and mythical functions. The natural attributes of these sites and the development of the physical environments within the sanctuaries created surroundings to help achieve healing and renewal. Edward Tick writes: "People from all over the ancient world who sought healing from dream incubation in Asklepion sanctuaries had severe physical, psychological, or spiritual ailments that had proven intractable to other treatments" (*Practice* 4).

The rituals for preparation involved seeking clarity and purity of both mind and body. Charitonidoa notes that pilgrims to the sanctuary "were supposed to know that they were entering a holy place to surrender themselves, body and soul, to the mercy of the god" (13). Rituals involved cleansing at the Sacred Fountain and offering a sacrifice to "Apollo and Asklepious" (13). With preparations completed, priests led the pilgrims into the Abato, where they would spend the night awaiting the dream and the visit from Asklepios (13).

According to Tick, "The abaton was the sleeping chamber"; the name literally means "the place not to be trodden" (*Practice* 4). The seeker was placed in a "womblike chamber" and waited for hours or days for a healing dream or vision where Asclepius appeared. At some point, Asclepius, who could be disguised as a god, bearded man, boy, snake or dog, appeared and touched the afflicted part of the person, sometimes offering advice and providing instructions (*Practice* 5). Tick observes, "Thus a cure was effected. It was the epiphany, the visit of the god through a dream, that healed" (*Practice* 5).

Over time the concept of healing at Epidaurus was transplanted to other locations throughout Greece and the ancient world. The transfer of the cult to new localities "was almost always effected by transporting one of the sacred serpents of Epidaurus to the new location" (Meier 10). In many mythologies, serpents, which shed their skins, represent a symbol of the renewal of life and are associated with both water and the earth. The serpents create an interaction in healing practices involving the exterior physical world of the earth and the inner spiritual world.

Within these sanctuaries, what roles do dogs play in the healing practices? Meier observes that "sources constantly emphasize that Asclepius cares for *so'ma kai psyche*," both body and mind ... and that "bodily sickness and psychic defect were for the ancient world an inseparable unity" (iv). Meier's observations reflect the intertwined aspects of both physical and psychological conditions on illness. In the case of Asclepius, dogs take an active role in the mythology associated with dreams and the licking of wounds and sores to promote healing.

The concept of a dog's healing powers from licking wounds continues from the ancient past up to the present day. In contemporary times, the French address the practice with this saying: "*Langye de chien, langue de médecin*" which translates to "A dog's tongue is a doctor's tongue" (Coren 3). According to Stanley Coren, "wound licking is an instinctive response in humans and many other animals to an injury" (2).

Archetypal imagery of guide, guard, and healer, in the relationships of people and dogs, are both interactive and accumulative throughout history. This accumulative nature is one of the major reasons that the bond between people and dogs continues to expand within the context of human development. Mythological stories about dogs provide psychological and spiritual connections framed within the earthly realm of the living and the spiritual realm of the dead. The importance of these connections in the evolution of the bond between dogs and people cannot be overstated. This book now turns to consider the role of dogs as guides and healers in contemporary cultures.

7

Psychological Journeys
Bridges Between the Past and Present

In the book *Healing Dreams and Ritual*, Meier discusses the different ways dreams are viewed in ancient Greece, beginning with Homer and continuing with Plato and Aristotle, whom he calls "the most powerful authority on dreams" (113). He notes that almost all Homeric dreams come from Zeus and that from ancient literature ... "it is apparent that everybody was convinced that dreams were messages from the gods" (112). This belief represents a founding concept in the development of the Asklepion practices in the healing sanctuaries throughout Greece.

Meier also discusses Plato's concept that dream content is determined by a particular part of the psyche that is active. According to Plato's *Phaedrus* 250, "in sleep the soul is freed from its tomb (the body) whereby it is sensitized and so is able to perceive and converse with higher beings, a thought that was also held by the Pythagoreans" (Meier 112). Aristotle adds to Plato's concepts noting that doctors can predict reactions in the physical world based on the dreams of patients. According to Aristotle, "during sleep the dreamer is much more sensitive to small disturbances of an organic nature. A skilled doctor can therefore predict illness, cure, or death from such dreams" (Meier 114). In addition, dreamers can gain knowledge concerning "the future actions" of significant people in their lives, and possible future courses of action to take, based on the study of their dreams (114).

How do these observations relate to contemporary psychology? What are the connections between the study of dreams in ancient cultures and the archetypal characteristics of guide and healer in dogs? The connections unfold based on the importance of dreams and the interactive nature of body and soul in some healing practices.

After further discussion of the Greek gods, Meier states: "I am strongly disposed to believe that almost all of the observations of the Greeks on dreams still hold good" (119). He also observes that "it is this chthonic origin of dreams" that survives down to contemporary time "in the practice of incubation" (113). In many healing rituals sleep represents a descent into death, into the depths of an unconsciousness to reality, and into the world of dreams. Subsequently, the patient or pilgrim awakens to rebirth, new awareness, and possibly healing. Scholars continue to explore theories on how the psyche functions during sleep up to the present day.

Although the sanctuaries and the healing practices of Asclepius are set in ancient times, many aspects of his healing methods and temple complexes are applicable to modern-day medicine and places of healing. Tick writes: "The Asklepian tradition says that any condition of the mind, body or spirit can be treated by these holistic practices" ("On Asklepios" 67). He illustrates these ideas in discussing his practice of dream healing, which involves what C.G. Jung calls "big dreams" ("On Asklepios" 68). Although most dreams are "little dreams," sometimes a person can have a big dream... "which is a breakthrough from the collective unconscious or from the transpersonal dimensions" (68). Tick feels "Asklepian healing is a 'particular medical/spiritual practice that combines the principals of both naturopathic medicine and sacred practice'" ("On Asklepios" 69).

According to the *Oxford American Dictionary and Thesaurus*, naturopathy is "a system of alternative medicine including the treatment or prevention of diseases by diet, exercise, and massage rather than by using drugs" (861). Naturopathy seeks to heal through physical practices including touch. In Asklepion sanctuaries, dogs provide a naturopathic and spiritual function through the physical connections of licking the wounds of patients and their spiritual association with Asclepius. During incubation in the abaton, dogs represent the sacred aspects of Asclepius as his companion and often manifestation of the god.

Meier also discusses C.G. Jung's thoughts on healing. He notes: "Jung has empirically discovered something which offers a close point of contact with the ancient healing cults" (127). According to Meier, these facts are as follows: "(1) The human psyche has an autochthonous spiritual function. (2) No patient in the second half of life has been cured without that patient finding an approach to this spiritual function" (127). This statement provides a bold perspective concerning the importance of spiritual and terrestrial connections to the underworld, or death, both physical and psychological. In many ancient mythologies one of the major aspects in healing practices centers around the importance of dreams.

7. Psychological Journeys

Archetypal Imagery and the Theories of Jung

In contemporary times, the nature and importance of dreams are also a focus of C.G. Jung and James Hillman in the practices of analytical

Saint Francis of Assisi (CC0 1.0 Universal).

psychology and archetypal psychology, respectively. Both of these modern psychologists inform their work based on interactions of the psyche with nature as evident in archetypal imagery.

In his work, Jung notes that everyone is connected by their "unconscious humanity" which he calls "the collective unconscious" (*Earth* 14). Jung describes the collective unconscious "as consisting of mythological motifs or primordial images" which he calls "archetypes" (Jung, *Essential* 16). Why is the concept of archetypes important within the human/dog bond? This book proposes that *dog archetypal images* contribute to the interspecies bond between people and dogs. In addition, such images possess a continuous spiritual energy which has evolved within the human/dog relationship, beginning with prehistory and continuing up to the present time. These responses are linked to the experiences of past ancestors extending back into ancient times. As Jung notes, "Our souls as well as our bodies are composed of individual elements which were already present in the ranks of our ancestors. The 'newness' in the individual psyche is an endlessly varied recombination of age-old components" (*Earth* 141).

Jung senses that the presence of archetypes creates a "numinous" impact on the individual which has profound spiritual significance (*Essential* 16). In his writings, Jung addresses the importance of a connection to nature through a framework of "matter and spirit" (*Earth* 80–81). Jung also addresses the connections between nature and psychological studies of the unconscious. He notes that the *lamen naturae* is the natural spirit "which can be now observed through psychological research concerning the unconscious" (81). According to Jung, "consciousness performs a selective function and is itself the product of selection, whereas the collective unconscious is simply Nature—and since Nature contains everything it also contains the unknown. It is beyond truth and error, independent of the interference of consciousness" (82). In his writings, Jung considers the existence of people and animals in nature and their mutual existence in the world of the "unknown" (*Memories* 67).

Jung addresses the impact of nature on both individuals and cultures throughout human development. He laments that with the advancement of technology and increased scientific research, people have lost the connection to ancient myths and nature itself. In this process, the ancient myths with their symbolic meanings in nature have been banished as superstitions and misguided stories of uninformed past generations (*Earth* 85). Jung describes how scientific reasoning replaces the symbols of nature as spirit and reduces nature to physical and biological "matter" (85). Jung discounts this reasoning and notes that "nature is not matter only, she is also

7. Psychological Journeys

spirit. Spirit seems to be the inside of things ... the soul of objects" (*Earth* 78). This statement reflects Jung's observation concerning the duality of nature, with nature possessing both physical matter and spiritual impact. Jung addresses this complexity from the perspective of nature's universal impact on the world and nature's personal impact on the individual. How do Jung's concepts of nature, spirit, and the individual psyche provide insights concerning the human/dog bond? The continuity of the bond between people and dogs and the instinctive understanding between these two species are influenced by aspects of these interactive spheres.

Jung also writes about his perspectives concerning the impact of nature within his own life. In the spring of 1957, at 83 years old, Jung agreed to write a memoir of his life. This book, *Memories, Dreams, Reflections* resulted from a collaboration between himself and his editor Aniela Jaffé, who describes their collaboration in the following manner. It was "only after a long period of doubt and hesitation" did he agree to this endeavor (*Memories* v). Jaffé writes: "Jung's distaste for exposing his personal life to the public eye was well known" (v). She adds: "It had been proposed that the book be written not as a 'biography,' but in the form of an 'autobiography,' with Jung himself as the narrator" (vii). At first, Jaffé asked questions and recorded Jung's replies. Their collaboration proceeded, with Jung writing some chapters and Jaffé utilizing the recordings of their conversations to supplement the chapters he wrote, and to expand "his sometimes terse allusions" (vii). In this manner, she compiled the chapters of the manuscript which Jung reviewed and approved, sometimes "correcting passages" or adding new material (viii).

Several of his reflections and experiences invoke the importance of nature and the impact of nature on the individual and the universal intertwined existences of people and animals throughout history. In this book, Jung also reveals his personal thoughts concerning God and nature. Jaffé observes: "This book is the only place in his extensive writings in which Jung speaks of God and his personal experience of God" (xi).

Jaffé notes, "He did not regard these memoirs as a scientific work, nor even as a book by himself. Rather, he always spoke and wrote of it as 'Aniela Jaffé's project' to which he made contributions" (*Memories* ix). Perhaps, viewing the book's creation from this perspective allowed Jung more freedom to reveal his intensely personal story through his own memories, dreams, and reflections. In addition, Jung specifically requested that the book not "be included in his *Collected Works*" (ix).

Jung describes his autobiography in this manner: "Thus, it is that I have now undertaken in my eighty-third year, to tell my personal myth"

The Dog as Guide, Guard and Healer

(*Memories* 3). He states: "Myth is more individual and expresses life more precisely than does science. Science works with concepts of averages which are far too general to do justice to the subjective variety of an individual life" (*Memories* 3). In this endeavor, Jung turns not to specific dates, places, or even people to tell his story, but rather back to the inner psyche, his own psyche, as well as the collective unconscious of humanity.

The following reflections from *Memories, Dreams, Reflections* illustrate his thoughts concerning the relationships of both individuals and humanity with nature and specifically animals. These observations highlight threads which also run through other works of Jung, notably his writings compiled in the book *The Earth Has a Soul: C.G. Jung on Nature, Technology & Modern Life*. Significantly, these reflections occur at important junctures in Jung's life. The first reflections occur during the time Jung spends in the city for his studies, and the second reflections during his time at his retreat in Bollingen. The third reflections combine aspects of the previous reflections seen through the perspective of time and age. He presents those thoughts at the end of his life.

In 1958, Jung completed the first three chapters of the book which covered "his childhood, school days, and years at the University" through his medical studies (*Memories* vii). During his school years, Jung compares city life with his childhood days in the country, drawing contrasts between that rural environment versus his new perspectives of reality in the city. He writes: "I had grown up in the country, among rivers and woods, among men and animals in a small village bathed in sunlight, with the winds and the clouds moving over it and encompassed by dark night in which uncertain things happened" (60). He adds, "It was no mere locality on the map, but 'God's world,' so ordered by Him and filled with secret meaning" (66).

Jung's thoughts focus on the importance of an interconnected world framed by the earthly terrestrial environment, the celestial movements in the sky, and the changing rhythms of weather. In this context, Jung observes the interactions of people and animals in rural environments and contrasts that world with the realities of city life.

In doing so, Jung provides observations concerning people and animals intertwined in an earthly and spiritual world, not bound by linear time beginning with birth and ending in death. Jung observes that people in the city did not appear to see the connections between both animals and people which transcend daily life. He contrasts this to the awareness and appreciation that people experience within rural environments, living with nature in close proximity to animals of all kinds both wild and

7. Psychological Journeys

domestic. In addition, Jung points out the interconnections of people and animals within the temporal and spiritual worlds and the links that nature provides for these connections.

Jung's observations of the intertwined world of animals and people transcend daily existence. Jung observes that people did not see these connections between themselves and animals. They did not understand "that they dwelt in a unified cosmos, in God's world, in an eternity where everything is already born and everything has already died" (*Memories* 67). These observations reflect the ideas prevalent in many mythologies concerning the continuity of life after death, with life giving away to death and subsequent renewal in new life. Several of the mythologies discussed previously present examples of these ideas.

Jung also provides these observations concerning animals: "Because they are so closely akin to us and share our unknowingness, I loved all warm-blooded animals who have souls like ourselves and with whom so I thought, we have an instinctive understanding" (*Memories* 67). The connections between people and dogs, which they have shared for thousands of years, are based, in part, on some aspects of instinctive understanding. Jung continues: "We experience joy and sorrow, love and hate, hunger and thirst, fear and trust in common—all the essential fortunes of existence with the exception of speech, sharpened consciousness, and science" (*Memories* 67).

While Jung speaks of animals in general, his observations are insightful in viewing the interactions and bond between people and dogs. Scientific researchers continue to explore the bond between these two species and the physiological and psychology aspects of this bond. Some examples of this research are presented in a subsequent chapters of this book.

The second selection from *Memories, Dreams, Reflections* comes from the chapter "The Tower." In 1927 Jung added "a tower like annex" to the stone home he built in Bollingen located on Lake Zurich (224). Jung worked on this retreat, built by hand, from the time he was 48 through the rest of his life (*Earth* 3). This retreat offered proximity to nature as well as privacy for Jung. In this setting, he develops many of his thoughts on the importance of nature in the lives of people and his personal responses to all forms of nature, both terrestrial and celestial. He observes: "At times, I feel as if I am spread out over the landscape and inside things and am myself living in every tree, in the splashing of the waves, in the clouds and the animals that come and go, in the procession of the seasons" (225).

One of Jung's most insightful observations occurs on the last page of *Memories, Dreams, Reflections* in the chapter titled "Retrospect." At the end of his life, Jung writes: "This is old age and a limitation. Yet there is so much that fills me: plants, animals, clouds, day and night, and the eternal in man" (359). Jung speaks of the importance of both earthly and celestial elements as observed in the physical and the spiritual aspects within his own life.

Several of Jung's concepts concerning the interactions of spirit and nature are pertinent to the interactions within the human/dog bond. Examples, in numerous cultures including Egyptian, Greek, Zoroastrian, and Hindu mythologies, illustrate the importance of dogs in the spheres of spirit and nature. In addition, stories involving celestial elements and mythical dogs highlight the interactions both personal and universal between people and dogs. Jung's personal reflections, and specifically his thoughts on archetypal imagery, help illustrate the psychological basis for the bond between people and dogs.

Animals, Nature and Soul Through the Perspectives of Hillman

In his work, James Hillman considers the importance of Jung to the modern field of depth psychology. Hillman notes that in following Jung, he uses "the word *fantasy-image* in the poetic sense, considering images to be the basic givens of psychic life, self-originating, inventive, spontaneous, complete and organized in archetypal patterns" (*Essential* 23). In addition, Hillman moves and expands the perspective of archetypal psychology "to envision the basic nature and structure of the soul in an imaginative way" (23). He describes archetypes "*as the deepest patterns of psychic functioning*, the roots of the soul governing the perspectives we have of ourselves and the world. They are the axiomatic, self-evident images to which psychic life and our theories about it ever return" (23).

As envisioned by Hillman, archetypal psychology exists in a nexus influenced by cultural and mythological concepts of human development, but more significantly the interior world and psyche of the individual. He develops a psychology theory informed by Renaissance philosophers and alchemists and framed in ancient mythology (*Essential* 2). In addition, when he speaks of religion, Hillman seeks to provide a new language for the discussion of religion (*Essential* 2). The concepts of archetypal imagery and the soul weave through Hillman's work. He looks to the philosophers and scholars of the past and seeks to create a new perspective for addressing concerns of the present day (*Essential* 2). Hillman's archetypal

7. Psychological Journeys

The Festival of Psyche, with Mercury from a set of Mythological Subjects after Giulio Romano (Metropolitan Museum of Art, CC0 1.0 Universal).

psychology provides this new perspective framed within the underlying concepts of psyche and soul.

How does this psychology offer potential insight into the relationships of people and dogs and the human/dog bond? Archetypal psychology expands the perspectives of how people may interact with dogs, and perceive dog archetypal imagery within those interactions. For instance, the archetypal characteristics of guide, guard, and healer exist throughout the evolution of the human/dog bond. These patterns, evident in the mythologies of civilizations and the cultures of societies, open doors to new conversations about *how* and *why* this unique bond exists.

Hillman explores the basis and impact of archetypal patterns and the presence of these patterns through philosophies from ancient times up to the present. He notes that the Greek philosopher Heraclitus "was the earliest to take psyche as his archetypal first principle, to imagine soul in terms of flux and to speak of its depth without measure" (*Essential* 22). Hillman notes that while the modern field of depth psychology focuses on the "unconscious levels of the psyche—that is, the deeper meanings of the soul," the association with depth extends to ancient philosophies (22).

According to Heraclitus: "You could not discover the limits of the soul (*psyche*), even if you traveled every road to do so; such is the depth (*bathun*) of its meaning (*logos*)" (qtd. in Hillman, *Essential* 22). Hillman adds, "Ever since Heraclitus brought soul and depth together in one formulation, the dimension of soul is depth (not breadth or height) and the dimension of our soul travel is downward" (22). Several of the mythologies discussed herein focus on the journey of the soul and the importance of dog archetypal imagery in this journey.

Some of Hillman's most significant work is associated with images of animals which occur in dreams. He began a collection of animal dreams "at the Jung Institute in Zurich in 1959 for a study group to inquire into animal motifs in dreams" (*Animal* 12). The collection, which grew over the years, forms part of the basis for his book *Animal Presences*. Hillman views "the dream animal without benefit of therapeutic intentions or psycho-dynamic concepts more like a complex image, a depiction in words, an imaginative *poesis* of what Jung called the objective psyche" (*Animal* 13).

In this process, Hillman discovers "another kind of dreamwork: an *essentialist approach to the dream*—toward what is essentially going on in the image" (13). He adds that "the animals led us to this approach, as if they were the essentials of the dreams, perhaps even essences" (13). The animals are the guides, just as in many mythologies dogs serve as guides in spiritual journeys and as messengers in healing practices. Dream animal imagery provides one method for viewing how internal images may transition into a framework for impacting external relationships between people and animals.

Hillman speaks not only of animal images in general, but also specific species including dogs (*Animal* 183). For instance, he notes that in Asklepion healing practices, the god appears in a dream as a dog licking the wounds of the patient and not as a symbol to be deciphered. Rather in these healing practices "it would have been a genuine appearance by the god in animal form" (183). In fact, according to Moore, "Hillman argues strongly against all symbolic and allegorical translations of dream imagery into ideas, concepts, and humanistic application" (*Essential* 6). He argues that dreams possess value within the world of dreams, which is different than the external world and as such, dreams do not have to "follow the laws of nature" (6).

Hillman expands his theories to include Henry Corbin's terminology "of the *mundus imaginalis*, an imaginal world that is neither literal or abstract and yet is utterly real, with its own laws and purposes" (*Essential* 6). According to Moore, "This imaginal world is the matrix of all Hillman's theorizing" (6). Hillman seeks to discover the meaning in images

7. Psychological Journeys

and experiences of the images rather than dividing experiences "dualistically into mind and matter" (8). He offers a perspective where images are encountered "as they present themselves, embodied in their own imaginal, yet precise, detail" (*Essential* 8).

Experiencing images within an intertwined framework of both physical matter, or nature, and psychological perspectives of mind impacts the relationships between individuals and dogs. This process provides one framework for the development of the human/dog bond and the impacts of dog archetypal imagery within this bond. Dog archetypal imagery of guide, guard, and healer, among others, exists at the nexus of these experiences within the relationships between people and dogs.

In his essay "A Psyche the Size of the Earth," Hillman explores the nature of the individual's psyche in relationship to the all-encompassing earth, and what he calls "the borders of the field of psychology" (xviii). He poses a question central to the interactions of the individual human psyche with nature: "What is the cut between 'me' and 'not-me'"? (xviii). With increasing scientific and medical study, this cut line continues to blur: "Today more and more 'human-like' attributes, some even superior to human consciousness, are being teased out of animals, so that the cut itself has come into question" (xviii).

Research studies continue to delve into the similar attributes shared by people and animals. In addition, studies seek to uncover interspecies links due to these similar attributes. Hillman considers these links and shared attributes from the perspective of depth psychology. Hillman notes that by the term "psychology," he means: "the study or order (*logos*) of the soul (*psyche*)" ("Psyche" xviii). He frames psychology as depth psychology because "it assumes an inside intimacy to behavior, dealing with moods, reflections, fantasies, images and thoughts" (xviii). Significantly, "moods, reflections, fantasies, images and thoughts" are some of the psychological aspects that facilitate the bond between humans and dogs and thus opportunities for guidance and healing associated within this bond (xviii).

Hillman also asks: "Where does psyche stop and matter begin?" ("Psyche" xix). He provides historical perspective by stating: "The deepest levels of the psyche merge with the biological body (Freud) and the physical stuff of the world (Jung)" ("Psyche" xix). Hillman reviews these basic perspectives, "to show that the human subject has all along been implicated in the wider world of nature" (xix). He further states, "the human subject is composed of the same nature as the world" (xix).

The context of the bond between people and dogs is framed within the world of nature. Over the course of history, the human/dog bond evolves framed within the intertwined spheres of mind and culture within nature. In this process, dog archetypal images of guide, guard, and healer impact interactions between people and dogs. As noted by numerous scholars, scientific research is essential to move the conversation forward concerning both *how* and *why* people and dogs express this bond and the value of this bond. Ongoing research explores this bond from the perspectives of quantitative research as well as the analysis of the qualitative aspects of this relationship. Specific quantitative and qualitative studies concerning these interactions are discussed in Chapters 9, 10, and 11. For instance, Müller et al. investigate whether or not dogs can differentiate facial cues based only on human emotional expressions (601). Topál et al. consider the "attachment behavior of dogs" utilizing a modified Ainsworth Strange Situation test (219).

During an interview with John Stockwell, Hillman offers some of his thoughts on animals when he discusses the interface between humans and animals. He states: "I have been trying to foster self-recognition of human being as animal being" ("Human Being" 164). In this interview, Hillman discusses his essay "The Animal Kingdom in the Human Dream," where he addresses events constituting "a momentary restoration of Eden," where "for that short eternal while, there is an original co-presence of human and animal" (167). Hillman's comments concerning "that short eternal while," in which there is "an original co-presence of human and animal," offer a context for viewing the human-dog bond (167). He speaks of an experience that anyone can have, noting examples of playing with a cat, listening to a horse breathing, or hearing a bird call. According to Hillman, this offers "An extraordinary chord of communion, that I believe, must also be sensed by the animal, maybe even the bird" (168).

This "chord of communion" weaves throughout the relationships of people and dogs and helps facilitate the connection and subsequent bond between these two species. Both ethological attributes of communication and psychological parameters of this communion frame aspects of the human/dog bond.

Thomas Moore writes about Hillman: "Above all, he re-visions psychology, taking it back from those who use it as a science of behavior, to treat it as an art of the soul" (*Essential* 2). Hillman's perspectives concerning the concept of soul are central to archetypal psychology. Moore observes that Hillman "likes the word" soul "for a number of reasons" (5). Concerning the word soul, Moore writes: "It eludes reductionistic definition; it expresses the mystery of human life; and it connects psychology to religion, love, death, and destiny" (*Essential* 5). Moore adds, "Whenever

Hillman uses the forms *psychology, psychologizing* and *psychological*, he intends a reference to depth and mystery" (5).

Hillman observes, "By *soul*, I mean, first of all, a perspective rather than a substance, a viewpoint toward things rather than the thing itself" (*Essential* 20). He suggests the word *soul* "refers to that unknown component which makes meaning possible, turns events into experiences, is communicated in love, and has a religious concern" (21). Later in his work he adds "three necessary modifications" to what he calls "these four quantitative qualifications" (21). He writes: "First, *soul* refers to the *deepening* of events into experiences; second, the significance *soul* makes possible, whether in love or in religious concern, derives from its special *relation with death*" (*Essential* 21). His third modification addresses the "imaginative possibility" within the nature of human experience. Hillman describes this possibility as "the experiencing through reflective speculation, dream, image, and *fantasy*—that mode which recognizes all realities as primarily symbolic or metaphorical" (21).

Both Jung and Hillman provide perspectives for considering dog archetypal imagery and the processes of how such images are interpreted by people. Hillman notes that Jung "reintroduced the ancient idea of archetype into modern psychology" and adds that Jung "insisted upon their indefinability" (*Essential* 23). Hillmans' concepts on soul offers perspective on how relationships between people and dogs can turn daily routines, and other interactions, into experiences which communicate love and meaning. Psychologists and other scientific researchers continue to explore the pathways and processes by which both people and dogs interact and the impacts of these interactions. These interactions create the environment and thought processes which lead to both increased meaning and subsequent happiness in the human/dog bond. Aspects of mythology and psychology merge in this process.

Synchronicity and the Network of Dog Archetypal Images

Joseph Cambray also offers insight into the interconnected spheres of nature and the psyche in the book *Synchronicity: Nature & Psyche in an Interconnected Universe*. In viewing field theory and synchronicity, Cambray explores Jung's theories concerning the interconnected spheres of nature and psyche through the perspectives of science, influenced by cultures and framed by religious perspectives. David Rosen notes: "Cambray

The Dog as Guide, Guard and Healer

Festival of Tihar at the second day of celebration called Kukur Tihar. Nepalese police officers worship a dog during the dog festival as part of celebrations of Tihar at Central Police Dog Training School in Kathmandu, Nepal (Navesh Chitrakar / Reuters Pictures).

defines synchronicity and links it to Jung's discovery of a science of the sacred, when nature and psyche come together" (XI). Cambray explores, from Jung's perspective, "the significance of field theories, in their classical and relativistic forms" (2). In addition, Cambray provides "amplifications that point to the archetypal background of these ideas" (2).

Cambray's observations concerning Jung's theories offer insight into the influences of archetypal imagery in the interactions between individuals and dogs. According to Cambray, "Jung was radically transgressive" (2). He did not isolate and confine his work in separate disciplines, but rather "sought the most profound patterns in mind, culture, and nature, what he called 'archetypes'" (2). From ancient times until the present, the patterns of mind, culture, and nature interact and influence the foundation for the human/dog bond. Aspects of various cultures, both scientific and spiritual, continue to impact the development of relationships between people and dogs.

Jung also addresses the interactive nature of science and religion. In Jung's view, "Science and religion were not inherently opposed, and he discovered a science of the sacred, especially in his clinical work"

7. Psychological Journeys

(Cambray 2). Later in his life, Jung reflects on the impacts of science and religion in his own personal myth (*Memories* 3). In this process, he returns to the continuous threads of nature and psyche in his life, from both an individual and universal perspective.

Jung provides "three key elements in his understanding of synchronicity: meaningful coincidence, acausal connection, and numinosity" (Cambray 12). In this hypothesis, "Jung aimed at expanding the Western world's core conceptions of nature and the psyche" (1). Jung wished people "to go beyond the readily explainable, beyond the restrictions of a cause—effect reductive description of the world, to seeing the psyche embedded into the substance of the world" (1).

Jung's concept that the impact of the psyche is both personal within an individual life and universal within the life of the world is pertinent to the human/dog bond throughout history. Both the *personal* and *universal* are imbedded within the experiences of people and dogs. Specifically, these influences surface in dog archetypal images such as guide, guard, and healer and in the responses of people and dogs to each other.

Cambray observes that "Jung's monograph on synchronicity was the product of years of thinking; and he only published it in the last decade of his life" (32). He elaborates on a central aspect concerning Jung's model of the psyche and "the archetypes of the collective unconscious" (34). Cambray writes: "Virtual, empty forms in themselves, they're imagined as structuring all psychic life; when constellated, as through a matching of environmental and internal cues, they tend to manifest in archetypal imagery" (34). The collective influences of the external environment and the human psyche provide these opportunities.

In considering Jung's archetypes, Cambray adds, "They are psychosomatic entities linking body and mind. Taken together they form a highly interconnected polycentric network'" (34). These observations enlighten one of the major theories of this book concerning the human/dog bond. The relationships between people and dogs evolve within a "highly connected" network of spheres including mind, culture, and nature. The influences of these spheres present the opportunities for people to experience dog archetypal imagery including guide, guard, and healer.

Cambray's observations concerning amplification and Jung's methods provide further insight. Cambray writes: "Amplification, the bringing of historical and cultural associations to bear on unconscious processes for the purpose of illuminating the deeper roots at play, became one of Jung's key methods" (35). Jung's observations on myth illustrate this point. For instance, Jung writes: "For it is to one of the typical qualities of a myth to fabulate, to assert the unusual, the extraordinary, and even the impossible" (*Earth* 131). Furthermore, myths cannot be treated as superstitions or illogical assumptions because they cannot be proven based on scientific research or enlightened understanding.

Jung illustrates the premise of viewing myth from a restrictive perspective of natural science and proven scientific concrete facts is misguided. Concerning myth he adds, "It describes, in figurative form, psychic facts whose existence can never be dispelled by mere explanation" (*Earth* 131). How are these observations relevant to the interactions between people and dogs? When viewed together, the spheres of myth and scientific knowledge offer increased insights into the relationships of people and dogs.

A field theory provides one lens to view the interconnected spheres of mind (psyche) and culture from a scientific perspective framed within nature. Jung's perspectives on both synchronicity and the impact of archetypal imagery amplify aspects of the intertwined spheres of mind, culture, and nature. For instance, in *Symbols of Transformation*, Jung writes: "Emotional manifestations are based on similar patterns and are recognizably the same all over the earth. We understand them even in animals, and the animals themselves understand each other in this respect, even if they belong to different species" (*CW V*, para. 234). The concepts of what emotions people and dogs share continue to be analyzed by scholars from numerous disciplines. Some examples of this research are presented in a subsequent chapter of this book.

According to Cambray, "Field theories are generally derived from studying interactions; whatever discipline uses such a theory, its application focuses on manifestations or expressions of an underlying connecting principle" (Cambray 42). He adds: "By moving to a field model Jung's view of the archetypes of the collective unconscious can be reformulated. Each archetype can be seen as a node embedded within the larger context of a polycentric whole, with sets of links or connections weaving the archetypes into a network..." (43).

Archetypal imagery exists as one connecting principle within the interspecies bond between people and dogs. This imagery is evident in the interconnected spheres of mind, culture, and nature. Aspects of mind (psychology), culture (comparative mythology) and dog ethology (nature) provide insight into the evolution and significance of the human/dog bond. In addition, the combined impact of these spheres is *greater* than the influence of each sphere separately.

Aristotle offers some perspective on the sum of various parts in his

7. Psychological Journeys

work *Metaphysics*. He states: "In the case of all things which have several parts and in which the totality is not, as it were, a mere heap, but the whole is something besides the parts, there is a cause" (qtd. in Cambray 32). Cambray adds, "or in the shorthand of gestalt psychology: 'the whole is greater than the sum of the parts'" (32). The *Oxford American Dictionary & Thesaurus* defines gestalt as "an organized whole that is perceived as more than the sum of its parts" (546).

The bond between people and dogs is framed by multi-faceted interactive archetypal characteristics of guide, guard, and healer. Disciplines such as comparative mythology, psychology, and dog ethology provide a framework for the study of the human/dog bond. Yet, there exists an undefinable essence at the center of this bond greater than the individual parts. This essence helps create the unique bond between these two species, humans and dogs. Jung's theories, Hillman's concepts concerning dream imagery and the soul, and the observations of Cambray provide paths for considering the various parts of this interactive bond.

The questions of *how* and *why* people and dogs communicate lie at the center of the human/dog bond. Characteristics of guide, guard, and healer weave throughout the fascinating theories, expanding conclusions and yes, some answers to these questions.

8

Social Skills

Impacts of Awareness and Intentions

On the earth there are many languages and only one of these languages is human speech. The earth speaks with a sense of place, with the voices of the land, sky, and sea. Residents of the earth including mammal, fish, and fowl all speak their "own" languages. Yet, while humans and nonhuman beings communicate amongst themselves with different patterns, movements, and sounds, they share an existence on the earth that is linked with the energy of life. For instance, research finds that humans and some other species share similar motivations in vocal communications as evident in "Morton's motivation-structural rules" (Yin and McGowan 349). Humans and dogs share different forms of communication as well as some motivations and meanings behind the communication. In addition, the abilities to focus both attention and awareness are central to these communications. One way to achieve these interactive communications is to lessen the overpowering desire to reason and to increase the desire to feel.

In *The Spell of the Sensuous*, Abram explores the framework of different types of communication and meaning within nature and between different species. He notes there is an intelligence in nonhuman nature that has the ability "to instill a reverberation in oneself that temporarily shatters habitual ways of seeing and feeling, leaving one open to a world all alive, awake, and aware" (19).

Abram proposes that when people interact with nonhuman inhabitants and listen to the moods and rhythms of the earth, they are more aware of the energies of the earth (*Spell* 46). In addition, Abram suggests that objective reality is not the ultimate framework for interpretation of human existence. Rather, he asks, "Is the human intellect rooted in, and secretly borne by, our forgotten contact with the multiple nonhuman shapes that surround us?" (49).

According to Abram, "phenomenology is the Western philosophical

8. Social Skills

tradition that has most forcefully called into question the modern assumption of a single, wholly determinable objective reality" (*Spell* 31). The works of Abram as well as Hillman insist on expansion of the perspectives of what constitutes reality. Exploring dog archetypal imagery provides one way to expand perspectives framed by philosophy, psychology and direct experience.

While Abram speaks eloquently of the languages of the earth and nonhuman beings, he does not specifically address the bond between humans and dogs. Yet, the concepts he proposes concerning direct experience and awareness provide two aspects for considering the human/dog bond. Specifically, viewing communication between people and dogs in this manner enhances opportunities to study the ways people and dogs communicate. In addition, direct experience and awareness create two avenues for considering archetypal aspects of the dog as guide, guard, and healer within the human/dog bond.

The discipline of phenomenology provides one pathway to explore these concepts. Edmund Husserl developed the early initial concepts of "the philosophical discipline of phenomenology" (Abram, *Spell* 35). This philosophy focuses on direct experience, turning attention "toward the world as it is experienced in its felt immediacy" (*Spell* 35). Phenomenology does not seek to "explain the world" with "mathematics-based sciences" (*Spell* 35). Rather, this philosophical discipline seeks to "describe as closely as possible the way the world makes itself evident to awareness, the way things first arise in our direct, sensorial experience" (*Spell* 35).

Phenomenology stresses two of the major components required for communication between dogs and people, attention and awareness. As noted by Abram, paying attention to the "realm of subjective experience" opens up participants to be aware of the "rhythms and textures" and "ever-shifting patterns" of direct experience (*Spell* 32). Attention and awareness, framed by perception, help facilitate communication within the world of direct experience.

According to Abram, "The event of perception, experientially considered, is an inherently interactive, participatory event, a reciprocal interplay between the perceiver and the perceived" (*Spell* 89). This concept provides a fundamental basis for communication between people and between people and dogs. Communication is both interactive and participatory. The ways that people and dogs interact in participatory communication impacts these communications.

The Dog as Guide, Guard and Healer

Interactive Aspects Within a Unique Niche

Over time, the bond between people and dogs has developed framed within the interactive aspects of their relationship. Uncovering the mechanisms for dog cognition, as evident in dog behavior, helps illuminate the interspecies basis for this bond. Dogs, as the oldest companions of people, have developed cooperative and communicative skills within their shared environment. As a result, "dogs are thought to have evolved cognitive-emotional traits analogous to the social skills that differentiate humans from other primates" (Range and Virányi 183). These observations highlight two significant aspects concerning the human/dog bond involving how dogs *communicate* and *cooperate* with people.

Contemporary research collects data seeking the ontogenetic and evolutionary origins of these abilities, in addition to "underlying mechanisms" (Range and Virányi 201). In this research, scholars explore how people and dogs communicate back and forth. In addition, they consider how their various forms of communication impact these interactions. People and dogs communicate in numerous ways including utilizing visual and auditory signals (Range and Virányi 139). They gather information and respond with communications involving visual expressions, notably facial expressions, body language including direct physical cues, and vocal information.

Studying various types of communication skills between these two species provide better understanding of the roles these skills and subsequent interactions play within the human/dog bond. In addition, exploring the underlying mechanisms of dog cognition skills in dog behavior, and the similarities between people and dogs concerning some social skills, provides significant insight concerning the development of this bond.

Range and Virányi observe that "the domestic dog offers a special opportunity to hypothesize about the evolutionary changes that contributed to the cognitive abilities of both dogs and humans" (183). They write: "Recent intensive research focusing on dogs' social interactions and communication with humans has revealed that dogs perform more like humans in some communicative and cooperative tasks than any other animal species" (183). People and dogs share an interconnected bond based on the domestication of dogs and evolutionary influences of the relationship between people and dogs. The framework of this relationship lies, to a great degree, in the communication methods between the two species and their interactions based on some similar skills of social cognition.

8. Social Skills

Significantly, this book suggests that through various means of communication, dog archetypal guide, guard, and healer characteristics impact this relationship. In addition, the presence of these characteristics helps further communication and enhance positive aspects within the individual relationships between people and dogs.

Many scholars are interested in dog cognition and canine science including the similarities between dog cognition and human cognition. Communication skills shared by people and domestic dogs are beneficial to the individual lives of people and the interactions and impacts of dogs within society as a whole. Range and Virányi note: "Because of the unique evolutionary and individual histories of dogs, the scientific study of their cognition and behavior is mainly focused on searching for skills that may be analogous to human characteristics" (183). Research concerning communication forms reveals opportunities to explore both similarities and differences in how people and dogs interact.

Mechanisms of Social Learning

Within the niche inhabited by people and dogs, how and by what means do interactions and communications flow back and forth? How do the social contexts of these interactions impact the human/dog bond? The following scholars address aspects of these questions. John Bradshaw and Nicola Rooney offer insight concerning the social structure of dogs in the context of their evolution within human society. Therefore, Bradshaw and Rooney focus on the social interactions between people and dogs rather than comparing the social structures of dogs and wolves or domestic dogs and feral dogs (135). In this process, they "examine the main communication channels—sight, sound and smell—relating each to the likely social function of each signal, and paying special attention to play" (135).

Horowitz considers the "point of view of the dog" based on the concept of *Umwelt* (20). According to Horowitz, German biologist Jakob von Uexkull changed "the scientific study of animals ... in the early twentieth century" with the concept of *Umwelt* (20). She writes: "What he proposed was revolutionary: anyone who wants to understand the life of an animal must begin by considering what he called their *Umwelt* (OOM-velt): their subjective or 'self-world'" (von Uexkull qtd. in Horowitz 20). Horowitz observes that "umwelt captures what life is like *as* the animal" (20). The concept of viewing communication between dogs and people from the

The Dog as Guide, Guard and Healer

Greetings (Nancy Wong, CC BY-SA 4.0).

dog's perspective helps create an interactive approach to the human/dog bond.

Bradshaw and Rooney provide additional perspectives noting that "communication is not an entirely straightforward concept, especially when dogs are exchanging information with humans" (139). They analyze communication channels utilizing the following definition of communication "…a stylised signal or display by one individual modifying the response of another" (Barnard qtd. in Bradshaw and Rooney 139). Significantly, they observe that there is an "emerging consensus that domestic dogs have evolved a unique sensitivity to human gaze and gesture" (139). For instance, Range and Virányi (2017) and Kaminski et al. ("How dogs know" 2012) explore research concerning social skills in dogs based on responses to eye contact and gestures. Research which contrasts how dogs and wolves communicate with people also provides insight into dog cognition skills. For instance, Kaminski et al. (2019) and Horowitz (2009) provide examples of how these differences impact the interactions between people and dogs.

Range and Virányi review dog cognition research by "using a structure based on the current categorization of human cognitive skills" (184).

8. Social Skills

In this process, they explore the following questions concerning social cognition and the emotions underlying dog behavior: (a) How do dogs develop their observation skills? and (b) "Whom do they observe?" (184).

What are the more simple social skills that people and dogs share? What are the dog behaviors utilized in order to share these skills? The underlying mechanisms associated with the dog social skills of observation, social learning, and referential communication create pathways for these interactions. Aspects of these skills facilitate how dogs communicate with people and subsequently how people communicate with dogs.

According to Range and Virányi, "In social species, one of the most crucial sources of information is the behavior and interactions of other individuals" (184). For dogs, the complexity of the human world and the bombardments of information and situations require dogs to be very selective in what they pay attention to (184). How do dogs observe information and how do they process this information as communication directed at them? Both the influences of familiarity and quality of relationships impact the daily interactions between people and dogs within the context of human society. While such findings might appear predictable, these concepts provide a foundation for considering the mechanisms of social learning in dogs. In both people and dogs, the ability to focus attention is one of the critical aspects in the ability to learn.

How a dog approaches an object "can be strongly influenced by the way humans manipulate the object while communicating with the dog" (Range and Virányi 191). This mechanism is an example of referential communication. This type of physical referential communication is very different from how people converse with each other, referencing persons and objects that are not even present (191). A great deal of human communication focuses on abstract ideas, whether presented by verbal communications or in other manners. In addition, people communicate not only with words, "but also other symbols (e.g., sign language, traffic signs) to recall different referents (objects, persons, situations, etc.) in others minds" (191). Range and Virányi note that "in contrast, dogs do not communicate with symbolic language" (191).

However, studies do show that dogs produce "context-specific barks" (Yin and McCowan, 2004) which present people a form of vocal communication (Range and Virányi 191). In addition, Pongrácz et al. find that "dogs barks carry emotional information for humans" (Pongrácz et al. 223). For instance, the barks can convey "aggressiveness, fear, despair, playfulness, and happiness based on varying situations" (Pongrácz et al. 228).

These findings are significant because they provide insight into communication links between people and dogs concerning the emotions of fear, aggression, despair, and happiness. From an anthropocentric perspective, these emotions appear to present specific responses and interactions found within both species and in interactions between both species. It should be noted that the interpretations of the meanings of the barks in the above studies are obviously made by humans. Scholars continue to explore what dogs actually think and what emotions they experience. According to Horowitz, "the subjective experience of animals is notoriously difficult to get at scientifically" (145). She adds, "No animal can be asked to relate its experience in voice or on paper, so the behavior of the animals must serve as the guide" (145).

People infer that the emotions of aggression, fear, distress, and happiness are present in dogs because they experience the communications through the lens of human perspective. Aggression is not always a negative behavior and in many situations can lead to positive outcomes. For example, barking dogs can sound aggressive while being protective and territorial in hunting and guarding situations. Chapters 1 and 3 discuss the importance of dogs in these situations. According to Range and Virányi, "Dog barks are functionally informative" in situations such as hunting and guarding (191). The communicative aspects of playfulness and happiness, in the relationships between people and dogs, are also pertinent to this book for several reasons. While this chapter explores the *ways* that people and dogs communicate with each other, subsequent chapters consider the importance of these communications in the human/dog bond.

Signals and Senses

The importance of the five senses, vision, hearing, smell, touch, and taste, vary between people and dogs concerning gathering and communicating information. For people, vision surpasses all other senses for gathering information followed distantly by hearing. (Horowitz 122). Both vision and hearing are part of nearly every human experience and are essential for gathering information and interpreting communications from others (122). Smell and touch vie for third and "taste runs a distant fifth" (122).

The hierarchy of importance for the five senses differs for dogs. Horowitz observes that "snout beats eyes and mouth beats ears" (122). Dogs possess outstanding "olfactory acuity" and vision plays a secondary role (122). Horowitz adds that "when a dog turns" its head toward a person,

8. Social Skills

Tug of war (PxHere).

"it is not so much to look" at the person with their eyes but rather to have their nose look at the person (122). Yet, how dogs use their eyes are central to interactive communications between dogs and people. Horowitz observes that dogs "have at least two critical uses of their eyes: to complement their other senses" and to look at people (123).

Eye contact and gazing are two of the major forms of communication between people and dogs. While people and dogs gather and process sensory information differently, priorities of how people and dogs utilize vision rank close to the top as a means to facilitate communication *between* the two species.

In communicating with humans, dogs "utilize the same repertoire of signals used for intraspecific communication, but the context is distinct and hence some meanings may have changed" (Bradshaw and Rooney 145). Dogs possess many forms of communication which serve various intentions based on the context of the interactions.

According to Horowitz, dogs communicate with "a language of the body," which involves "rumps, heads, ears, legs, and tails" (109). She adds, "The dog uses his body expressively: communications writ through movement" (113). It might be dryly noted, by some, that people with their human language and restricted body movement do not possess quite such an expressive repertoire. Communications between people and dogs hinge on a combination of signals sent and received. For both species, posture provides communication, and "For an animal with a limited vocal repertoire, posture is even more important" (Horowitz 109).

The nuances or intents of posture signals vary based on what dogs wish to signal such as possible engagement with peeked interest or stating a case for dominance (Horowitz 110). She notes that "for dogs, posture can announce aggressive intent or shrinking modesty" (109). When dogs "stand erect, at full height, with head and ears up," they announce "readiness to engage, and perhaps to be the prime mover in the engagement" (108–109). In contrast, "the opposite body posture, crouching with head down, ears down, and tail tucked away, is submissive" (110).

A review of dog signals during play also illustrates several communication methods including visual and auditory communication as well as physical gestures. According to Bradshaw and Rooney, "Play is an important aspect of the social behavior of dogs" (150). They note several positive aspects of play that are significant concerning the human/dog bond. These aspects involve play between dogs and play between dogs and people. Concerning the benefits to dogs, "Playing is not only intrinsically pleasurable and self-rewarding" (150). The benefits of play between dogs also occur in the responses of people and dogs during play. These benefits include enhanced well-being, reduction of social tension or stress, enhanced positive health benefits from exercise and increased happiness (190). Play is joyful whether you are a dog or a person.

Bradshaw and Rooney observe that play between dogs includes visual signals such as play panting, as well as growling and barking (151). As noted in research by Yin and McGowan, acoustic variables "can be used to separate disturbance barks, isolation barks, and play barks" (346). Horowitz observes that dogs possess their own type of laughter (124). She notes "The dog laugh is a breathing exhalation that sound like the excited burst of panting" (103–104). She describes this panting as "*social panting*: it is a pant only heard when dogs are playing or trying to get someone to play with them" (104). These observations illustrate how dogs use different types of communication skills with varying nuances of social intention in play situations.

Rooney and Bradshaw observe that "dogs communicate play to humans using many of the same signals, but also make use of learned behaviors: for example, toy presentation, physical contact and specific vocalizations" (151). They add, "Play solicitation signals such as the 'play bow' all convey the most recognized types of dog behavior" (151). Research has found that humans communicate with some of the same signals as dogs in play situations (151). For instance, people communicate with vocalization and a "play face" (151). People signal the desire to play with smiling and laughter while dogs use vocalizations and body movements to convey excitement at the prospects of play.

In what other ways do people communicate their desire to play with dogs? Bradshaw and Rooney write: "Humans commonly initiate at and maintain play with dogs using a repertoire of over thirty actions" (151). In addition, "Individual signaling repertoires which are unique" to specific relationships between individuals and dogs may indicate examples of "ontogenetic ritualization" (151). The authors define ontogenetic ritualization as "the process of mutual anticipation by which particular social behaviors come to function as intentional communicative signals" (151). In other words, in these situations, the interspecies communications between individuals and dogs create a mutual objective based on predicted responses and desired interactions. Play between people and dogs provides an excellent example of the social skills of intentional communication.

Vocal and Visual Patterns

The following research studies provide examples of *how* vocalization, comprehension, and attention interact within communications between people and dogs. The first study analyzes different types of dog barks utilizing spectrograms. The second study, which includes both people and dogs as participants, considers how people interpret dog barks in various contextual situations. This research explores ethological aspects of the interconnections between dogs and people and reveals scientific links between the two species' communication skills.

Communicative interactions form one of the major foundations of the human/dog bond and aspects of these communication skills exist within a unique niche. The word "unique" should be judiciously used and is very often overused. Yet, in the case of the bond between dogs and people forged over the span of human history, the word "unique" accurately expresses this interactive relationship.

Barking provides the most direct form of vocal communication between dogs and people. Dogs bark sometimes excessively and in large variations within different situations (Yin and McCowan 343). These characteristics have "led some investigators to conclude that barks are primarily an attention-seeking vocalization rather than a context-specific form of communication" (343). The desire or need for attention is prevalent in both people and dogs, but that motivation varies from trying to communicate context specific information from one to the other. The desire to communicate context specific information focuses on achieving different objectives. Numerous research studies now confirm that dogs seek attention and inform people.

Scholars find that dog barks provide information to people concerning the contexts of various situations. In addition, research finds that people can interpret specific situational conditions as well as identify individual dogs from their barks. For instance, in a 2003 study, Yin and McCowan conducted experiments to explore situational contexts and interpretation

Howl of a Husky (CC0 1.0 Universal).

of dog barks (343). Their study focuses on three questions: "First, can dog barks be classified into subtypes, based on context?" (344). Second, if so, then what "acoustic variables" define the barks within different contexts? (344). The third question investigates specific dog vocal patterns methods, asking "can individual dogs be identified by their barks?" (344).

The study involved various breeds with a propensity to bark including Australian cattle dogs, Australian Shepherds, an English Springer Spaniel, a Labrador Retriever mix and German Shorthair Pointers (344). All of the subjects lived in households as pets with ages ranging from three to 13. Three situations were repeated at least five time for each dog over a three-month period. In this process, Yin and McCowan analyzed spectrograms of 4672 barks, "that took 60 sequential frequency measurements and 60 sequential amplitude measurements along the length of the call" (343).

Yin and McCowan "measured harshness, or the harmonics-to-noise ratio on 3922 barks" in these situations utilizing "a software program developed for speech analysis" (346). Significantly, they analyze the spectrograms, or voice prints, of the dogs' vocal communications with similar methods used to analyze speech patterns in humans. Their work explores scientific methods to reveal links between communication patterns of dogs and the interpretation of these vocal communications. In their findings the dogs provide consistent behavioral responses in situations involving danger, fear of separation, as well as play.

The subjects "were recorded in three contexts: (1) a disturbance situation in which a stranger rings the doorbell, (2) an isolation situation in which the dog was locked outside or in a room isolated from its owner and (3) a play situation in which either two dogs or a human and dog played together" (Yin and McGowan 345). The selected situations are pertinent since they illustrate three major areas of interactions between people and dogs. In the first context the situation and subsequent reactions illustrate aspects of guarding or protecting. The second situation underscores the cognitive understanding and fear of being separated from a significant person. The third situation presents behavioral responses associated with play and happiness, two of the most significant aspects underlying the human/dog bond.

Yin and McCowan utilized "discriminant function analysis (DFA) to determine which acoustic variables could be used to discriminate between barks used in different contexts" (346). According to Yin and McCowan, "Discriminant function analysis determines the combination of independent variables that best discriminates groups from each other" (346). In their research, DFA determines "which variables or sets of variables can best be used to separate disturbance barks, isolation barks and play barks" (346).

Yin and McGowan write: "Mean frequency, minimum frequency and location of the minimum frequency were the most important variables for discriminating the identity of the barking dog, whereas amplitude range, minimum frequency and duration were the most important variables for discriminating context" (352). They add, "Despite myriad potential confounding factors and sources of variation, discriminant function analysis did robustly classify barks to specific individuals" (352).

According to the statistical analysis, "Dogs barks are graded vocalizations that range from harsh, low-frequency calls to harmonically rich, higher-frequency calls" (Yin and McCowan 349). They also conclude that "barks are context specific for different dogs, even though these dogs come from diverse developmental environments" (353). In addition, they find "that dogs can be identified by their barks and that the same acoustic parameters can be used to identify individuals within a given context" (352). This research illustrates that dogs convey both informational responses in specific situations and information concerning their individual identities based on their vocal signatures.

The above study analyzes dog barks utilizing spectrograms and DFA analysis. Subsequent research expands on these findings with ethological studies that include both people and dogs as participants. In the following study people assign emotions and interpretations to specific situations based on the sounds of dog barks. Research by Pongrácz et al. shows that people can identify individual dogs utilizing only the sounds of their barks and "dog barks carry emotional information for humans" (228). Pongrácz et al. consider the behavioral responses involving the emotions of danger, fear of separation, and play. People, as the participants, interpret what the bark sequences mean based on their perspectives of the dogs responses. These interpretations occur independent of situational context where the participants (people) could anticipate the types of behavioral responses.

Pongrácz et al. found that "acoustic parameters, like tonality, pitch and inter-bark time intervals, seemed to have a strong effect on how human listeners described the emotionality of these bark vocalizations" (228). They also investigated if the "human understanding of different barking vocalizations of dogs was based on the common mammal heritage following Morton's structural motivational rules" (230).

In addition, Pongrácz et al. considered whether "dog human communication via acoustic signals can be a new case of spontaneous interspecific communication" (230). In their research, "People with different experience with dogs were asked to describe the emotional content of several artificially assembled barking sequences" (228). These emotional states included "aggressiveness, fear, despair, playfulness," and happiness (228).

All of the barks were collected from the Mudi breed, a working style of dog traditionally used to herd sheep and cattle in the countryside (Pongrácz et al. 231). This breed is also known for being a "vigilant" watchdog and "is characterized by the extensive use of barking" (231). The bark recordings were collected from 15 Mudis ranging in ages from one to nine years, all kept as pets by owners in homes and apartments.

The tests used acoustic bark samples to avoid referential situations

8. Social Skills

where the people participants interacted with the dogs. The individual barks were selected "solely on the basis of their pitch (low, medium and high) and harmonic to noise ratio (HNR) (low, medium and high)" (Pongrácz et al. 230). The barks were then "joined together into sequences where the inter-bark interval (pulsing) was also manipulated (short, medium and long)" (230).

The barks were recorded in the following six test situations: stranger, dog attacks human, alone, walk, ball, and play (231–232). In the first case, a stranger approaches the door of the house while the owner is away or in another room. In the second situation, a trainer (rather than the owner) acts aggressively toward the dog, encouraging "the dog to bark and bite the glove on the trainer's arm" (231). Situations one and two create environments requiring guarding or territorial behavior.

In another test the owner ties the dog's leash "to a tree in a park" and walks away "out of sight of the dog" (Pongrácz et al. 232). Three other situations involve tests where the dog anticipates activities such as walks and play. In one test the owner prepares to take the dog for a walk moving toward the leash or door. In another situation the owner holds a favorite ball or toy out in front of the dog. The last situation involves creating games of play between the owner and dog, such as "tug-of-war, chasing or wrestling" (232).

Pongrácz et al. did find that "the scoring of the emotional content of the bark sequences was in accordance with the so-called Morton's structural-acoustic rules" (228). They also "found that the inter-bark intervals had a strong effect on the emotionality of dog barks for the human listeners: bark sequences with short inter-bark interactions were scored as aggressive, but bark sequences with longer inter-bark intervals were scored with low values of aggression" (228–229). In addition, "High pitched bark sequences with long inter-bark intervals were considered happy and playful, independently from their tonality" (229). "Pongrácz et al. also observe that people with different levels of experience with dogs described the emotional context of the bark sequences quite similarly" (228).

Significantly, these research examples show that the motivation and frequency of dog vocalizations reflect similar responses of other non-human creatures, both mammal and birds. Yin and McCowan write: "The changes in harshness and frequency with context are consistent with Morton's motivation-structural rules, which state that birds and mammals use harsh, relatively low-frequency sounds when they are being hostile and higher-frequency, or more tonal sounds when they are approaching in an appeasing or friendly manner, or when they are frightened" (349).

The Dog as Guide, Guard and Healer

These findings provide another scientific link of how mammals communicate within the natural ethological environment and the cultural environment of people. In addition, Yin and McGowan, as well as Pongrácz et al., find that people appear to comprehend the information and intent of dogs' vocalizations within varying contexts.

Why are these findings significant to understanding the bond between dogs and people? These studies illustrate how interspecies communication *between* dogs and people facilitate aspects of the human/dog bond. The studies also reveal aspects of how dogs interpret context and how they seek to inform people. For instance, "by understanding the communicative aspects of barking, dog owners can gain better appreciation of their dogs' communicative abilities and may be more successful at modifying barking-related problem behaviors" (Yin and McCowan 344). In addition, Yin and McGowan note: "Covariation between context and bark structure suggests that dogs may perceive meaningful differences between contexts and adjust their bark accordingly" (353). The word covariation highlights the behavioral mechanisms where dogs responding to varying situations provide informational barks.

Significantly, research suggests that dogs may *adjust* vocal communications to *specifically inform* people of varying situations. As such, vocal communications appear to provide both referential and social intentions, two of the aspects found in human communications. In addition, dogs possibly adjust their vocal communications based on *what they perceive* as the responses of their owners or others. In other words, dog vocalizations provide one method for the interactive communication path between these two species.

From a different perspective, it is also important to consider how direct experience affects shared communication between people and dogs. Abram provides insight with the following reflections. He observes that meaning "remains rooted in the sensory life of the body—it cannot be completely cut off from the soil of direct, perceptual experience without withering and dying" (*Spell* 80). He adds "to affirm that linguistic meaning is primarily expressive, gestural, and poetic, and that conventional and denotative meanings are inherently secondary and derivative, is to renounce the claim that 'language' is an exclusively human property" (80).

Abram's description of linguistic meaning reflects aspects of the shared communication within the human/dog bond. He adds that "if language is always in its depths, physically and sensorially resonant, then it can never be definitively separated from the evident expressiveness of bird-song, or the evocative howl of a wolf late at night" (*Spell* 80). Abram

8. Social Skills

writes: "Language as a bodily phenomenon accrues to *all* expressive bodies, not just to the human" (80). Dogs share a language of meaning with people, framed by direct experience as evident in numerous forms of communication. Dogs and people also share surprising similarities concerning behavioral responses and motivations forged by the evolutionary niche they share and framed by their interactions with each other.

9

Observations, Communications and Viewpoints

A Two-Way Street

Dogs interact with human communications continuously. The question arises, can dogs differentiate when communications are directed toward them or not? What cues by people facilitate the communicative interactions of dogs toward people? According to research, "In recent years it has become clear that, among animals, domestic dogs (*Canis faimiliaris*) tune into human communication in special ways" (Kaminski et al., "How dogs know" 223). Domestication and the evolutionary niche that dogs inhabit, due to their close proximity to people, frame these communications. Research offers several theories, some of which overlap, concerning the nature of these special dog cognitive skills and their impact on communications with people.

Human communication occurs on several different levels and involves varying intentions (Kaminski et al., "How dogs know" 222). For example, Kaminski et al. observe that "the communicator typically intends the recipient to attend to something (the referential intention) and then to know, do, or feel something as a result (the social intention) in the terminology of Tomasello, 2008. Another important level is the so-called communicative intention (or Gricean communicative intention) in which the communicator intends that the recipient recognize…" that the communication is directed at them (222).

Aspects of intentions, both referential and social, impact dog cognition. The abilities of dogs to interact with people utilizing referential and social cognitive skills create one basis for their interspecies communication. Several questions concerning these interactions are pertinent to this discussion. For instance, how unique are these communication skills in the animal world and what is their significance to the formation of the human/dog bond? Are dog cognitive skills the result of initial domestication, ontogeny, evolution based on the shared history of human and dogs,

9. Observations, Communications and Viewpoints

or a confluence of all three? Scientific research in dog ethology continues to probe and seek answers to these complex questions.

Kaminski et al. explore some of these questions in "How dogs know when communication is intended for them" (221). According to Kaminski et al., "Domestic dogs comprehend human gestural communication in a way that other species do not" ("How dogs know" 222). The authors set up test situations to determine how dogs react to *specific* communication cues from people. For instance, people typically address communications to other individuals by utilizing eye contact or calling their name (222). Research finds that eye contact, and to a lesser extent calling the dog's name, also facilitate communication between people and dogs (222). There also appear to be some cognitive similarities with young human infants' sensitivity to eye contact and whether their names are called, especially in a high pitched tone (222).

Kaminski et al. analyzed which types of specific cues facilitate dog communication skills in their interactions with people. The authors created four studies in which adult dogs and young puppies were confronted utilizing object choice tests where an individual points or gazes at one of two opaque cups. The researchers "varied whether the communicator made eye contact with the dog in association with the gestures (or whether her back was turned or her eyes were directed at another recipient) and whether the communicator called the dog's name (or the name of another recipient)" (Kalminski et al. 222).

The first study with 26 dogs explored "whether dogs would differentiate intentional communicative acts from similar but 'non-intentional' behaviors directed toward target hiding locations" (Kaminski et al., "How dogs know" 225). In these types of tests a food reward is placed in one of the two opaque cups. Pointing and gazing cues are then directed from the human to the dogs concerning which cup holds the desired food objects.

In the first study, "eye contact provides the main cue for intentional communication by humans" (225). This finding reinforces the importance of eye contact in the development of interactive communication—important, but not absolutely essential, as further studies reveal.

The second and third studies "were designed to investigate further the role of eye contact in dogs' following of human communicative gestures, and also to explore an additional ostensive cue: the calling of the dog's name (in a high pitched speech register)" (Kaminski et al., "How dogs know" 225). These studies, which include 70 dogs, consider the combination of both eye contact and vocal communications between people and dogs.

The Dog as Guide, Guard and Healer

During these tests, the individual provided verbal intentional communications but kept their back turned so the dog could not see any facial cues including eye contact (Kaminski et al., "How dogs know" 225). The second test involved three different situations: (a) where the person called the dog's name, (b) where they called a strange name other than the dog's name, and (c) where they address someone else now sitting in the room other than the dog (225). The results of the study demonstrated that eye contact was not necessary for dogs' to know a communicative gesture was directed toward them (227). In addition, calling the dog's actual name was not a necessary cue in these object choice tasks (231). Rather, dogs may be responding to the higher pitch voice tones humans typically use when addressing dogs (231). Kalminski et al. write: "In the first study, eye contact was the major distinguishing feature between the intentions and non-intentional, and in the second and third studies eye contact were clearly the strongest cue when all the different conditions were compared" (231).

They add that "dogs' sensitivity to the intentional dimension of human communicative gestures is not an artifact of some species-specific, inflexible reactions to specific cues, but rather constitutes a more general and flexible comprehension" (231). These findings indicate that dogs possess flexible comprehension in their interactions with people. In addition, the ability to comprehend intent as well as act on intent helps create the unique interactive exchanges shared by people and dogs.

The fourth study considers what role ontogenetic influences play in the communicative interactions between people and dogs. This test involves 84 puppies utilizing the same point and gazing conditions as per previous tests. Kalminski et al. find that the dog puppies' performance is striking ("How dogs know" 231). The puppies were still with their mothers and had experienced little human contact (231). However, the puppies' performance is comparable to how adult dogs performed in the tests (231). Kaminski et al. observe "This suggests that traditional learning processes are not the major factor in the ontogenetic emergence of these communicative skills in dogs" (231). "One implication for human development is that special attunement to such things as eye gaze and high-pitched voices may in principle emerge in ontogeny without extended learning" (231).

These test studies illustrate that dogs interact with people with intentional communications based on the various cues presented and that dogs comprehend what the intentions imply. In addition, the findings indicate that dogs respond to the same high-pitched tones adults use to communicate with young children (Kaminski et al., "How dogs know" 225).

9. Observations, Communications and Viewpoints

Similarities in communication patterns between people and dogs, and mothers and children are discussed in Chapter 11. The interactive communications between people and dogs form a significant basis for the human/dog bond. Furthermore, contemporary research is finding increasing similarities in the social skills used to form the mother/infant bond and the human/dog bond.

Pathways to Shared Communication

Horowitz also addresses the importance of eye contact for communication between dogs and people. In addition, she notes differences in how wolves interact with people versus how dogs interact with people. She finds that one of the most significant behavioral differences between dogs and wolves involves their eyes (Horowitz 45). Horowitz writes: "The difference is this: dogs look at our eyes" (45). In contrast, "Wolves avoid eye contact" (45).

She adds that dogs look at people for information—"about the location of food" and study people's faces seeking information on their emotions (Horowitz 45). Dogs seek information "about what is happening"

Path to communication (PxHere).

within the social environment group of people (45). Eye contact and visual exchange of information occur in both people and dogs with the information flowing from one to the other.

The ability of dogs to gain and process information from eye contact and facial expressions is one of the most significant differences which separate dogs from other species within the human social environment. According to Horowitz, this ability "serves as a foundation for their skill at social cognition" (46). This communicative process is interactive between people and dogs and represents an essential element within the human/dog bond. Eye contact can also be threatening to dogs and people. For example, dogs and people share a mutual dislike of excessive or aggressive staring. However, although dogs "have inherited some aversion to staring too long at eyes, dogs seem to be predisposed to inspect" people's faces "for information, reassurance, for guidance" (46).

Horowitz observes that when people look at dogs, dogs return their gaze (139). She writes: "The importance of the dog's gaze, when it is directed at our faces, is that gaze implies a frame of mind" (139). She adds, a dog's gaze "implies attention," both to the individual and also "possibly" to what the individual is paying attention to (139). As previously noted, paying attention is essential in determining the intent of communications by others and learning new skills by imitation.

People and dogs interact in a world where they are constantly bombarded with stimuli. Within this context, both people and dogs focus on stimuli by using visual attention and auditory attention (Horowitz 139). According to Horowitz, "what distinguishes dogs from other mammals, even other domestic mammals, is the way that their attention overlaps with ours" (140). She finds that dogs study the "subtle movements, moods, and most avidly" the faces of humans (140–141).

The ability of dogs to focus their attention, their subsequent behaviors, and their interactions with people revolve within the human social world. As a result, the human/dog bond exists within both individual and larger social environments. In addition, the ability of dogs to pay attention in the human world and their interactions with people provide major impetus for contemporary dog cognition studies (Horowitz 144). To learn about the social skills and behavioral responses of *dogs* in situations with humans opens up avenues to learn more about *human* behavioral responses with humans. In this process, scholars continue to expand their understanding of the human/dog bond. For instance, links between motivation and attachment provide insights into interactive communication between people and dogs. (See Chapter 11.)

9. Observations, Communications and Viewpoints

Canine Perspectives and Human Viewpoints

Huber and Lonardo "address the question whether dogs have the ability to take the perspective of others and thus come to understand what others can or cannot perceive" (275). If dogs can understand what others see or not see, can they "infer what others know and use this to anticipate what others do next?" (297). Can dogs perceive what others see or not in certain situations, infer from that what others know, and then, even more difficult, "anticipate what others will do next?" These questions address essential aspects of perspective-taking in humans and perhaps in dogs: the abilities to *comprehend* what others know in certain situations, *understand* what that knowledge implies, and then *anticipate* subsequent actions by others based on that knowledge.

According to Huber and Lonardo, "Dogs have solved several perspective-taking tasks instantly and reliably across a large number of variations, including geometrical gaze-following, stealing in the dark, concealing information from others, and Guesser/Knower differentiation" (275).

Huber and Lonardo review numerous studies "about the perspective-taking ability of domesticated dogs" to evaluate the perspective-taking abilities of dogs (275). They consider sensitivity to others' gaze, sensitivity to others' attention, and visual perspective-taking. Research by Bradshaw and Rooney (2017), Horowitz (2009), and Range and Virányi (2017), explore aspects of attention in the social skills of dogs (See Chapter 8). Dog social skills concerning attention to humans cues are essential in their perspective-taking abilities. Studies discussed below by Maginnity and Grace and Catatla et al. consider perspective-taking abilities of dogs utilizing the Guesser-Knower task. Huber and Lonardo expand this discussion with review of autocentric perspective-taking and how dogs react to their perceptions of true or false beliefs tasks.

Based on previous research, "In sum, dogs recognize and react appropriately to many different cues of visual attention, have some understanding of humans' visual field, and can make use of this information in a functional way both in cooperative (e.g., begging, obeying a command) and competitive contexts (e.g., stealing)" (Huber and Lonardo 287).

Huber and Lonardo add it's not known "whether their concept of seeing can abstract beyond observable behavior and environmental cues" (287). Can dogs utilize received information to infer what others, their human companions know in a given situation, and furthermore, can they project how their companions might react to a situation based on that information?

The Dog as Guide, Guard and Healer

The following studies provide insight into essential dog cognitive skills concerning sensitivity following gaze direction, interpretation of others attention, and sensitivity to the reaction of others' visual fields. Significantly, this sensitivity focuses not on the dog's behavior, but how the dogs *interpret* the behavior of people. Huber and Lunardo develop tasks to test not only if dogs recognize "the association between certain behavioral or environmental cues, and a likely outcome or reaction, but also whether they can correctly infer others' differential perceptual access in the absence of differential behavioral or environmental cues between conditions" (287).

Primatologists invented the Guesser-Knower task, which "requires the observer to distinguish between knowledgeable and ignorant others by appreciating their differential access to a hiding event (Poninelli and Eday 1996)" (Huber and Lonardo 289). In this task, "While one informant (the Knower) either hides the food her/himself or watches someone else hide the food, the other (the Guesser) is out of the room or otherwise cannot see the baiting" (Huber and Lonardo 289).

Recent studies utilize the Guesser-Knower task to explore whether or not dogs possess Level 1 perspective-taking, a basic cognitive ability associated with the Theory of Mind in humans (289). Catala et al. write: "Currently, there is still no consensus about whether or not animals can ascribe mental states (Theory of Mind) to themselves and others" (581). They add: "Showing animals can respond to cues that indicate whether another has visual access to a target or not, and that they are able to use this information as a basis for whom to rely on as an informant, is an important step forward in this direction" (Catala et al. 581).

Key questions concerning this concept revolve around what dogs perceive from different cues and how do they interpret this information? Can dogs, utilizing visual and behavioral cues of humans, infer information, and interpret behaviors from these cues? And significantly, can they use this information to act in various situations requiring decisions based on this information? How do these abilities impact the dog's archetypal characteristics of guide, guard and healer in the interactive bond between people and dogs?

Studies utilizing "Domestic dogs (*Canis familaris*) with human informants are an ideal model, because they show high sensitivity towards human eye contact, they have proven able to assess the attentional state of humans in food-stealing or food-begging contexts, and they follow human gaze behind a barrier when searching for food" (Catala et al. 581). Three key social cognition skills, associated with the Theory of Mind, revolve around *perception, interpretation,* and *decision making.*

9. Observations, Communications and Viewpoints

Dogs and Guesser-Knower Tasks

The following studies explore dogs' visual perspectives and social cognition skills involving perception and decision making. The first study by Maginnity and Grace utilizes the Guesser and Knower task in four experiments involving food baiting with hidden food. The second study by Catala et al. further considers potential behavior reading in dogs and whether or not dogs possess the behavior-reading "skills of geometrical gaze following and perspective taking" (Catala et al. 581). Why are these studies significant to the human/dog bond and interactions of dogs with people?

This research explores the possibilities that dogs do possess some basic Level 1 characteristics of Theory of Mind. In addition, these studies offer insights into the interactive relationships of people and dogs and dog archetypical characteristics. The abilities of dogs to utilize cognitive and social skills of gaze followings, and directing attention to their human companions create pathways for dog archetypal characteristics of guide, guard, and healer within individual relationships.

Taking a break between tests (PickPik).

The Dog as Guide, Guard and Healer

The social cognitive skills of dogs to follow pointing and gazing behavioral cues by humans are central to the interactive communications between people and dogs. These experiments explore how dogs perceive these cues and utilize this knowledge. In addition, this research considers the potential links of dogs' perception-taking skills and the possibilities they possess some basic levels of Theory of Mind. If these hypotheses prove accurate, they reveal another link to *how* the bond between people and dogs is unique and imbedded in human development throughout history.

Dogs possess remarkable assessment and sensitivity skills concerning attention to their human companions. How significant are these skills in the human/dog bond? The following studies utilizing versions of the Guesser-Knower task address aspects of these skills.

Maginnity and Grace create a study to evaluate the visual perspective-taking skills of dogs. They test 16 domestic dogs utilizing a Guesser-Knower task in four experiments, each with 24 test trials (Huber and Lonardo 285). Maginnity and Grace "manipulated the informants' perceptual access, participation, and knowledge state regarding the food baiting in an attempt to determine the cues used by dogs" (1377). In the four experiments, two informants utilize pointing and gazing gestures with increasingly controlled testing aspects to eliminate any other possible behavioral cues by the informants (1377).

A brief summary of the purposes of the four experiments follows. In the first experiment, Maginnity and Grace "wanted to establish whether dogs could respond correctly in a Guesser-Knower task modeled after Povinelli et al.'s (1990) procedure" (1381). If the dogs respond correctly to the Knower, they "wanted to determine whether performance depended on cues that were correlated with the informants' knowledge of the food location, associative cues related to the food handling, or both" (1381).

The experiments are set up with a screen which could be easily raised or lowered. When raised, the upper body and faces were visible, but the dogs could not see the food containers or the informant's hands (1378). Four opaque and sound proof containers are utilized for the experiments. A hidden piece of food in the soundproofed fabric assures that all the containers smell like food. At the start of each trial, the owner leads the dog to the center of the room, restrained by a lead or collar (1380). The screen is lowered, and the knower points to the baited container whereas the guesser points to an unbaited container. After the informants provide the pointing and gazing cues for two seconds the owner releases the dogs during the choice phase (1380).

9. Observations, Communications and Viewpoints

According to Maginnity and Grace, results of the first trial confirm "a significant preference for the knower" (1382). In the second experiment, a third person does the food baiting while the informants sit passively by. In the experiment two trials, "the knower covered her cheeks with her hands and the guesser covered her eyes" (Huber and Lonardo 285). In the third experiment, the informants used only the direction of their gazing to indicate in which container the food was hidden (Maginnity and Grace 1383). In this trial, "the knower looked at the baiting and the guesser looked at the ceiling" (Huber and Lonardo 285). Experiment four was structured with two new conditions involving equal knowledge of the food location and pointing. In this trial both the knower and guesser were present during the food baiting and knew if the food cues contained food or not (285).

In summary, "When informants had different perceptual access to the baiting, dogs preferred the location indicated by the knower from the start of the testing even when baiting was done by a third experimenter" (Huber and Lonardo 285). They write… "this study confirmed that dogs have a remarkable sensitivity to cues relating to humans' attentional state, in this case, the visibility of the humans' eyes and their gaze directions" … (290). Yet, the question remained if dogs possess the skills for geometric gaze following? (290). According to Huber and Lonardo, "Cognitively more sophisticated mechanisms are required for 'geometrical gaze following' in which subjects track others' gaze direction geometrically behind visual barriers (Tomasello et al. 1999)" (277). A further question involves whether the "dogs' assessment of a human's knowledge would go beyond *directly observable differences* between two informants" (296). The following study by Catala et al. addresses these questions.

According to Catala et al., "It is still an open question if dogs can use geometrical gaze following as a perspective-taking mechanism, to assess what a human can see and therefore know" (582). They develop a study with two purposes to evaluate perspective-taking in dogs. First, they want to try and replicate the Maginnity and Grace (2014) study to further verify the results in that study utilizing a Guesser/Knower task (582). Their second goal centers considers checking "whether the dogs' assessment of a human's knowledge can go beyond directly observable differences between two informants" utilizing a "variant of the Guesser-Knower task" (582).

Catala et al. create a "task in which both human informants behaved identically: they both looked in the same direction but differed in whether they could see the baiting process" (582). Significantly, the tests were arranged where the dogs could not see the "object of interest to the human" and therefore, would not be able to use line of sight connections from the informant's eyes to the object ("eye-object line") (582). Instead, the dogs "must infer from the humans' gaze direction what they can see or not, i.e. geometrical gaze following" (582). The informants' exchange roles "repeatedly in each test" to avoid the dogs' using any unintended cues (582).

Aspects of this test are designed to increase the difficulty for the dogs to make decisions, based on the type of informant's cues. As noted by Huber and Lonardo, the "active use of others' gaze cues has been considered a crucial step towards an understanding of mental states like attention and intention (Tomasello et al. 2005)" (277). They add "Following human gaze in dogs can be considered a socially facilitated orientation response, which in object-choice tasks is modulated by human-given ostensive cues" (277).

The results of these research studies illustrate that dogs utilize human pointing and gazing cues in order to make decisions in object choice tasks. Furthermore, the perspective-taking abilities of dogs to evaluate what humans know or do not know help frame numerous interactions in the human/dog bond including their roles as working dogs and companions. These types of studies also expand opportunities to explore fascinating questions concerning whether or not dogs possess some characteristics associated with Theory of Mind.

Dogs possess amazing abilities to communicate with people, framed by social cognition skills which include referential gestures. Dogs' *attention* to communicative cues and *interpretation* of those cues is one of the central aspects of how dogs communicate with people and a foundational aspect of the human/dog bond.

Aspects of Referential Gestures

As noted by Worsley and O'Hara, "Referential gestures are used by a signaler to draw a recipient's attention to a specific object, individual or event in the environment" (456). They write that "domestic dogs (*Canis familiaris*) ... provide an ideal non-primate candidate for investigating referential signaling due to their unique relationship with humans that centers on non-verbal communication with frequent interaction" (456).

Numerous studies illustrate how dogs respond and interpret cues from people. These cues help communicate what humans desire dogs to see, understand, and do. But, what about studies that consider what

9. Observations, Communications and Viewpoints

Gestures and goals (PickPik).

the dogs want people to do? As noted by Worsley and O'Hara "Thus far, dog-human communicative research has tended to focus on dogs' ability to understand human-given gestures" (458). What activities do dogs wish people to provide in everyday situations and how important are referential gestures in these communications? What gestures by dogs help frame communications of people and dogs in the daily interactive rhythms of their lives together?

Worsley and O'Hara develop a study "by observing gestures that pet dogs direct to their owners during everyday communicative bouts to investigate referential gesturing and humans' ability to understand gestures performed by dogs" (458). This study illustrates how specific communicative gestures by dogs reflect referentiality and inform their owners what they wish them to do.

Worsley and O'Hara note that "for a gesture to be considered as referential in function, it must conform to five features" (457). They add that "referential gestures are non-accidental" (457). Referential gestures have specific purposes and characteristics that reflect intentionality (457). In these communications, an individual provides a goal-directed gesture towards the recipient (457–458). The recipient must satisfy the signaler with the desired response. The signaler can repeat the gesture, or incorporate new gestures from their repertoire of gestures if the recipient does not respond or their response is slow (458).

A referential gesture "must show at least some of these attributes of intentionality; in particular persistence and elaboration (Woodruff and Premack 1979)" (458). Worsley and O'Hara illustrate how dogs utilize their repertoire of gestures to direct attention and achieve desired responses from their owners. Previously this book discussed how dogs communicate with people, with physical movements, eye contact, and gazing cues. Referential gestures reflect various combinations of these communication skills framed by elaboration, persistence, and repetition (458).

Worsley and O'Hara recruit "the owners of 37 domestic dogs (16 female, 21 male, aged 1.5–15 years) who have lived with their owners for a minimum of 5 months before the start of the study" (458). In order "to maximize the quantity of data" accumulated they utilized a "citizen science method" (458). They add that "this citizen science approach was founded on the method utilized by Horowitz and Hecht (2016) in their 'play with your dog' study" (458). Wolsey and O'Hara ask their participants "to film their dogs performing 'everyday' communicative bouts (e.g., requesting food and doors to be opened, playing and requesting to be scratched)" (459). Prior to commencing the study, the researchers show the owners pre-collected footage by the researcher, illustrating "the kinds of things" they were interested in (459). No limit is "placed on the collection and the same kinds of communicative bouts could be recorded multiple times" (459).

What types of gestures do dogs exhibit in their portfolio of referential gestures? Worsley and O'Hara note: "Gestures were categorized as per their apparent satisfactory outcome (ASO). ASOs are deduced from a plausible desire and signaler satisfaction (Hobaiter and Byrne 2014). They produce an outcome that results in the termination of the communication" (459). Analysis of the gathered data provided "four ASOs which yielded the highest frequency of observation to decipher potential referential gestures" (459). "These actions included limb, head and whole body movement but not facial expressions or static body stances. (Hobaiter and Byrne 2011, 2014)" (459).

"The four ASOs with the highest observational frequency were 'Scratch me!,' 'Give me food/drink,' 'Open the door' and 'Get my toy/bone' resulting in 242 bouts of communication" (Worsley and O'Hara 460). The analysis of these communicative bouts revealed gestures with referential criteria ultimately yielding 1016 bouts demonstrating "hallmarks of intentional production…" (460–461).

9. Observations, Communications and Viewpoints

Wolsey and O'Hara then analyze how the four highest ASO dog gestures "confirm to the five features of referentiality" (460). The criteria for referential gestures, summarized below, also reflects aspects of interaction and communicative dog social skills previously discussed in this book. The observed dog gestures are evaluated based on the following five criteria for referentiality.

Gestures are "directed towards an object or specific area" and are performed at the location of the specific goal. Examples include standing at the food bowl or "pressing the nose or face against the recipient" as in please feed me or scratch me (Worsley and O'Hara 465). Other gestures involve leading the recipient toward the goal such as going to a door the dog wants opened (460).

The second and third criteria involved how the communication gestures are directed to the recipients. In the Worsley and O'Hara study, all gestures are aimed at the recipient since the recipient was filming their dog's gestures, and the gestures "receive a voluntary response" (460). In this study, "all gestures when performed individually and within a portfolio promoted a voluntary response from the intended recipient" (460).

Referential gestures require assistance from the recipient and "are mechanically ineffective" (Worsley and O'Hara 460). Dogs perform the gestures "with the apparent aim" of recruiting the recipient "to attain an ASO" (460). In other words, if the dogs could achieve their goals by themselves, they would not be asking for help.

In this study, the hallmarks of intentional production include the following: (1) The dogs exhibited goal oriented behavior to achieve an ASO; (2) The "dogs were persistent in their performance of gestures until the apparently desired outcome was achieved and all communication was directed to the appropriate audience" (Worsley and O'Hara 460). In addition, the dogs exhibited "persistence and elaboration of gestures" when the receiver did not provide the ASO or was not "sufficiently quick to respond" (460).

Other findings include "The most common gesture observed involved gaze alteration (head turn) gestures, recorded 381 times over all four ASOs" (461). Of the 37 dogs, 35 used the head turn gesture (Worsley and O'Hara 461). In addition, the "high occurrence of gaze alternation (Head Turn)" ... "was not limited to one ASO" (461). The results illustrate how social skills involving gazing and visual perspective-taking impact the communications. The results also "revealed that the size of the individual's referential gestural repertoire is directly proportional to the number of people who live with the dog" (465). It appears that the larger number

The Dog as Guide, Guard and Healer

of people dogs have to interact and communicate with, the larger "portfolio of gestures" they possess and utilize in interactions with "their human social partners" (Worsley and O'Hara 465).

The perspective-taking skills of domestic dogs significantly impact their behaviors and the subsequent interactions between people and dogs. In addition, these behaviors influence individuals' perceptions of dog archetypal characteristics of guide, guard, and healer within individual relationships. Interactive communication between people and dogs create pathways for shared experiences framed by dog archetypal characteristics.

These characteristics manifest themselves as dogs interact with people as companions and as guides through different psychological experiences and within the physical world. Dogs serve as therapy dogs, service dogs, as well as guides on treks though the outdoors. Throughout history, they work closely with their human companions as haulers, herders, hunters, and retrievers. In addition, dogs provide individual feelings of security in various situations from guarding properties to leading the way on walks. The loyalty and talents of dogs in their shared environmental niche with humans cannot be overstated. The spheres of psychology and culture link dogs and people in the evolutionary journey of both species from prehistory until now.

10

Interactions

Aspects of Emotion and Empathy

People and dogs utilize social intention and cognitive skills to communicate attachment, emotion, and motivation. In addition, research suggests that empathic responses reside in some of these interactions and are reinforced by the bond between people and dogs. How do people and dogs perceive these interactions and what are impacts on the human/dog bond? Thought processes in both humans and dogs are complex and behavioral studies offer one avenue to reveal aspects of emotion and empathy.

Significant to this conversation are several questions concerning what dogs think and feel as expressed in their behavior towards people. What emotions do dogs experience? A subjective follow up question revolves around whether or not dogs experience emotions in their interactions with people in similar ways as people. Do dogs feel the emotions of happiness, sorrow, guilt, love, empathy? This book suggests that a vast majority of individuals, who share their lives with dogs, would reply of course they do. Others caution, however, such responses come from the anthropocentric human perspective which views dog behavioral responses and emotions from the perceptions of human emotions.

The following perspectives and research studies illustrate the complexity of these questions. According to Range and Virányi, "Empathy, the ability to understand and vicariously experience the emotional and motivational states of others, is thought to be an important prerequisite for social interactions and especially cooperation" (197). Empathy, as described above, focuses on the cognitive abilities to *understand* and also vicariously *experience* both the emotions and motivations of another. Aspects of dogs' cooperation and social skills weave throughout the interactions between dogs and people. Yet, do dogs possess the ability to experience *some* aspects of empathy in their interactions with individuals? Research including studies by Custance and Meyer (2012), Annika Huber et al. (2017), and Müller et al. (2015) suggest that dogs do possess the ability to vicariously experience some aspects of emotional intentions and empathetic behavior within the human/dog bond.

Consideration of these questions highlights the complexity and unique nature of the bond between people and dogs. The human/dog bond exists at a nexus, which is more than the sum of the parts, framed by ethology, psychology, and mythology, as well as numerous other influences. In addition, an undefinable central core or essence resides within the interactive bond shared between individuals and dogs which cannot be precisely defined, or scientifically proven, just as an archetype cannot be precisely defined. Furthermore, dog archetypal imagery of guide, guard, and healer offer some insight into interactions between people and dogs.

Obviously, not all phenomena in life are explainable by scientific research. For instance, psychological responses involving emotional reactions between two people cannot be defined by strict scientific evaluations of cause and effect. In relationships between people and dogs, the interplay of companionship, contentment, and happiness cannot be precisely quantified. Yet, studying the behavior of dogs, including social interactions and emphatic responses from scientific perspectives, provides essential insights into various aspects of this bond. While the challenges are formidable, scholars continue to pursue scientific research to better understand the Human-Animal Bond or HAB. The potential rewards and importance of such pursuits are immense for individuals, dogs, and larger social groups.

For instance, the Duke Canine Cognition Center founded by Brian Hare, an evolutionary anthropologist, "is dedicated to the study of dog psychology" (Duke). Researchers are "studying how dogs understand communicative intentions, the effect of domestication of their psychology, how they form trusting relationships, navigate, and form memories" (Duke).

In what ways do dogs perceive people as *social partners*? What perspective-taking cues help dogs relate to people as social partners in their shared world? According to Correia-Caeiro et al., "Comparative studies of human-dog cognition have grown exponentially since the 2000's" (727). However, studies focused on how dogs view people and other dogs "as social partners is a more recent phenomenon despite its importance to human-dog interactions" (757). Correia-Caeiro et al. address three areas concerning research on visual perceptions of dogs involving emotion cues. Their study includes an initial brief summary of "the current state of research in visual perception of emotion cues in dogs and why this area is important" (727). They "then critically review its most

10. Interactions

commonly used methods, by discussing conceptual and methodological challenges and associated limitations in depth" (727). Based on that analysis, the authors "suggest some possible solutions and recommend best practices for future research" (727).

According to Correia-Caeiro et al., "Typically, most studies in this field have concentrated on facial emotional cues, with full body information rarely considered" (727). They write: "There are many challenges in the way studies are conceptually designed (e.g., use of non-naturalistic stimuli) and the way researchers incorporate biases (e.g., anthropomorphism) into experimental designs, which may lead to problematic conclusions" (727).

These observations reflect several concepts in this book about the challenges in gathering and interpreting data concerning emotion cues and empathy in the relationships of dogs with people. Dog communication methods do include overall movements as well as visual, vocal, and facial interactions. The three spheres of mind (psychology), culture (e.g., cultural environments of individual and larger collective groups), and dog ethology frame communications methods between people and dogs. Exploring the interactions and shared influences of these spheres provides insights for research concerning visual perception of dogs. Motivations for behavior in both humans and dogs are multifaceted, complex, and shifting based on the circumstances in given situations and the background of the individuals.

Why are these observations pertinent to aspects of guide, guard, and healer dog archetypal characteristics? Analyzing social interactions and interpretation of emotion cues highlight the complexity of research concerning *human/human* and *human/dog* communications. For instance, in research with people, even with all their verbal language skills, the underlying contexts and responses to emotion cues are multi-layered and often hard to ascertain. Correia-Caeiro et al. contrast the difference between emotions and emotion cues as follows. They write: "Whilst *emotions* are internal states and arise from multi-component complex biological and perceptual processes" (and thus are subjective and hard to measure as a single concept) "*emotion cues* are variably present on a sender, may be observable by a receiver, and belong to distinct modalities (and thus can be objectively quantified)" 729.

A "critical review of methodology" such as the study by Correia-Caeiro et al. provides context for analyzing complex questions concerning visual perceptions and emotion cues in dogs (726). This type of research impacts the understanding of the human/dog bond including aspects of empathetic responses in both people and dogs. Correia-Caeiro et al. write: "Solving conceptual and methodological challenges in the field of emotion perception research in dogs will not only be beneficial in improving research in dog-human interactions, but also within the comparative psychology areas, in which dogs are an important model specie to study evolutionary processes" (726).

An explosion in interest and scientific studies has moved the domestic dog to the forefront concerning research about similarities with people in social skills, some cognition abilities, and interpretations of behaviors including emotion cues. According to Correia-Caeiro et al., this increased number of studies "has been changing the status of the domestic dog in biological research, from inadequate/irrelevant for 'real biology' due to its domestication, to an ideal model species…" (727).

Continuous research highlights *how* cognition and social skills of the domestic dog impact the unique relationship of people and dogs, and the evolution of the human/dog bond. Correia-Caeiro et al. observe that numerous recent studies "reveal this species is highly sensitive to visual social cues, particularly when it comes to human-dog communication" (730). For example, perspectives of Miklósi (2014) and Huber and Lonardo (2023) offer insight on how the domestic dog has become "an ideal model species" for research (727). Research studies by Yin and McCowan (2004), Topal et al. (1998), and Kaminski et al. (2016) highlight the domestic dog's unique relationship and interactions with people. For example, research by Kaminski et al. (2012) explores how dogs "understand human intentions" and the impacts of this understanding on the human/dog bond (See Chapter 8).

This book utilizes these studies and others to explore the evolution in communications and cooperative endeavors between humans and dogs and the profound impacts of their shared companionship in the developments of human history. Aspects of psychology, culture, and ethology meet at the nexus of the communication and cooperative skills of the domestic dog, the oldest companion of people.

An overview by Huber and Lonardo et al. (2023) discusses how dogs understand people based on different levels of sensitivity to human communication cues (202). Research illustrates that "dogs have solved several perspective-taking tasks instantly and reliably across a larger number of variations including geometrical gaze–following" … "and Guesser/Knower differentiation" (Huber and Lonardo 297). Studies by Maginnity and Grace (2014) and Catala et al. (2017) evaluate the perspective-taking abilities of dogs in object choice tests (see Chapter 9). In addition, research

10. Interactions

by Worsley and O'Hara (2018) explores the types of communicative gesture cues dogs direct towards people. Their work evaluates what the various gestures in the dog's repertoire mean and how certain gestures illustrate "the five features of referentially" (400). Some of these studies consider whether dogs possess some characteristics associated with the Theory of Mind in humans.

The ability to experience empathy and the subsequent responses provided in different situations also serve to increase the basis of the human/dog bond. Considerations can be given to what emotions people experience as their dogs offer them comfort and solicitation. The emotional feeling that someone or some other living creature cares about an individual is one of the lynchpins that facilitates feelings of well-being within individuals. People determine whether or not they experience empathy from others and that includes their perceptions of the responses from their dog companions. Emphatic behavior moves back and forth between the two species.

Research offers insight into various foundational aspects of this bond. The following four research studies explore aspects of emotion and empathic behavioral responses between dogs and people. The first, second and third studies consider empathetic responses of dogs when presented with distress by their owners and strangers. These studies highlight behavioral responses concerning interactions between people and dogs. Significantly, when faced with these situations, dogs must evaluate the situations, make decisions on how to proceed, and then offer various responses to the owners and strangers present in the experiments. In addition, these studies are framed by both the dogs' behavioral responses and subsequent interpretations of these behaviors by people. A fourth study explores the ability of dogs to understand facial expressions irrespective of human perceptions. This experimental procedure considers if dogs can discriminate human emotional expressions without any behavioral cues from humans.

Perspectives Concerning Emotions and Empathy

Two of the most important emotions people experience involve happiness and sadness. Both of these emotions reside at the center of each individual's perceptions concerning their well-being or lack of well-being. People often express the emotions of happiness and sadness with behavioral responses of laughter and, in contrast, crying. In many cases, these emotions are couched in emphatic concerns for others. Pertinent to this discussion, can dogs also experience empathy in their relationships with their human companions?

According to the *Oxford American Dictionary and Thesaurus*, "empathy is the ability to understand or share the feelings of another person" (417). This definition can be expanded to consider whether or not dogs possess the ability to *understand* and *share* feelings within the human/dog bond.

Empathy differs from sympathy which involves "the feeling of being sorry for someone who is unhappy or in difficulty" (*Oxford American* 1326). These observations highlight comments by Horowitz, as well as Range and Virányi. Horowitz considers the difficultly of analyzing "the subjective experience of animals" without the benefit of verbal responses (145). Range and Virányi observe that human cognitive skills involve both simple and more complex skills (126–127). Expressions of empathy do not require verbal responses, but rather can be evident in dog behavioral responses. These observations do not preclude dogs from being able to respond to some levels of empathy. Empathic responses involve different degrees of complexity.

According to Custance and Mayer, "Empathy covers a range of phenomena from cognitive empathy involving metarepresentation to emotional contagion stemming from automatically triggered reflexes" (1).

Companionship (Chris McBrien, CC BY-SA 2.0).

10. Interactions

Significantly, the necessity of verbal explanation, required with some higher levels of cognitive abilities, does not preclude dogs from sharing empathy utilizing less complex social skills. Scholarly research continues to explore the responses and thoughts of people toward their dogs and dogs toward people. Countless people extol the certainty that dogs do feel and express empathy toward their human counterparts, through various behaviors, based on the contexts of different situations. Empathic responses occur, not just between human individuals, but also between humans and dogs.

The following three studies highlight the behavioral responses of dogs to human emotions. The first, by Custance and Mayer, considers how dogs respond to human behaviors of distress in various physical situations. The second, conducted by Yong and Ruffman, explores how dogs respond to stress and crying based on "auditory stimuli" (155). Subsequently, these studies consider whether or not dogs feel empathy toward people in certain situations. A third study by Huber et al. evaluates responses of dogs to "gain insights into intra- and interspecies empathy" (714). In this study, empathetic responses of both dogs and people are interpreted.

In their work, Custance and Mayer evaluate potential empathic responses of dogs to distress in humans. When presented by distress in humans, dogs can respond either with curiosity or to seek comfort for themselves from the person exhibiting the distress (Custance and Mayer 3). Neither of these responses provides an expression of empathic concern (3).

Custance and Mayer conduct the following tests utilizing a modified version of the Strange Situation Test to evaluate the possibility of empathetic responses in dogs. The tests involve four situations centered on differentiating the types of responses dogs provide when confronted with human distress. In the procedures, the subjects include both the dog and their owner as well as a stranger. Two-minute periods of talking between the owner and stranger separate each individual test situation. The dogs were exposed to four separate experimental test conditions, including (1) when their owner cried; (2) a stranger cried; (3) their owner hummed; and (4) when the stranger hummed in a high-pitched rapid manner (Custance and Mayer 3). The humming test, with the high-pitched hum by the stranger, was designed to investigate if the dogs would express curiosity at such an unusual occurrence.

The tests occurred in the dogs' living rooms so that the environments would be as normal as possible. The study included 18 medium size dogs of various breeds from the North West United States which are all household pets (Custance and Mayer 2). The owners and stranger remained seated throughout the experiments approximately six feet apart. The same person who played the stranger in all the tests was completely unfamiliar to all of the dogs prior to testing (Custance and Mayer 3). She ignored the dogs upon entry, did not look at them directly, or call their names. Subsequently, the dogs showed little interest in the stranger prior to the testing procedures. During the tests, a third person discretely recorded the dog's behavior with a camcorder from the corner of the room.

Two observers (the second author of the study) and an observer unaware of the study's hypothesis, scored a total of six different behavioral categories (Custance and Mayer 4). These behavioral categories included if and how the dog approached, looked at or contracted the owner and stranger (4). The other responses involved if the dog walked around the room, engaged in playing alone or remained passive (4). These procedures highlight the dogs' decision-making processes, based on their behavioral responses whether to engage or disregard the owner and stranger in each of the four situations.

The authors also considered the types of emotional responses exhibited in the above conditions (Custance and Mayer 3). Four pen drawings, with brief descriptions of emotional postures, were created to reflect the approach options as calm, submissive, alert, or playful (5). They note: "Observers, unaware of experimental hypotheses and the condition under which dogs were responding, more often categorized dogs' approaches as submissive as opposed to alert, playful or calm during the crying condition" (Custance and Mayer 1). Significantly, the dogs approached the crying individual whether it was the dog's owner or the stranger (7). "When the stranger pretended to cry, rather than approaching their usual source of comfort, their owner, dogs sniffed, nuzzled, and lick the stranger instead" (Custance and Mayer 3).

The combination of the experiments with the owners and stranger, highlighted by the outside observers' reviews, points to potential recognizable expressions of empathy by the dogs. According to the authors, "The dogs' pattern of response was behaviorally consistent with an expression of empathetic concern, but it is more parsimoniously interpreted as emotional contagion coupled with a previous learning history in which they have been rewarded for approaching distressed individuals" (1). The perceived ability of dogs to share empathic responses with their companions highlights one of the most significant aspects of the interactive bond between people and dogs and includes aspects of dog archetypal characteristics.

Several studies focus on whether dogs and people experience similar physiological and behavioral responses when faced with situations involving distress in others. Do these two species share empathy in such situations? For instance, Yong and Ruffman utilized ... "three auditory stimuli: a human infant crying, a human infant babbling, and computer generated 'white noise' with the latter two stimuli acting as controls" to test responses from the participants (155). These test included 75 canines and 74 humans. They found that dogs and humans showed similar physiological responses based on significant increased cortisol levels ... "only after listening to the crying" (155). The humans also exhibited increased alertness. In addition, the dogs "showed a unique behavioral response to crying, combining submissiveness with awareness" (155). The authors write: "These findings suggest dogs experience emotion contagion in response to human crying and provide the first clear evidence of a primitive cross-specie empathy" (155).

Emotional Contagion and Emphatic Responses

An investigation by Annika Huber et al. further evaluates the responses of dogs to "gain insights into intra- and interspecies empathy" as well as differences in responses to positive and negative emotional sounds (714). The study evaluates responses of 53 dogs "to acoustic stimuli of different meaning" based on three dimensions (703). These dimensions include "Emotionality" by contrasting non-emotional sounds in the dogs' environment with emotional sounds in humans (laughing and crying) and sounds of other dogs (barks and isolation whines) (726). The second dimension "Species" contrasts acoustic stimuli of humans and dogs. The third dimension "Valence" compares dog behavioral responses to positive and negative sounds of humans and other dogs, as well as non-emotional stimuli (715).

This investigation adds insight into the empathetic responses of dogs generated by emotional versus non-emotional reactions in their human companions and the impacts of negative and positive sounds from other dogs. In addition, these responses highlight opportunities for understanding shared empathy between people and dogs.

Why are these three dimensions significant to archetypal characteristics of guide, guard and healer within individual relationships between people and dogs? What aspects of these dimensions facilitate and resonate within interactions involving dog archetypal characteristics? Huber et al. note that emotional contagion is "a basic component of empathy" defined as "emotional state-matching between individuals" (703). They write: "Preston and de Waal (2002) proposed a multi-level concept of empathy, whose most basic level is emotional contagion, defined as an automatic and unconscious emotional state–making between two individuals…" (703).

Research concerning empathy notes the importance of emotional contagion in the ability to experience empathy. In this study, the three dimensions of emotionality, species, and valence address behavioral interactions significant to how dogs interact with people in situations involving empathy. These three areas are also pertinent to how people experience empathy. For instance, why is emotional contagion important in relationships between people involving empathetic reactions? Huber et al. note that emotional contagion "may well be important in personal relationships because it fosters behavioral synchrony and the moment-to-moment tracking of other people's feelings even when individuals are not explicitly attending to this information" (Hatfield et al. 1993, p. 96) (702). These observations are also pertinent to the interactions between people and dogs.

The aim of this investigation "was to further shed light on emotional contagion in dogs to acoustic stimuli of different meanings" (704). Huber et al. set up a playback study which analyzed "the three dimensions simultaneously…" (704). The testing took place in two identical rooms, each room containing three wooden separation walls "arranged in a semi-circular manner…" (704). The separation walls concealed a wooden box hiding an external loudspeaker. Each room contained one loudspeaker, connected by an audio cable to a laptop outside the room. Opposite the walls, a blanket was placed on the ground for the dog, next to a chair for the owner (703). At the beginning of each trial, the owner "entered the room though the connection door with the dog on leash and sat down on the chair" (702). After a five minute accommodation period, the dog was unleashed. The speaker stimuli sounds were then shifted from box to box, randomly throughout the testing and each sound was played for two minutes with the dog able to move freely around the room (707). The locations for the trials were alternated between the individual rooms and the speaker position was switched from one position to another while the dog was in the other testing room. "This experiment consisted of two sessions, four trials each" with four different acoustic stimuli, played back in each trial (706). "All tests were video-taped with three cameras in each room, and subsequent analysis of the dogs' behavioral response were made from the videos" (Huber et al. 707).

Huber et al. grouped the behavioral variables into the following three

10. Interactions

categories: (1) *Owner-oriented* behavioral comprised of two variables: "Look at Owner" and "Approach the owner"; (2) *Loudspeaker–oriented* behavior comprised two categories "Look at loudspeaker" and "Approach the loudspeaker"; and (3) *"Indicators for arousal and negative emotional states"* (708). The third category provided data concerning ten variables of communication including vocalization (barking, whining), and other facial movements (yawning, lip licking, and panting) (709). Body communication movements of shaking, stretching, immobility/freezing, and tail wagging round out these variables (709).

Huber et al. found that "the dogs' behavioral responses differed between emotional and non-emotional sounds for nearly all analyzed variables" (710). For the second behavior category, loudspeaker oriented: "Specifically, in trials with emotional sounds, the dogs looked significantly longer toward the loudspeaker areas where the playback oriented from…" (710). "They also observed differences in the human trials with emotional and non-emotional sounds for both variables" (710). In the third behavior category "*Indicators for arousal and negative emotional states*," the ten behavioral variables were pooled to add a new variable "Relative Reactivity Score" ("RRS"). This variable "represents the dogs' overall behavioral response in terms of arousal and negative emotional valence" (708).

Huber et al. note that two previous studies (Custance and Mayer 2012) and (Yong and Ruffman 2014) "investigated emotional contagion in dogs" by analyzing "the emotional tone of the subjects' behavior in terms of emotional state postures…" (712). In those experiments, "they applied a rather qualitative behavior analysis by coding emotional displays on the basis of the dogs' overall body postures" (712). In contrast, the Huber et al. study "applied a quantitative behavioral analysis by focusing on single predefined behaviors" (712). According to Huber et al., "Interpreting the dogs' behavior responses in terms of certain valanced states is generally a challenging task…" (712). They add: "However, it is a prerequisite for labeling behavioral responses as triggered by empathy (Edgar et al. 2012)" (712).

Significantly, Huber et al. found in comparing positively with negatively valanced sounds, "that, independent of the species from which the sound originated, dogs expressed more behavioral indicators for arousal and negatively valanced sounds after hearing negative emotional sounds" (703). They add: "This response pattern indicates emotional state-making or emotional contagion for negative sounds of humans and conspecifics" (703). "It furthermore indicates that dogs recognized the different valences of the emotional sounds, which is a promising finding for future studies on empathy for positive emotional states in dogs" (703).

In addition, aspects of "emotional state-matching" provide perspectives on how dog archetypal characteristics impact relationships with people (703). Dogs can match the emotional states of their human companions in situations involving potential empathic responses and possess the social skills to provide these types of responses. Dogs concentrate on interpreting cues from their human companions from moment to moment watching and evaluating perspectives-taking cues in their interactions with people.

The capacity to share feelings of both happiness and distress resides at the highest level of the human/dog bond. In addition, a dog's companionship during such experiences with their human counterparts often creates a sense of *mutually shared experience*. In many situations, individuals and dogs experience and share the emotional impacts of situations *as they occur*. Furthermore, these communications between individuals and dogs exist within an interactive cord.

The above research examples illustrate how people and dogs communicate through interactions involving attachment, motivation, and empathy. At the center of these interactions lies interpretation of behaviors by *both* species. People and dogs interpret these behaviors framed by an individual and universal bond that continues to unfold.

Facial Expressions and Emotional Intentions

Previously, this book explores different communicative methods people and dogs utilize, including physical, visual, and vocal cues. The following research seeks to eliminate all such cues which might affect whether or not dogs "can discriminate emotional expressions of human faces" (Müller et al. 600). This research explores "the question of whether animals have emotions and respond to the emotional expressions of others" (601). The authors note that prior to their 2015 study, "no study has convincingly shown that animals discriminate between emotional expressions of heterospecifics, excluding the possibility that they respond to simple cues" (601).

Mueller et al. highlight the significance of research concerning interspecies communications between people and dogs. They write: "The most promising species pair for investigating emotion recognition between heterospecifics are domestic dogs and their human owners" (601). They

10. Interactions

Empathy (Free Range Stock).

observe "On the one hand, emotional expressions are best understood in humans, and on the other hand, a wealth of data shows that dogs excel at reading human behavioral cues" (601).

Dogs interpret behavioral cues of people in various situations. This research considers whether dogs can differentiate the emotions of people based *only* on facial cues. In their research, Mueller et al. set up "a meticulously controlled experiment that the subjects could only solve by discriminating the emotional expressions in the presented human faces" (601). The experimental procedures for this research are briefly summarized below. Originally, the subjects included 24 adult pet dogs with 18 Border Collies, two mixed breed dogs, and one Fox Terrier, Golden Retriever, Sheltie, and German Shepherd (Müller et al. Table S1: Subjects). According to the authors, "All subjects had prior experience with a touch-screen apparatus and had at least learned to solve a two-choice task that required them to discriminate two geometrical figures presented simultaneously on the computer screen (a square and circle)" (Müller et al. Supplemental Experimental Procedures). In addition, "Six of the subjects had previously participated in a study in which they were rewarded for discriminating between two unfamiliar faces, or elements of the two faces, presented on the touch-screen monitor" (Supplemental Experimental Procedures).

The computer testing apparatus included a three-sided box with touch-screen at the end. The apparatus was designed so the touch-screen was visually shielded with panels on the sides and top "to ensure that the dogs' choices would not be influenced by the owners or experimenter" (Müller et al. Material). The dogs' owners sat at the opposite end of the room. Behind the monitor box was a feeder box with an automatic feeder, the computer, and the experimenter who was not visible to the dogs.

The test procedures involved pre-training, training, and four probe trials. The pre-training sessions with the subjects involved presenting "picture pairs of a face with a neutral expression and the back of the head of the same person" (Müller et al. 601). The dogs then "learned to discriminate between faces of the same person with a happy or angry emotional expression presented on a touch-screen monitor" (601). Significantly, "in this training phase, the subjects were only shown the upper halves or the lower halves of the pictures" (601). According to the authors, "If the subject chose the correct stimulus by touching it with their nose" a pleasant tone was played and a food reward dispensed (Müller et al. Procedure). They added "if the subject chose the incorrect stimulus" a less pleasant tone was played and a red screen was presented for three seconds (Procedure).

During this phase, the dogs learned "to discriminate between happy and angry human faces in 15 pairs, whereby for one group only the upper halves of the faces were shown and for the other group only the lower halves of the faces were shown" (601). The pictures included only "the presence or absence of simple cues such as teeth or frown lines" (602). These facial cues are also central to how people convey emotions of happiness and anger between each other.

The dogs "proceeded from the pre-training to training phase once they had reached a learning criterion of at least 24 correct choices in three consecutive sessions" (Müller et al. Procedure). Eleven of the 18 subjects then proceeded "to the test phase after they reached a learning criterion of at least 23 correct choices in 4 out of 5 consecutive sessions" (Procedure).

During the probe trials, the authors "could subsequently test the subjects' ability to spontaneously categorize novel pictures that shared with the training stimuli only the emotional expression as the distinguishing feature" (Mueller et al. 601). The four types of probe trials included pictures of upper and lower half of novel faces which the dogs had not seen, as well as pictures of upper half and left half faces previously shown in training sessions (602). Ten pairs of stimulus pictures were included in each probe (602).

The results of this study are significant in several ways. The authors "found that dogs for which the happy faces were rewarded learned the discrimination more quickly than dogs for which the angry faces were rewarded" (601). The authors note: "This would be predicted if the dogs recognized an angry face as an aversion stimulus" (601). In addition, the authors found that "the dogs performed significantly above chance level in all four probe conditions and thus transferred the training contingency to novel stimuli that shared with the training set only the emotional expression as a distinguishing feature" (601). Significantly, Müller et al. concluded "that the dogs used their memories of real emotional human faces to accomplish the discrimination task" (601).

While definitely fascinating, why is this research important in understanding social skills of dogs? The research by Mueller et al. focuses on the abilities of dogs to retain memories of human expressions (happy, sad, and angry) based only on the communication cues of facial expressions. Three social skills of discernment, evaluation, and subsequent actions are all evident in this research. These three abilities are also central to communications between people. The ability to determine implications of memories and subsequently interpret emotional expressions provides another example of how dogs utilize their social skills. These social skills provide fundamental elements within interactive relationships between dogs and people

The Dog as Guide, Guard and Healer

Companionship Within Individual and Social Environments

The American Veterinary Medical Association defines the Human-Animal Bond or HAB as "a mutually beneficial and dynamic relationship between people and other animals that is influenced by behaviors that are essential to the health and well-being of both. This includes, but is not limited to, emotional, psychological, and physical interactions of people, other animals, and the environment" (qtd. in Fine and Beck 5). Interactions between people and dogs, framed by dogs' communication and social skills, are significant within both individual relationships and larger social environments.

Love (Naina dsc, CC BY-SA 4.0).

10. Interactions

For example, Salmon and Salmon conducted a large-scale study in Melbourne, Australia, concerning the nature of individual relationships between people and their dogs. This study considers emotional and psychological interactions between dogs and individuals, as well as physical characteristics in these relationships. Their objectives involved investigating "...the differential role of pets for people at different stages of the life cycle; the benefits and problems associated with pet ownership and the level of pet owners' knowledge about municipal regulations and the responsibilities of pet ownership" (Salmon and Salmon 246). The 1980–81 study included personal interviews "in 308 households, representing a total of 1063 people..." with "396 dogs, 197 cats and 193 other pets" (246). The structure of the questionnaire included four variables: person-related and pet-related demographics, factual, attitudinal, and level of knowledge (Salmon and Salmon 247).

Person-related demographics addressed questions about household composition, household location ("inner, middle, or outer suburb"), sex, age, and marital status (247). Pet-related demographic questions included the number, types, breeds, age, sex, and if the pet had been spayed or neutered (247). The factual variable addressed "Length of ownership" and which members of the family assumed "caretaking responsibilities" for the pets (247). Level of knowledge questions included the owner's knowledge of regulations in their municipality and ownership responsibilities such as registration and leash laws (247). Several aspects of the attitudinal variables are discussed in more detail below, noting archetypal and motivational influences for different age groups of participants and stages of life.

The questions were formulated to determine how much the four variables influence the role of the pet in the family and to explore the different roles pets play for different ages and groups (Salmon and Salmon 247). These two functions, the roles dogs play in the interactive family relationships and the varying importance of dogs for different age groups and life cycle stages illustrate the multi-faceted niches of *how* people and dogs interact within the human/dog bond (259). The research and responses concerning interactions between individual family members and their dogs reveal several aspects pertinent not only to the overall human/dog bond but also specific aspects concerning dog archetypal characteristics of guide, guard, and healer. Metaphysical and temporal aspects frame these interactions couched in the influences of psychology and cultural considerations.

The authors utilized various questions constructions "...to elicit information including Likert scales, the semantic differential, rating

The Dog as Guide, Guard and Healer

scales, and simple open-response questions" (Salmon and Salmon 247). For example, one question addressed the owners' perceptions of their dogs based on the open-ended question "How would you describe your dog's behavior?" (253). This question received 91 percent positive responses that "...gave a favorable image of the dog such as obedient, well-behaved, good dog, gentle, quiet, affectionate, loving, good watch dog, good with children, and intelligent" (Salmon and Salmon 248).

What interactions and perceptions help create such positive responses from people concerning their dogs? A further series of cross-tabulations on the rating scales data "...showed some variations among people despite the extremely 'favorable results' in the sample as a whole'" (254). The authors noted that possibly "...people see their dog as an extension or projection of themselves and thus describe it according to their own self-concept. This possibility is not surprising when one considers the enormous amount of generalization that takes place in human relationships" (Salmon and Salmon 254).

A factor analysis of the descriptive adjectives data also revealed "...an underlying pattern of relationships existed among these descriptions" (Salmon and Salmon 254). "This analysis yielded three major factors: acceptance/trust, love/friendship, and intelligence/obedience" (254). Salmon and Salmon write: "This analysis showed that pet owners described their dogs according to three components or dimensions that form a conceptual image which people have about their pets. This image, in turn, governs their relationship with the pet" (254).

From a different perspective, dog archetypal characteristics of guard, guide, and healer emerge in these findings. The findings reveal interactions and accumulative perceptions of people toward their dogs framed by these archetypal characteristics. How do these interactions occur and flow between dogs and people? What characteristics and attributes of dogs help facilitate and influence these responses?

In the Salmon and Salmon et al. study, several questions and responses for the attitudinal variable reflect behavioral and motivational influences between dogs and people. Significantly, many responses reveal motivations concerning fulfillment of the five basic needs described in Maslow's Theory of Motivation. The two basic needs of love and self-esteem significantly mirror the first two major factors noted above of acceptance/trust, and love/friendship. Aspects of the third factor, intelligence/obedience, illustrate characteristics of guide and guard within the human/dog bond including the basic need of safety. For instance, three quarters of the respondents "felt the need to be physically protected by a dog" ... and

10. Interactions

that their dogs protected their homes from burglary (Salmon and Salmon 256). Here the dogs provide physical protection for the individual as well as property and psychological protection resulting in a reduction of fear or insecurity.

Results from this survey reveal significant connections between the individual's desire for fulfillment of basic needs and the unique bond between people and dogs. Salmon and Salmon write: "…the main needs satisfied by dogs were companionship, protection and happiness/pleasure" (255).

Dogs and people share a relationship framed with the influences of love, support, and the presence that dogs provide and share with their human companions. These perceptions move back and forth between people and dogs. The social skills, perspective-taking abilities, and physical skills of dogs underpin these interactions. At the center of this relationship lies the bond of companionship, couched in a unique essence that remains undefinable and extends back through time into prehistory. This central essence weaves through the past, present, and future journey of people and dogs.

11

Links Between Motivation, Companionship and Social Capital

Aspects of motivation, companionship and social capital reside and interact within the nucleus of the human/dog bond. Motivation, a complex and dynamic concept with wide ranging causes, provides an essential link within this bond. Significantly, motivation creates similar responses impacting observation, communication, and social interactions between people and dogs. At the nexus of these shared interactions lies attachment. How does attachment occur, evolve, and weave through individual relationships between people and dogs? Why is it so important in the human/dog bond? And, what link does motivation play in interaction between people and dogs?

The perspectives of humanistic psychology provide several concepts pertinent to motivation and attachment within the human/dog bond. For instance, the work of Maslow highlights human psychological needs including love, belonging, and esteem. These needs, as well as attachment, influence interactions between people and dogs. In 1943, Maslow published "A Theory of Human Motivation" which presents "at least five sets of goals" defined as basic needs ("Theory" 12). In this theory, "Human needs arrange themselves in hierarchies of pre-potency" (1). He observes that "the appearance of one need usually rests on the prior satisfaction of another, more pre-potent need" (1). In addition, he notes that people "are motivated by the desire to achieve or maintain the various conditions upon which these basic satisfactions rest and by certain more intellectual desires" (12).

Maslow describes these basic needs as "physiological, safety, love, esteem, and self-actualization" ("Theory" 12). A brief overview of Maslow's first four level of needs follows. This book focuses somewhat on the motivational need for safety, but more specifically on the needs for love and

11. Links Between Motivation, Companionship and Social Capital

esteem and the impact of these needs on the bond between people and dogs.

The first priority in basic needs involves physiological requirements. Physiological responses include homeostasis "the ability to maintain a relatively stable internal state that persists despite changes in the world outside" (Lanese 2). Lanese adds "All living organisms, from plants to puppies to people, must regulate their internal environment to process energy and survive" (Lanese 2). Physiological processes involve such items as the contents of water, salt, sugar, protein, fat, calcium, oxygen and other physiological requirements of the human body (Maslow, "Theory" 2). Other physiological needs include "sexual desire, sleepiness, sheer activity and maternal behavior in animals" (Maslow, "Theory" 2).

The second group of needs involves the desires for safety (Maslow, "Theory" 2). For the most part within functioning societies, "its members feel safe enough from wild animals, extremes of temperature, criminals, assault, murder" and tyranny ("Theory" 5). The motivation for safety arises when an individual faces a personal threat or global threat, an emergency such as "war, disease, natural catastrophes, crime waves, societal disorganization" as well as some psychological disturbances (5).

On an individual level, within the relationships of people and dogs, there are situations where a dog's presence helps alleviate some of the fears involved in personal safety. The interactions between people and dogs in areas of safety and security have been a significant element in the historical development and evolution of the human/dog bond. Since their early interactions with people, prehistoric dogs provide guard duties and people provide food and inclusion within their camps. These interactions continue up to the present day and dogs continue to provide guard and protection duties. In addition, as people interact in contemporary societal groups, dogs can also provide personal feelings of security.

According to Maslow, "If both the physiological and the safety needs are fairly well gratified, then there will emerge the love and affection and the belongingness needs" ("Theory" 6). The basics needs for love, esteem, and belonging described by Maslow are central motivations within the human/dog bond. These basic needs help frame interactive responses in the relationships between people and dogs. The cognitive abilities of dogs, the behaviors of dogs, and the responses of people toward these behaviors impact this bond.

Maslow adds further insight concerning motivation and behavior. He emphasizes "that the basic principle" in this motivation theory is neither the instigation nor the behavior, "but rather the functions, effects, purposes, or goals of the behavior" (11). Various aspects of attachment between people and dogs can be viewed through the perspectives of this motivation theory. For instance, relationships between dogs and people create a sense of purpose for individuals, the sense of being needed and belonging. Interactions with dogs offer opportunities for increased self-esteem and reciprocated love.

Maslow's motivational theory stresses and centers "itself upon ultimate or basic goals rather than partial or superficial ones, upon ends rather than means to these ends" ("Theory" 1). Maslow notes that such an emphasis implies "a more central place for unconscious than for conscious motivations" (1). In addition, "There are usually various cultural paths to the same goal" (1). Subsequently, he observes that due to such opportunities, "conscious, specific local-cultural desires are not as fundamental in motivation theory as the more basic unconscious specific goals" (1).

Aspects of Maslow's theory of motivation reinforce some of the unconscious influences concerning how motivations are expressed within the human/dog bond. For instance, unconscious motivations can be expressed through responses to dog archetypal images within interactions between people and dogs. As such, the human/dog bond reflects aspects of guard, guide, and healer imagery in the perceptions of individuals and their responses to dogs. People seek safety, the desire for belonging, love, and self-esteem within their lives. Dogs serve as guides and partners to help achieve these goals and enhance positive aspects of their fulfillment from a psychological perspective and a physical presence.

Significantly, Maslow finds that "motivation theory is not synonymous with behavior theory" ("Theory" 2). In addition, "motivations are only one class of determinants of behavior" (2). Maslow writes: "While behavior is almost always motivated, it is almost always biologically, culturally and situationally determined as well" (2). Behavior between people and dogs within the human/dog bond is also motivated by these influences as evident in psychology and dog ethology.

Maslow addresses two additional characteristics of basic needs that impact the human/dog bond. He describes these characteristics as the "Unconscious character of needs and the 'Cultural specificity and generality of needs'" ("Theory" 10). Concerning "the character of needs" he observes that "these needs are neither necessarily unconscious nor conscious" (10). Maslow adds that, for the most part, unconscious motivations would be rather "more important than the conscious motivations" (10). In addition, "basic needs are very often largely unconscious" (10).

Pertinent to the human/dog bond are *why* and *how* these motivations influence interactions between people and dogs. The archetypal characteristics of guide, guard, and healer reside, to some degree, within the unconscious desires for fulfillment of some basic needs. In addition, both seeking and fulfilling these needs is not static but rather interactive and evolving based on psychosocial parameters of each individual. In this process patterns of behavior and motivational influences create pathways to fulfillment of basic needs within the human/dog bond.

Maslow's theory also considers "the relative unity behind the superficial differences in separate desires from one culture to another" ("Theory" 10). Maslow does not suggest that his classification of needs is "ultimate or universal for all cultures" (10). Rather, he suggests that this classification of needs is relatively more ultimate, more universal, more basic, than the superficial conscious desires from culture to culture (10). The concept of universality also occurs in the interconnected spheres of the human/dog bond.

Why are these observations important to the human/dog bond? Observations concerning basic needs and subsequent motivations highlight unconscious desires across cultures and time and the impacts these motivations inspire. These motivations, which are interactive within various situations, inspire and fortify aspects of the bond between people and dogs. Cultural and psychological responses inform these desires. In addition, dog archetypal imagery of guide, guard, and healer reside within these interactions and subsequent responses.

Motivation for achievement of basic goals creates one link in the continuity of the human/dog bond throughout history. For instance, links between motivation and attachment provide insight into the interactive communication between people and dogs. What role does motivation play in attachment and social interactions between people and dogs? How do aspects of communication weave throughout these interactions? The following pages explore these questions framed by selected dog ethological and psychological studies. These studies lead to significant results and fascinating insights concerning the bond between people and dogs.

Aspects of Companionship

In January 1980, the British Small Animal Veterinary Association held an international symposium on The Human–Companion Animal Bond. Scholars from the fields of psychology, sociology, ethology, anthropology and psychiatry, together with veterinarians, presented papers. The

The Dog as Guide, Guard and Healer

book *Interrelations Between People and Pets*, a product of the symposium, highlights the interrelated threads between these disciplines concerning the nature and importance of the human-companion animal bond.

Michael Fox, former director of the Institute for the Study of Animal Problems in Washington, D.C., presents a paper titled "Relationships Between the Human and Nonhuman Animals." He notes that one of the greatest values of pets "is to help people regain their 'animal/nature connection': to become more fully human by an interspecies relationship that can break down egocentric and humanocentric perceptions and valuations" (30). In arriving at this conclusion, he focuses on four categories of owner–pet relationships: Object-oriented relationships, utilitarian relationships, need-dependence relationships, and the actualizing relationship (32–33). Object oriented relationships address owning a pet because "the family has always had a pet," or owning a pet as a status symbol (30). Functions, such as "guard, bird dog, guide for the blind, for show, obedience trials, and for breeding purposes" involve utilitarian relationships "… in combination with varying degrees of need-dependence and object oriented relatedness" (31).

The third category of "interpersonal intimacy" involves need-dependency relationships. According to Fox, this type of relationship "is perhaps the major reason why people have pets, especially dogs and cats; it is also a common underlying emotional mode in many relationships between people" (32). In addition to being companions, dogs provide "an unconditionally affectionate and accepting emotional support; a link with nature, with natural, uninhibited and honest emotions and responses; a refreshing break from the vacuous impersonal and often dehumanizing human transactions" (32). This description highlights some of the answers to why humans desire and seek the companionship of dogs.

Aspects of need-dependency also impact other influences within the relationships of individuals and dogs. Here lie great opportunities and risks. Utilizing Fox's perspective, dogs are easier to relate to and do not carry "the insecurities, ego defenses and associated expectations" of humans (33). These characteristics are absent or minimal in a dog, as well as small children, allowing the opportunity to establish "a natural, transpersonal relationship" (33). The risk is that "this unconditional openness and receptivity in the pet (or child) can lead to a need-dependency relationship, satisfying such human needs as to mother and indulge or dominate and control" (33). Here are two seemingly opposite responses: the need to mother and indulge versus dominate and control. Both of these responses appear in psychological research concerning early human

11. Links Between Motivation, Companionship and Social Capital

mother/child relationships. Researchers also find similar responses in some types of relationships between humans and dogs.

Michael Fox then defines the fourth category of the human-companion animal relationship as a mature, actualizing relationship between pet and owner. He writes: "Here the pet is related to essentially as a respected 'significant other'; its intrinsic worth being appreciated for itself instead of for reasons of status, utility, or emotional support" (33). Within this category, "The person's perception and understanding of the pet shifts from one of dependency to one that is self-actualizing, less egocentric, and more transpersonal" (33). This level of interactions, between humans and pets, reflects Maslow's research concerning self-actualization. Maslow notes self-actualization is defined in several ways. He adds: "All definitions accept or imply, (a) acceptance and expression of the inner core of self, i.e., actualization of these latent capacities, and potentialities, 'full functioning,' availability of the human and personal essence" (Toward 163).

Constance Perin, a cultural anthropologist, discusses similarities between the human-dog bond and the mother-child bond in her paper "Dogs as Symbols in Human Development." Perin notes that bonding between people and dogs is characterized by "super abundance" (77). This bond "is often seen to represent an *excess of love* having no rightful place in human relationships, supersaturated feelings people are not able to or not allowed to bestow on other people" (77). Perin also states that "dogs enter into our deepest feelings without our having to use speech" (77). This observation illustrates David Abram's observations that humans possess the capacity to feel and understand nonhuman forms of speech. Hillman also notes, "We find nature in our mutual wordless relation with the dog" (133).

Perin offers an observation that with dogs, humans turn to another species to receive "unquestioning devotion, utter adoration, a total absence of judging, unspeakably overwhelming trust, unspoken understanding, and unbounded love" (81). Human relationships cannot possibly match this list of superlatives. Perin sees the anticipation or fulfillment of "such supernatural expectations" by dogs as a symbol of "something transhuman or metaphysical" (81). Dog archetypal imagery of guide and healer reside within shared experiences, both conscious and unconscious within interactions between people and dogs. Sensing these archetypal presences, and desires for human fulfillment, are major catalysts within relationships between individuals and their dog companions.

The Dog as Guide, Guard and Healer

Characteristics of Attachment: Similarities Between People and Dogs

Topál et al. explore three aspects of attachment that are applicable to attachment between people and dogs. These aspects involve the importance of emotional ties, the desire to maintain close physical proximity, and the establishment of a bond that reflects a long-term emotional connection. Previous research studies highlight these interactions between people. For instance, attachment has been "considered a hypothetical factor that ties individuals together (Lorenz, 1966) or a behavior system that results in one individual seeking and maintaining proximity to another individual (Bowlby, 1972). Cohen (1974) defined *attachment* as a special affectional relationship between two individuals that is specific in its focus and endures over time" (Topál et al. 219). These descriptions originally addressed attachments between people, but they also are relevant to attachments between dogs and people and reflect specific characteristics within the human/dog bond.

In 1970, Mary Ainsworth "developed a standardised experimental procedure aimed at characterizing attachment relationships in human infants based on Bowlby's theories: the Strange Situation" (Emanuela and

Attachment (CC BY-SA 4.0).

11. Links Between Motivation, Companionship and Social Capital

Prato Previde and Paola Valsecchi 169). This test provides a significant methodological approach for evaluating aspects of attachment (Topál et al. 219). Topál et al. create a modified version of the Strange Situation test to analyze dog attitudinal behavior in various situations (219). Their study offers perspectives on three behavioral factors: attachment, anxiety, and acceptance (219).

"According to Ainsworth (1989), affectional bonds fulfil the following criteria: (1) endure over time; (2) involve a specific individual which is not interchangeable with anyone else (the 'reference figure'); (3) are emotionally significant"; ... (Previde and Valsecchi 168). The additional criteria include (4) "promote proximity—and contact—seeking behaviors towards the reference figure; and (5) are characterized by a distress reacting when involuntary separation from the reference figure occurs (Cassidy, 1999)" (Previde and Valsecchi 168). Significantly, the attachment bond includes one additional criterion "that is unique of the attachment bond: the individual seeks security and comfort in the relationship with the partner and yet 'has the ability to move off from the secure base provided by the partner, with confidence to engage in other activities'" (Ainsworth, 1989, p. 711), quoted in Previde and Valsecchi (168).

Why are research findings concerning attachment between infants and caregivers pertinent to the human/dog bond? Research suggests that similarities exist between the caregiver/infant bond, framed by attachment, and the bond between dogs and their human companions. In addition, the nature of these attachments, including anxiety and acceptance, provides some of the catalysts for the interactions between humans and dogs.

These behavioral responses are evident in the following Topal et al. study conducted concerning attachment behaviors between dogs and their owner or caregiver. As noted above, the Strange Situation test focuses on the attachment behavior of infants activated by their responses to separation and reunion with their attachment figures (Topál et al. 219). According to the authors, "Infant responses to this situation are customarily classified as fitting into one of three overall patterns of behavioral organizations: 'secure, insecure-avoidant, and insecure-resistant'" (219). In the first category, *secure*, "the infant shows signs of missing the parent upon separation, greets the parent actively upon reunion, and then settles and returns to play" (219). The second category of behavior is described as "*insecure-avoidant* (the infant shows little or no distress of separation from the parent) and actively avoids and ignore the parent upon reunion" (219). The third category is define as "*insecure-resistant* (the infant is highly distressed by separation,) and seeks for contact or reunion, but cannot be settled by the parent and may show strong resistance" (Topál et al. 219–220).

In their study, Topál et al. explore similar situations between dogs, owners, and strangers based on the parameters of the Strange Situation test. The tests involve eight episodes including an initial session and seven experimental test sessions (220). Their ethological method utilizes 50 owner-dog pairs from kennel clubs, with the owners' ages 13 to 60 years (220). The dog participants include 20 different pure breeds as well as seven mixed breeds in the sample. The tests are set up to evaluate the behavioral aspects involved in separation and *how* the dogs react to both separation from their owner and reunion with their owner (Topál et al. 219).

Topál et al. create an environment and experimental protocol to replicate as close as possible the Ainsworth et al. Strange Situation test (Topál et al. 220). The tests occur in a fairly empty room which contains two chairs for the owner and stranger and a door. At the end of the room (opposite the door), they provided toys for the dogs (220). After an introductory episode, the sessions involve two-minute episodes where the dogs interact in situations with both the dog's owner and the stranger in the room, the owner and dog alone in the room, the dog alone with the stranger, and two different episodes when the owner and dog are reunited (Topál et al. 221). When the stranger and dogs are alone, the stranger attempts to play or pet the dog in order to discourage him or her from entering the door (221). Later, the videotaped sessions are analyzed based on eight behavior categories by trained observers (221).

According to Topál et al., "The results demonstrate that adult dogs (*Canis familiaris*) show patterns of attachment behavior toward the owner. Although there was considerable variability in dogs' attachment behavior to humans, the authors did not find any affect of gender, age, living conditions, or breed on most of the behavioral variables" (219). The results of the secure-base episodes included increased exploration and playing when their owners or caregivers were present (220). In contrast, during "the separation episodes, dogs stood at the door for considerable length of time; the fact that this behavior was not reduced by the presence of the stranger suggests dogs' strong preference to their owners in stress situations" (Topál et al. 226).

Why is this research significant concerning the bond between dogs and people? Similarities between the mother/infant bond and human/dog bond provide some of the most significant scientific data concerning the basis of the human/dog bond. The structure of the research and responses

11. Links Between Motivation, Companionship and Social Capital

of the participants illustrate several aspects of the attachment between dogs and people. Topál et al. hypothesize "that for dogs in strange situations, as for children, it is not only the separation from the attachment figures (owner) but the reunion with him or her that activates the dogs' attachment behavior" (220). Their study provides insight into the behavioral mechanisms of interactions and the nature of attachments between individuals and their dogs. Dogs respond to the presence of their owner or caregiver in unknown situations, or the lack of their presence, based on trust, companionship, and reliability in their shared relationship.

In their review of several research studies, Hart and Yamamoto discuss characteristics of communicative behavior and companionship between dogs and people. According to a study by Beck and Madresh, "Pets are a consistent source of attachment and security; relationships with dogs are scored as more secure than those with partners on several measures" (Hart and Yamamoto 249). In one study, "Humans were found to be more effective in offering instrumental aid, affection, and admiration, whereas dogs were better at providing companionship, opportunities for nurturance, and reliable alliance, according to 90 informants" (249). Hart and Yamamoto observe that "the dog may better provide for its owner in areas where humans are lacking, and vice versa" (249). These interactive aspects help reinforce the bond between people and dogs and provide flexibility in how individual relationships adapt to changing conditions.

Dogs communicate with a language of movement that conveys and evokes a wide range of behavioral responses. For instance, Darwin describes behavior patterns in dogs' physical movements which are as evident today as in the 1800s. These behavior pattern include moving their heads and wagging the tail and body, trying to lick their owner's face, hands, or ears, and nestling their body up to their owner (Hart and Yamamoto 250). Often these gestures indicate happiness as they greet their human companions (250). In addition, a dog's body language can reveal underlying emotional responses which communicate expressive intent. Aspects of these expressions create soothing and calming responses in their human counterparts.

Hart and Yamamoto also explore the importance of dogs as companions in different stages of people's lives. The reliability and comfort of a dog's behavior is one of the essential aspects in the establishment and the continued enrichment of the bond between an individual and dog. According to Salmon and Salmon, "it is apparent that dogs satisfy more of the needs of widowed, separated, and divorced people than those at other stages of life" (257). With less family framework, the importance of the dog as a companion increases. For example, the dog becomes "...more of a close friend to them, more like a child, makes them feel safer, and provides them with the greater opportunities for exercise" (257). Significantly, "Dogs seek out their owners for mutual contact and provide affection that is not contingent upon the owner's success or appearance" (Hart and Yamamoto 251). A dog provides an unconditional source of affection that is sometimes neither assured nor expressed between individuals in society.

In many ways, the attributes of well-being and associated behaviors are difficult to define. Perceptions of what constitutes well-being vary from person to person and within societies as a whole. Yet, some behaviors appear to be generally accepted as positive aspects conducive to well-being. For instance, the behavioral patterns associated with displays of affection, loyalty, devotion, and the importance of the tactile interactions of touch and play enhance aspects of well-being between dogs and people.

According to Hart and Yamamoto, "Almost all dog owners in a US study reported playing with their dogs (Stallones et al., 1998)" (251). In one study, observers found that when people were walking their dogs, "on 36% of the walks," people were playing different types of games such as fetch and tag with their dogs. (251). Such activities provide positive dual benefits of physical exercise and the joy of play. In addition, 73 percent of older couples, without children, felt that walking their dogs encouraged interactions with people, "compared with only 48 percent of people at other stages of life" (Salmon and Salmon 257).

Shared close proximity offers one of the most enjoyable and significant aspects of the relationships between people and dogs. For instance, Katcher and Beck conducted "an analysis of 1105 photographs of dogs or cats in a family setting submitted to a photograph contest" (Hart and Yamamoto 251). They "found that 97% of the pictures illustrated people and animals touching each other, generally with the heads of the animal and human close together" (251–252). In addition, 92 percent of the pictures showed "one person and one animal occupying the center of the photograph" (252). These pictures illustrate the smallest social group possible, the individual and their animal family member, which reinforces the importance of both physical closeness and the significance of a one-on-one relationship.

Dogs not only share physical and emotional relationships with individual family members but also offer social connectivity in larger groups of society. The abilities to offer individual enrichments and increase social

11. Links Between Motivation, Companionship and Social Capital

interactions highlight the communicative and social skills of domestic dogs. These characteristics illustrate significant aspects of attachment, emotion, and motivation within the human/dog bond.

Relationships and Rating Scales

The Monash Dog Owner Relationship Scale (MDORS), developed by Dwyer et al. provides "a multi-dimensional questionnaire with which to assess human-companion dog relationships. A multi-step process involving over 1,000 participants resulted in the development of a scale with 28 items, the Monash Dog Owner Relationship Scale or MDORS. The MDORS has three sub-scales, Dog-Owner Interaction, Perceived Emotional Closeness, and Perceived Costs" (243). These scales "appear to represent important and diverse aspects of the human-companion dog relationship" (243).

Elements of this research can also illustrate aspects of the dog archetypal characteristics of guide, guard, and healer as evident in the social skills of dogs and their interactions with their human companions. For instance, the MDORS considers characteristics of "social support, bonding, companionship, and unconditional love" in the relationships between people and dogs (250). Dwyer et al. write: "The starting point for the development of the scale was Social Exchange Theory, a well established

Social time (Carptrash, CC BY-SA 4.0).

psychology theory specifying that human relationships are maintained only when under the perceived costs and benefits are either balanced or when the perceived benefits outweigh the perceived costs" (245).

The study examines both positive and negative aspects of dog ownership. The authors initially "used literature searches and focus groups to help identify relationship dimensions believed to be relevant and then tested a large number of items on a small pilot sample" (245). "The first factor, Factor One, contained items tending to reflect the perceived emotional closeness associated with companion dog ownership. Items in the factor of 'Perceived Emotional Closeness' relate to social support, bonding, companionship and unconditional love" (250). In contrast, items in Factor Two, "Perceived Costs" relate to the negative aspects of companion dog ownership (250). Items in "Perceived Costs" address the costs of caring for a companion dog including monetary aspects, increased responsibility, and restrictions placed on the owner because of the dog (250). The final form of the MDORS provides a "28 item, pencil and paper scale that requires the respondent to simply select one of five possible responses for each item" (252).

The scale could also be utilized to explore dog archetypal characteristics of guide, guard and healer. For example, the three sub-scales assess the extent to which owners and dogs engage in shared activities, the perceived emotional closeness of the relationship, and the perceived costs for the dog owner (Dwyer et al. 252). In addition, the scale could provide further insights into the interconnected spheres of mind, culture and nature in individual relationships between people and dog companions.

The MDORS expands the scientifically based knowledge of aspects of the human/dog bond based on the "statistical priorities of the items as well as their theoretical relevance" (252). The scale includes "a comprehensive assessment of the perceived costs of companion animal ownership as well as the perceived benefits" (252).

The following research offers additional perspectives concerning companionship and attachment between individuals and their dogs. Dotson and Hyatt conduct an expansive survey of 749 dogs owners which "focuses on the dog-human relationship and the dog-related consumption expenses that come from such relationships" (Dotson and Hyatt 457). The authors investigate specific components and responses involved in companionship between individuals and their dogs and the "results that came from such interactions" (457).

Participants "filled out a self-administrated questionnaire in a mall-intercept setting (424) respondents, in a veterinarian waiting

11. Links Between Motivation, Companionship and Social Capital

room setting (219) respondents across five vet (offices), or a dog-owning internet-discussion-group (106 respondents)" (460). The questionnaire included 57 Likert-type exploratory questions which revealed 12 factors. Only seven of these factors "could be meaningfully interpreted and explained" ... "with a significant amount of variance in the data" (460). Therefore, those seven factors were utilized in analyzing responses concerning dog-human companionship dimensions.

The research by Dotson and Hyatt identifies the following seven underlying dimensions in dog companionship: "symbiotic relationship, dog-oriented self-concept, anthropomorphism, activity/youth, boundaries, specialty purchases, and willingness to adapt" (457). They write "Dog companionships has attitudinal, experimental, and behavioral components that underlie it" ... and the objective is ... "to uncover its underlying dimensions" (457). In this process, they consider "The nature and meanings of such relationships" from a quantitative rather than qualitative perspective (457).

This research offers several dimensions of companionship between dogs and their owners which also reveal links with underlying dog archetypal characteristics of guide, guard, and healer. Why are these dimensions and perspectives pertinent to aspects of the dog as guide, guard, and healer? Attitudinal and behavioral components frame aspects of dog archetypal characteristics. Several research studies in this book illustrate aspects of these dimensions within the human/dog bond.

Dotson and Hyatt write, "In present society, evidence points to the role that dogs play in satisfying human needs for companionship, friendship, unconditional love, and affection—all of which have become increasingly hard to satisfy in 'our nuclear families living impersonal suburban lifestyles' (Salmon and Salmon 1983)" (250).

The first four "dimensions of the dog-companionship experience" explore aspects which illustrate the importance of guide, guard, and healer dog characteristics (Dodson and Hyatt 460). These characteristics impact individuals but also provide benefits to dogs creating a positive interspecies bond. The Symbiotic Relationship dimension "describes the mutually beneficial bond between person and dog" (460). This dimension includes "...a combination of enjoying, the nurturing component of having a dog along with the benefits received by both parties. In such a relationship, the human is happier, less stressed, less lonely, safer and calmer, while the dog is treated as a child/person who is fed, cared for, and psychologically nurtured" (Dotson and Hyatt 460).

Symbiotic characteristics highlight the mutually beneficial psychological and physiological benefits within human/dog companionship. Numerous research studies, including work by Perin (1981) and Salmon and Salmon (1983), illustrate the interactive cords of this relationship.

The second dog-companionship dimension, Dog-Oriented Self-Concept, "focuses on the importance of the dog(s) to the human's self-concept and social self" (461). Aspects of this dimension also appear in research concerning the social capital of dogs and how people perceive their relationship with their dog companions in different life stages. In this variable, "The dog is both an extension of self and the human's best friend" (460).

Comments include "My dog(s) have helped me develop better relationships with other people" and "My dog is an extension of myself" (Dotson and Hyatt 461). The authors note that this variable provides a more "holistic," profound theme "then found in earlier research" (461). They add: "Dog owners who score high on this dimension are likely to see themselves as 'dog people' and their dogs will play more detailed roles in their lives" (461).

The third variable anthropomorphism reveals additional perspectives concerning how individuals relate to dogs, and how they perceive dogs relate to them. Dotson and Hyatt write: "the dog is seen as more of a person and less of an animal. The dog is perceived as a child surrogate or as a part of the family, who can be communicated with much like another human" (461).

Significantly, this variable addresses perceptions of the dog as a conversation partner who comprehends and interacts in various situations much like a human companion communicates. Dotson and Hyatt add: "Here, the dog owner has opportunities to learn from the dog" (461). Comment include "My dog is part of my family," and "I learn a lot from my dogs" (461). This dimension brings together several aspects concerning the social skills of communication and empathy in the companionships between dogs and people. This variable also highlights some of Perin's observations concerning aspects of the companionship bond and similarities to the mother-child bond (Perin 81).

The research by Dotson and Hyatt illustrates links and perspectives to previous observations by Fox concerning the four categories of owner-pet relationships. For example, the third category "interpersonal intimacy" illustrates the progressing and increasing complexity of how people relate to their dog companions. Fox notes that the fourth category of pet relationships is framed with the individual's increasing appreciation of their dog companion as "respected significant other" (33). The observations

11. Links Between Motivation, Companionship and Social Capital

correlate to aspects of the second and third dimensions of "Dog-Oriented Self Concept" and "Anthropomorphism" in Doston and Hyatt's work. These various psychological perceptions also highlight significant dog archetypal nuances in relationships of people with their dog companions.

In the Activity Youth Variable, responses highlight the positive aspects of exercise, play, and joy. Responses include "I feel like a kid when I'm playing with my dogs," and "My dog keeps me young" (Dodson and Hyatt 461). This variable illustrates aspects in Bradshaw and Rooney (2017) concerning the benefits of play and observations by Hart and Yamomoto (2017) concerning the benefits of dog companionship.

The fifth variable Boundaries evaluates boundaries or "rules" for dogs in the house. The sixth variable Specialty Purchases involves stopping for specific dog-related purchases and the seventh dimension Willingness to Adapt considers how owners adjust their purchases, schedules, and home environments based on their interactions with their dog companions (Dodson and Hyatt 462). Responses to the sixth and seventh dimensions concerning dog-related purchases and consumption point "to people's heightened involvement with their dogs" (Dodson and Hyatt 458). They also note, "The increased amount of time, energy, effort, and money that people spend in providing for their dogs results in significant lifestyle changes for dog owners" (458).

Dogs, People and Social Capital

Extensive research highlights the social and behavioral skills of dogs as companions with individuals. However, few studies consider if and how dogs facilitate and encourage "friendship formation or social support networks among humans" (Wood et al. 1). A recent study explores these questions, including how dogs serve as catalysts in social interactions. Wood et al. investigate "the indirect role of pets as facilitators for three dimensions of social relatedness: getting to know people, friendship formation and social support networks" (1).

Why are these potential roles of dogs significant concerning interactions and health benefits between people? According to current literature, "there is now compelling empirical evidence for the importance of social relationships and social support for both physical and mental wellbeing" (Wood et al. 1). How can dogs encourage more interactions between groups of people and reduce the disconnection sociologists observe in contemporary societies? Dogs possess several talents in their social interactions with

The Dog as Guide, Guard and Healer

Happiness (Делфина, CC BY-SA 4.0).

people, including descriptions ranging from serving as a social lubricant, a connection trigger between causal acquaintances, and a social icebreaker (2). While there are anecdotal and qualitative research studies concerning these roles, few empirically based studies have been conducted (Wood et al. 2).

Wood et al. provide a concept diagram of pet-facilitated social relatedness, illustrating types of interactions between pet owners and opportunities for social support. They divide the opportunities first into two types of interactions involving incidental social interaction and friendship formation (3). These two types of interactions create potential social support opportunities. The authors define social support in four categories: "(1) Informational—the provision of useful information; (2) Emotional—provision of empathy, affection or encouragement; (3) Instrumental—provision of practical help or favor; and (4) Appraisal—provision of advice/opinion" (3).

This study includes over 2600 residents from four cities, Perth, Australia and three cities in the United States, San Diego, Portland, and Nashville (Wood et al. 1). The study focuses on interactions in neighborhoods, with all participants initially asked about "getting to know people within

11. Links Between Motivation, Companionship and Social Capital

their neighborhood" (1). Pet owners are then provided "additional questions about the type/s of pet/s they owned, whether they had formed friendships as a result of the pet and if they had received any of the four different types of social support from the people they met through their pet" (1).

Results provide insight into the significance of dogs companions within these environments and potential for social supports. For instance, "Specifically dog owners were five times more likely to get to know people in their neighborhood than other pet owners" (8). The role of social icebreakers and the importance of dog walking were recurrent themes in the results (8). According to Wood et al., "Overall, 42.3% of pet owners received one or more types of social support" (11). In addition, "Compared to other pet owners, dog owners were more than three time more like to receive at least one type of social support from people met through their pet" (Wood et al. 11).

These findings help highlight dog archetypal characteristics of guides and healers, specifically as potential conduits for socially supportive networks within communities. Dog companions create opportunities for interactions between people, offering common interest connections and bridging distances between groups. As guides, they create social bridges between individuals and enhance support and wellbeing within communities.

These observations reinforce the importance of dogs in three significant areas: the central interactive nucleus of dogs and individuals, the potential for connectivity between individuals and strangers, and the perspectives of how individuals view their social interactions within a larger society. In addition, the non-judgmental reliability and affections of a companion dog can help create an environment conducive to increased calmness, feelings of acceptance, and subsequent perceptions of well-being within their human counterparts. The statements above reflect widely felt observations concerning the interwoven forms of the bond between people and dogs.

12

The Journey

*Framed by Aspects of Past,
Present and Future*

Throughout history, the interspecies bond between people and dogs continues to evolve, adapt, and grow. This bond resides at a nexus of influences from the prehistoric past leading through the development of civilizations, through the more immediate past, and into the contemporary present. In addition, the progression of the human/dog bond moves not only in a linear path forward, but rather continues to be influenced by the past as well as the present.

Dogs and people share an interspecies bond couched within nature, framed by social intention and cognitive skills, attachment, and shared communication. These influences exist within cultures throughout history, individual psychologies, and larger social groups. Within this bond, dog archetypal characteristics, including guide, guard, and healer, unfold framed by psychological and cultural influences. These characteristics are accumulative and impact both the perspectives of individuals and the perceptions of larger societies.

For instance, during prehistoric periods dogs served as guards for camps and later hunting companions. Subsequently, through their interactions, people discovered that dogs possess remarkable abilities as working dogs in herding livestock, as well as guarding individuals and settlements. Later, as a result of specific goals in breeding, training, and subsequent adaption, dogs provide specialized skills for police forces, military personnel, in animal therapy, and as companion guide dogs.

The three spheres of mind, culture, and nature weave throughout the human/dog bond and the journey of these two species. Aspects of comparative mythology, psychology, and dog ethology highlight the evolution and importance of the human/dog bond within these spheres. The journey of people and dogs begins with domestication and continues to evolve

12. The Journey

within an evolutionary niche in the human world. Cultural and dog archetypal characteristics impact this journey.

These characteristics exist within individual relationships and universal influences found in mythologies and cultural developments throughout history. Dog archetypal characteristics of guard, guide, and healer reside in these interactions within the human/dog bond. Dogs possess a psychological essence as well as a physical presence which resonates throughout these interactions. For instance, mythological stories from Egyptian, Greek, Roman, and Iranian cultures illustrate the spiritual and practical importance of dogs. From prehistory up until the present, dogs share companionship with people in spiritual, physical, and psychological journeys.

Reflections on the unique characteristics of the bond between people and dogs, based on scientific research, illustrates and reinforces the universal nature of this bond. In addition, within individual lives and society, the future holds promise for new scientific opportunities to consider the impacts of dogs' archetypal characteristics of guide, guard, and healer characteristics. Links between the social and communication skills of dogs and archetypal characteristics of guide, guard, and healer reinforce aspects of the human/dog bond. Aspects of attachment, empathy, and motivation within the human/dog bond impact these communications.

Different types and methods of communication between people and dogs frame their interspecies connections. Dogs possess amazing abilities to adapt, interact, and communicate with people. No two other species possess the abilities to communicate between each other as do dogs and people. Dogs communicate with people utilizing physical, visual, and vocal skills informed with aspects of social cognition and intention. These interspecies communications possess an elasticity, moving back and forth between people and dogs. For individuals, these communications can mitigate loneliness, enhance feelings of social connection, and encourage well-being.

Scientific studies continue to explore these abilities as well as the importance of the bond between individuals and dogs within larger society groups. Studies within the field of dog cognition offer enormous opportunities to uncover *how* dogs think and *what* they feel. This research will provide pathways to further understand how people feel and experience various aspects of companionship between each other.

Scholars also seek to document and understand the human/dog bond in order to uncover similarities in interactions between people, such as within the mother/child bond. Research continues to advance this knowledge not only by comparing interactions between people and dogs, but also similar interactions between humans. Yet, there will always be an essence in the human/dog bond which is universal and undefinable, an essence felt, couched in psychological and mythopoetic aspects of each individual relationship.

Perhaps, the most important aspects in this relationship revolve around the needs for belonging, regard and love, esteem, and companionship. The first paragraph of this book notes that people and dogs are social beings and that they choose to share their existence together, in part, because they want to be together. Over time, the bond between individuals and dogs often extends beyond companionship to include influences for positive social capital. Dogs offer not only love, trust, and loyalty to individuals, but also facilitate positive interactions between people in larger community groups.

People and dogs exist in a unique and symbiotic relationship and together they continue to traverse their journey. They share an existence intertwined within the spheres of mind, culture, and nature framed by the central essence of the human/dog bond. The bond between people and dogs, couched in the past and framed by the present, also resonates as vibrant and enormously significant for the future. The shared journey of people and dogs will continue to unfold, richly layered, fluid, and experienced in both the physical world of nature and the psychological parameters of the mind.

Bibliography

Abram, David. *Becoming Animal: An Earthly Cosmology.* Random House, 2011.

―――. *The Spell of the Sensuous.* Random House, 1996.

American Kennel Club. "The 7 AKC Dog Breed Groups Explained." June 2023. https://www.akc.org/expert-advice/lifestyle/7-akc-dog-breed-groups-explained/.

Anastasia. "Mesopotamian Cylinder Seals—Exploring Glyptic Images." *Ancient & Oriental,* 29 June 2022. https://www.antiquities.co.uk/blog/imagery-symbolism/mesopotamian-cylinder-seals-exploring-glyptic-images/.

Arkow, Phil. "Animal Therapy on the Community Level: The Impact of Pets on Social Capital." *Handbook on Animal-Assisted Therapy: Foundations and Guidelines for Animal-Assisted Interventions,* edited by Aubrey H. Fine, 4th ed., Elsevier, 2015, pp. 43–51.

"As It Happens: Nearly 8 Million Dog Mummies Found in Egyptian Catacomb." CBC Radio, 25 June 2015. www.cbc.ca/radio/asithappens/as-it-happens-wednesday-edition-1.3126363/-nearly-8-million-dog-mummies-found-in-egyptian-catacomb-1.3126379.

Atsma, Aaron J. "Keberos." *Theo Project,* www.theoi.com/Ther/KuonKerberos.html.

Barrientos, Alex. "Hunting Dogs in the Ancient World." *Classical Wisdom,* 2 Sept. 2020. https://classicalwisdom.com/culture/history/hunting-dogs-in-the-ancient-world/ https://www.fci.be/en/Presentation-of-our-organisation-4.html. Reproduced with permission.

Beck, Alan M. "The Biology of the Human–Animal Bond." *Animal Frontiers,* vol. 4, no. 3, July 2014, pp. 32–36. https://doi.org/10.2527/af.2014-0019.

Bradshaw, John. *In Defense of Dogs.* Penguin, 2012, pp. 52–53.

Bradshaw, John, and Nicola Rooney. "Dog Social Behavior and Communication." *The Domestic Dog: Its Evolution, Behavior, and Interactions with People,* edited by James Serpell, 2nd ed., Cambridge UP, 2017, pp. 133–159.

Brewer, Douglas, et al. *Dogs in Antiquity: Anubis to Cereberus: The Origins of the Domestic Dog.* Oxbow Books, 2011.

Buck, William. "The Lonely Encounter." *Mahabharata.* U of California P, 1973, pp. 353–369, 415.

Bulsara, Max K., et al. "More Than a Furry Companion: The Ripple Effect of Companion Animals on Neighborhood Interactions and Sense of Community." *Society & Animals,* vol. 15, no. 1, pp. 43–46. https://doi.org/10.1163/156853007X169333.

Cambray, Joseph. *Synchronicity: Nature and Psyche in an Interconnected Universe.* Texas A&M UP, 2009, pp. 1–42.

Campbell, Joseph. *Joseph Campbell: Historical Atlas of World Mythology: Volume 1: The Way of the Animal Powers, Part 1: Mythologies of the Primitive Hunters and Gatherers.* Harper & Row, 1988, pp. 1–125.

―――. *Joseph Campbell: Historical Atlas of World Mythology: Volume 1: The Way of the Animal Powers, Part 2: Mythologies of the Great Hunt.* Harper & Row, 1988, p. 129.

―――. *The Power of Myth with Bill Moyers,* ed. Betty Sue Flowers, MJF Books, 1988, p. 162.

Catala, Amélie, et al. "Dogs Demonstrate

Bibliography

Perspective Taking Based on Geometrical Gaze Following in a Guesser–Knower Task." *Animal Cognition* vol. 20, 2017, pp. 581–589. https://doi.org/10.1007/s10071-017-1082-x. http://creativecommons.org/licenses/by/4.0/.

Charitonidou, Angeliki. *Epidaurus: The Sanctuary of Asclepios and the Museum.* Clio Editions, 1978, pp. 1–51.

Clutton-Brock, Juliet. "Origins of the Dog: The Archeological Evidence." *The Domestic Dog: Its Evolution, Behavior and Interactions with People,* edited by James Serpell, 2nd ed., Cambridge UP, 2017, pp. 7–21.

Collins, Tim. "The World's First Images of Dogs Are Found on 8,000-Year-Old Rocks in Saudi Arabia—and They're Wearing LEASHES." *Daily Mail,* 20 Nov. 2017. https://www.dailymail.co.uk/sciencetech/article-5100327/The-worlds-images-dogs-wearing-leashes.html.

Coren, Stanley. "Can Dogs Help Humans Heal? Science Looks at Whether Dog Saliva Has Healing Properties." *Psychology Today,* 7 June 2013, pp. 1–8. www.psychologytoday.com/us/blog/canine-corner/201106/can-dogs-help-humans-heal.

Cornwell, Langley. "Superstitions about Howling Dogs." May 2014, www.canidae.com/blog/2014/05/superstitions-about-howling-dogs/.

Correia-Caeiro, Catia, et al. "Visual Perception of Emotion Cues in Dogs: A Critical Review of Methodologies." *Animal Cognition* vol. 26, 2023, pp. 727–754. https://doi.org/10.1007/s10071-023-01762-5. http://creativecommons.org/licenses/by/4.0/.

"Coursing." *Oxford American Dictionary and Thesaurus: Second Edition,* Oxford UP, 2009, p. 285.

Custance, Deborah, and Jennifer Mayer. "Empathic-Like Responding by Domestic Dogs (*Canis familiaris*) to Distress in Humans: An Exploratory Study." Department of Psychology, Goldsmiths College, London, 27 May 2012. www.academia.edu/1632457/Empathic-like_responding_by_domestic_dogs_Canis_familiaris_to_distress_in_humans_an_exploratory_study. Reproduced with permission.

"Cynosure." *Oxford American Dictionary and Thesaurus: Second Edition.* Oxford UP, 2009, p. 310.

Dale-Green, Patricia. *Lore of the Dog.* Houghton Mifflin, 1967, pp. 16–137.

Debroy, Bibek. *Sarama and Her Children: The Dog in Indian Myth.* Penguin Random House India, 2008, pp. ix–83.

Dotson, Michael J., and Eva M. Hyatt. "Understanding Dog–Human Companionship." *Journal of Business Research,* vol. 61, no. 5, 2008, pp. 457–466. ISSN 0148-2963. https://doi.org/10.1016/j.jbusres.2007.07.019. https://creativecommons.org/licenses/by-nc-nd/3.0/. Reproduced with permission from Elsevier.

"Dualism." *Oxford American Dictionary and Thesaurus: Second Edition.* Oxford UP, 2009, p. 392.

Duke Canine Cognition Center. Duke Trinity College of Arts and Sciences Department of Evolutionary Anthropology, 2021. https://evolutionaryanthropology.duke.edu/.

Dwyer, Fleur, et al. "Development of the Monash Dog Owner Relationship Scale (MDORS)." *Anthrozoös,* vol. 19, no. 3, 2006, pp. 243–256. https://doi.org/10.2752/089279306785415592. Reproduced with permission.

Edrey, Meir. "The Dog Burials at Achaemenid Ashkelon Revisited." Johannes Gutenberg U, 12 Aug. 2008, pp. 267–287. www.researchgate.net/publication/233672198.

"Empathy." *Oxford American Dictionary and Thesaurus: Second Edition.* Oxford UP, 2009, p. 417.

Farricelli, Adrienne. "What's the Difference Between Dog Howling and Baying?" Dec. 24, 2016, dogdiscoveries.com/difference-between-dog-howling-and-baying/.

Federation Cynologique Internationale. "Presentation of Our Organization." https://www.fci.be/en/Presentation-of-our-organisation-4.html.

Fine, Aubrey H., and Alan M. Beck. "Understanding Our Kinship with Animals: Input for Health Care Professionals Interested in the Human-Animal Bond." *Handbook on Animal-Assisted Therapy: Foundations and Guidelines*

Bibliography

for *Animal-Assisted Interventions*, edited by Aubrey H. Fine, 4th ed., Elsevier, 2015, pp. 3–10.

Foltz, Richard. "Zoroastrian Attitudes Toward Animals." *Society and Animals*, vol. 18, 2010, pp. 367–378. https://www.animalsandsociety.org/wp-content/uploads/2016/04/foltz.pdf.

Fox, Michael. "Relationships Between the Human and NonHuman Animals." *Interrelations Between People and Pets*, edited by Bruce Fogle, D.U.M. M.R.C.V.S., Charles C. Thomas, 1981, pp. 23–40.

Frydenborg, Kay. *A Dog in the Cave: The Wolves Who Made Us Human*. Houghton Mifflin Harcourt, 2017.

Germonpré, Mietje, et al. "Fossil Dogs and Wolves from Palaeolithic Sites in Belgium, the Ukraine and Russia: Osteometry, Ancient DNA and Stable Isotopes." *Journal of Archaeological Science*, vol. 36, no. 2, 2009, pp. 473–490. ISSN 0305-4403. https://doi.org/10.1016/j.jas.2008.09.033. Reproduced with permission from Elsevier.

"Gestalt." *Oxford American Dictionary and Thesaurus: Second Edition*. Oxford UP, 2009, p. 546.

Grimm, David. "Dawn of the Dog." *Science*, vol. 348, April 2015, pp. 274–281. DOI: 10.1126/science.348.6232.274. Reproduced with permission from AAAS.

———. "These May Be the World's First Images of Dogs—and They're Wearing Leashes." *Science*, 16 Nov. 2017. www.sciencemag.org/news/2017/11/these-may-be-world-s-first-images-dogs-and-they-re-wearing-leashes.

Grout, James. "Dogs in Ancient Greece and Rome." *Encyclopaedia Romana*. 13 Dec. 2010. https://penelope.uchicago.edu/~grout/encyclopaedia_romana/miscellanea/canes/canes.html.

Hart, Lynette A., and Mariko Yamamoto. "Dogs as Helping Partners and Companions for Humans." *The Domestic Dog: Its Evolution, Behavior and Interactions with People*, edited by James Serpell, 2nd ed., Cambridge UP, 2017, pp. 247–270.

Hausman, Gerald, and Loretta Hausman. *Canine Legend and Lore through the Ages: The Mythology of Dogs*. St. Martin's Press, 1977, pp. 75–78, 202–204.

Heberlein, Marianne T.E., et al. "Dogs' (*Canis familiaris*) Attention to Human Perception: Influence of Breed Groups and Life Experiences." *Journal of Comparative Psychology*, vol. 131, no. 1, 2017, pp. 19–29. https://doi.org/10.1037/com0000050. American Psychological Association. Reproduced with permission.

Hesoid. *The Works and Days: Theogony: The Shield of Herakles*. Translated by Richard Lattimore, Ann Arbor Paperbacks, U of Michigan P, 1991, pp. 169.

Hillman, James. *Animal Presences*. Spring Publications, 2008, pp. 10–13, pp. 150–187.

———. *The Essential James Hillman: A Blue Fire*. Introduced and edited by Thomas Moore in collaboration with the author, Routledge, 1998, pp. 1–35.

———. "Human Being as Animal Being: A Correspondence with John Stockwell." *Animal Presences*. Spring Publications, 2008, pp. 161–169.

———. "Let the Creatures Be: A Conversation with Thomas Moore." *Animal Presences*. Spring Publications, 2008, p. 183.

———. "A Psyche the Size of the Earth: A Psychological Foreword." *Ecopsychology*. Sierra Club Books, 1995, pp. xvii–xxiii.

Horowitz, Alexandra. *Inside of a Dog: What Dogs See, Smell, and Know*. Scribner's, 2009, pp. 13–160.

Huber, Annika, et al. "Investigating Emotional Contagion in Dogs (*Canis familiaris*) to Emotional Sounds of Humans and Conspecifics." *Animal Cognition*, vol. 20, 2017, pp. 703–715. https://doi.org/10.1007/s10071-017-1092-8. http://creativecommons.org/licenses/by/4.0/.

Huber, Ludwig, and Lucrezia Lonardo. "Canine Perspective-Taking." *Animal Cognition*, vol. 26, 2023, pp. 275–298. https://doi.org/10.1007/s10071-022-01736-z. http://creativecommons.org/licenses/by/4.0/.

Ikram, Salima. "Man's Best Friend for Eternity: Dog and Human Burials in Ancient Egypt." *Anthropozoologica*, vol. 48, no. 2, 1 Jan. 2013, pp. 299–307. https://doi.org/10.5252/az2013n2a8. Reproduced with permission.

Bibliography

Janssens, Luc, et al. "A New Look at an Old Dog: Bonn-Oberkassel Reconsidered." *Journal of Archaeological Science*, vol. 92, 2018, pp. 126–138. ISSN 0305–4403. https://doi.org/10.1016/j.jas.2018.01.004.

Jeffers, Jim. "Illustrated History of Greyhounds." FastFriends Greyhound Adoption of California, Inc. https://www.fastfriends.org/history-of-greyhounds. Reproduced with permission.

Jung, C.G. *Collective Works of C.G. Jung, Volume 11: Psychology and Religion: West and East*, edited by Gerhard Adler and R.F.C. Hull, Princeton UP, 1970, para. 6.

———. *The Earth Has a Soul: C.G. Jung on Nature, Technology & Modern Life*, edited by Meredith Sabini, North Atlantic Books, 2008.

———. *The Essential Jung*, edited by Anthony Storr, Princeton UP, 2013, pp. 16–19.

———. *Memories, Dreams, Reflections*, translated Aniela Jaffé, Random House, 1963.

Kaminski, Juliane and Patrizia Piotti. "Current Trends in Dog-Human Communication: Do Dogs Inform?" *Current Directions in Psychological Science* vol. 25, Sage Publications, 2016, pp. 322–326. Reproduced with permission of SAGE Publications.

Kaminski, Juliane, et al. "Evolution of Facial Muscle Anatomy in Dogs." *Proceedings of the National Academy of Sciences*, vol. 116, no. 29, 2019, pp. 14677–14681. doi:10.1073/pnas.1820653116. https://creativecommons.org/licenses/by/4.0/.

———, et al. "How Dogs Know When Communication Is Intended for Them." *Developmental Science*, vol. 15, no. 2, 2012, pp. 222–232. https://doi.org/10.1111/j.1467-7687.2011.01120.x. Reproduced with permission from Wiley.

Lanese, Nicoletta. "What Is Homeostasis?" *Live Science*, 2019, pp. 1–5. www.livescience.com/65938-homeostasis.html.

Lange, Karen E. "Wolf to Woof: The Evolution of Dogs." *National Geographic*, Jan. 2002, pp. 2–11.

Larson, Greger, et al. "Rethinking Dog Domestication by Integrating Genetics, Archeology, and Biogeography." *Proceedings of the National Academy of Sciences of the United States of America*, vol. 109, no. 23, 2012, pp. 8878–9983. doi:10.1073/pnas.1203005109.

Leach, Maria. *God Had a Dog: Folklore of the Dog*. Rutgers UP, 1961, pp. 1–170.

Lindow, John. *Norse Mythology: A Guide to the Gods, Heroes, Rituals, and Beliefs*. Oxford UP, 2001, pp. 1–135.

Maginnity, Michelle E., and Randolf C. Grace. "Visual Perspective Taking by Dogs (*Canis familiaris*) in a Guesser-Knower Task: Evidence for a Canine Theory of Mind?" *Animal Cognition*, vol. 17, 2014, pp. 1375–1392. https://doi.org/10.1007/s10071-014-0773-9.

Maslow, Abraham. "A Theory of Human Motivation." *Classics in the History of Psychology*, York University, Toronto, Aug. 2000, pp. 1–14. psychclassics.yorku.ca/Maslow/motivation.htm.

Manlow, Abraham H. *Toward a Psychology of Being*. Sublime Books, 2014, p. 163.

Meier, Carl A. *Healing Dreams and Ritual: Ancient Incubation and Modern Psychology*. 4th ed., Daimon Verlas, 2009.

Miklósi, Ádám. *Dog Behavior, Evolution, and Cognition*, 2nd ed., Oxford UP, 2015, pp. 124–152.

Miklósi, Ádám, and Eniko Kubinyi. "Current Trends in Canine Problem-Solving and Cognition." *Current Directions in Psychological Science*, vol. 25, 2016, pp. 300–306. https://doi.org/10.1177/0963721416666061.

Miller, Geoffrey David. "Attitudes Toward Dogs in Ancient Israel: A Reassessment." *Journal for the Study of the Old Testament*, vol. 32, no. 4, 2008, pp. 487–500. https://doi.org/10.1177/0309089208092144.

Moore, Thomas. "Prologue." *The Essential James Hillman: A Blue Fire*. Routledge, 1998, pp. 1–11.

Morford, Mark, et al. *Classical Mythology*, 10th ed., Oxford UP, 2014, pp. 221–235, 326, 379, 575.

Müller, Corsin A., et al. "Dogs Can Discriminate Emotional Expressions of Human Faces." *Current Biology*, 25 Mar. 2015, pp. 601–605. https://doi.org/10.1016/j.cub.2014.12.055. Reproduced with permission from Elsevier.

Bibliography

"Naturopathy." *Oxford American Dictionary and Thesaurus: Second Edition.* Oxford UP, 2009, p. 861.

Okunishi, Shunsuke. "The Four-Eyed Dog." https://cogito.ucdc.ro/2012/vol4n2/en/-13_the-four-eyed-dog.pdf.

Ornan, Tallay. "The Goddess Gula and Her Dog." *IMSA*, vol. 3, 2004, pp 13–30.

Parker, Heidi G., et al. "Genetic Structure of the Purebred Domestic Dog." *Science*, vol. 304, no. 5674, 2004 May 21, pp. 1160–1164. doi: 10.1126/science.1097406. PMID: 15155949. Reproduced with permission from AAAS.

Perin, Constance. "Dogs as Symbols in Human Development." *Interrelations Between People and Pets*, edited by Bruce Fogle, D.U.M. M.R.C.V.S., Charles C. Thomas, 1981, pp. 68–88.

Pinch, Geraldine. "Deities, Themes and Concepts." *Egyptian Mythology: A Guide to the Gods, Goddesses, and Traditions of Ancient Egypt.* Oxford UP, 2002, pp. 26–214.

Pongrácz, Péter, et al. "Acoustic Parameters of Dog Barks Carry Emotional Information for Humans." *Applied Animal Behaviour Science*, vol. 100, nos. 3–4, 2006, pp. 228–240. ISSN 0168-1591. https://doi.org/10.1016/j.applanim.2005.12.004. Reproduced with permission from Elsevier.

Previde, Emanuela Prato, and Paola Valsecchi. "The Immaterial Cord: The Dog-Human Attachment Bond." *The Social Dog: Behavior and Cognition*, edited by Juliane Kaminski and Sarah Marshall-Pescini, Elsevier, 2014, pp. 165–189.

Range, Friederike, and Zsófia Virányi. "Social Cognition and Emotions Underlying Dog Behavior." *The Domestic Dog: Its Evolution, Behavior and Interactions with People*, edited by James Serpell, 2nd ed., Cambridge UP, 2017, pp. 182–209.

Ridpath, Ian. *Star Tales.* Universe Books, 1988, pp. vii–43.

Ripley, Katherine. "Shih Tzu Facts You May Not Know." 20 Mar. 24. https://www.akc.org/expert-advice/lifestyle/fun-facts-shih-tzu/.

Rosen, David H. "Series Editor's Foreword." *Synchronicity: Nature and Psyche in an Interconnected Universe.* Texas A&M UP, 2009, pp. xi–xiv.

Salmon, Peter W., and Ingrid M. Salmon. "Who Owns Who? Psychological Research into the Human-Pet Bond in Australia." *New Perspectives on Our Lives with Companion Animals*, edited by Aaron Honori Katcher and Alan M. Beck, Pennsylvania UP, 1985, pp. 244–275.

Sax, Boria. *The Mythical Zoo: Animals in Myth, Legend, and Literature.* Peter Mayer, 2013, pp. 175–186.

Serpell, James. "From Paragon to Pariah: Some Reflections on Human Attitudes to Dogs." *The Domestic Dog: Its Evolution, Behavior and Interactions with People*, edited by James Serpell, 2nd ed., Cambridge UP, 1995, p. 254.

Sinding, Mikkel-Holger S., et al. "Arctic-Adapted Dogs Emerged at the Pleistocene–Holocene Transition." *Science*, vol. 368, 2020, pp. 1495–1499. DOI:10.1126/science.aaz8599.

Stahl, Peter W. "Old Dogs and New Tricks: Recent Developments in Our Understanding of the Human–Dog Relationship." *Reviews in Anthropology*, vol. 45, no. 1, 2016, pp. 51–68. https://doi.org/10.1080/00938157.2016.1142298.

"Sympathy." *Oxford American Dictionary and Thesaurus: Second Edition.* Oxford UP, 2009, p. 1326.

Tick, Edward. "On Asklepios, Dream Healing and Talking with the Dead." *Alternative Therapies*, vol. 10, no. 1, Jan./Feb. 2004, pp. 65–72.

———. *The Practice of Dreaming Healing: Bringing Ancient Greek Mysteries into Modern Medicine.* Quest Books, Theosophical Publishing House, 2001, pp. 1–40.

Topál, Józef, et al. "Attachment Behavior in Dogs (Canis familiaris): A New Application of Ainsworth's (1969) Strange Situation Test." *Journal of Comparative Psychology*, vol. 112, no. 3, 1998, pp. 219–229. https://doi.org/10.1037/0735-7036.112.3.219. American Psychological Association. Reproduced with permission.

vonHoldt, Bridgett M., and Carlos A. Driscoll. "Origins of the Dog: Genetic Insights into Dog Domestication." *The Domestic Dog: Its Evolution, Behavior*

Bibliography

and Interactions with People, edited by James Serpell, 2nd ed., Cambridge UP, 2017, pp. 22–41.

White, David Gordon. "Dogs." *Encyclopedia of Religion,* edited by Lindsay Jones, 2nd ed., vol. 4, Macmillan Reference USA, 2005, pp. 2392–2394. *Gale Virtual Reference Library,* go.galegroup.com/ps/i.do?p=GVRL&sw=w&u=carp39441&v=2.1&.

White, Ella. "What Is the Kennel Club?" *Front of the Pack.* 21 Dec. 2023, https://fotp.com/learn/dog-lifestyle/what-is-the-kennel-club.

Wood, Lisa, et al. "The Pet Factor—Companion Animals as a Conduit for Getting to Know People, Friendship Formation and Social Support." *PLoS ONE,* vol. 10, no. 4, 2015, e0122085, https://doi.org/10.1371/journal.pone.0122085. http://creativecommons.org/licenses/by/4.0/.

Worsley, Hannah K., and Sean J. O'Hara. "Cross-Species Referential Signalling Events in Domestic Dogs (*Canis familiaris*)." *Animal Cognition,* vol. 21, 2018, pp. 457–465. https://doi.org/10.1007/s10071-018-1181-3. http://creativecommons.org/licenses/by/4.0/.

Xenophon. *Cynegeticus: On Hunting with Dogs.* Biblioness, 2017, pp. 1–5, 57–61.

Yin, Sophia, and Brenda McCowan. "Barking in Domestic Dogs: Context Specificity and Individual Identification." *Animal Behaviour,* vol. 68, no. 2, 2004, pp. 343–355. ISSN 0003-3472. https://doi.org/10.1016/j.anbehav.2003.07.016. Reproduced with permission from Elsevier.

Yong, Min Hooi and Ruffman, Ted. "Emotional Contagion: Dogs and Humans Show a Similar Physiological Response to Human Infant Crying," *Behavioural Processes,* Volume 108, 2014, Pages 155-165, ISSN 0376-6357, https://doi.org/10.1016/j.beproc.2014.10.006.

Index

Numbers in **_bold italics_** indicate pages with illustrations

Abram, David 124–125, 138, 179, 195
Actaeon 47, 80, **_81_**
Aeneas 86, 88
The Aeneid 86, 88
Africa 41, 46, 52, 54, 56, 59–60, 68, 68, 73
agriculture 11, 14, 41–43, 52–53, 58
Alaskan Malamute 59, 68
American Kennel Club 14, 56, 69, 195
Anastasia 195
ancient breeds 15, 43, 53, 56, 60, 65, 67, 69–70
Anubis 33, **_34_**, 35, 90–91, 99, 195
Apollo 88, 103–105
archetype 110, 114, 119–122, 156
Arctic 55, 59–60, 68, 199
Aristotle 107, 122–123
Arkow, Phil 6, 195
Arrian **_50_**, 55
Artemis 47, 51, 80–81
Asclepius 102–106, 108, 116, 196
Ashkelon 12, 35–36, 45, 101
Asia 32, 60, 68, 73
Asklepion 104–105, 107–108, 116
Assyria 48–49
astronomy 72–74
Atsma, Aaron J. 86–88, 195
attachment 3–4, 29, 62, 95, 97, 118, 144, 155, 166, 174, 176–177, **_180_**, 181–183, 185–186, 192–193, 199

Babylonia 101–102
Barrientos, Alex 51, 54–55, 195
Basenji 54, 59, 68
basic needs 5, 172–177
Beck, Alan M. 5, 170, 183–184, 195–197
Bering Strait 41
Bradshaw, John 19, 127–128, 131–133, 145, 189, 195
breed groups 58, 60, 64–67, 69, 70, 195, 197

Brewer, Douglas 43, 45–46, 48–53, 195
Buck, William 98–99, 195
Bulsara, M. 195

Cambray, Joseph 119–123, 195
Campbell, Joseph 9–10, 13, 16, 31–33, 35–36, 81, 195
canine perspective-taking 64–67, 145–146, 148, 150, 153–156, 158, 173, 173
Canis major 73–76
Canis minor 73, 75–76
Catala, Ameilie 146–148, 158, 195
Cerberus **_84_**, 85–86, **_87_**, 88–90
Charitonidou, Angeliki 196
China 41, 58–59, 68
choice tests 64, 66, 141, 158
Chow Chow 39, 59, 67–68
Classical World 51–52, 58, 60, 70
Clutton-Brock, Juliet 12, 18–19, 23, 196
Collins, Tim 38, 196
communication cues 61, 141, 158, 169
companionship 5, 10–11, 20, 23, 33, 36, 39, 42, 45, 55, 57, 67, 70–71, 90, 99, 156, 158, **_160_**, 166, 170, 173, 178–179, 185–189, 191, 193–194, 196; *see also* Strange Situation test 180–183; "A Theory of Human Motivation" 174–177
constellations 73–75
Coren, Stanley 106, 196
Cornwell, Langley 78–79, 196
Correia-Caeiro, Catia 156–158, 196
coursing 45–49, **_50_**, 54–55, 196
Custance, Deborah 155, 160–162, 165–196
cynosure 104, 196

Dale-Green, Patricia 78, 80, 83, 85, 88, 92, 102–103, 196
Darwin, Charles 22–23, 183
Debroy, Bibek 92–93, 104, 196

Index

DNA 18, 24, 26–27, 197
dog barks 129, 130, 132–137, 163, 199
dog burials 33–37, 101, 196
dog cemeteries 34, 99, 103
dog cognition 6, 126–128, 140, 144, 156, 193
domestication 4, 6–7, 9, 11–28, 31, 37–39, 61–62, 97, 126, 140, 156, 158
Dotson, Michael J. 186–188, 196
dream incubation 104–105
dreams 75, 98, 104–109, 111–113, 116, 118, 123, 198–199
Driscoll, Carlos A. 13–14, 43, 55, 199
dualism 90, 195, 196
Duke Canine Cognition Center 156, 196
Dwyer, Fleur 185–186, 196

Edrey, Meir 12, 35–36, 196
Egypt 5, 12, 32, 36, 39, 43, 44–48, 50–52, 54, 58, 70, 82, 99, 114, 193, 195, 197, 199; *see also* Anubis 90–91; Ikram, Salima 33–35
emotion contagion 163–165
emotion cues 156–158, 196
empathetic responses 6, 156, 158–161, 163
empathy 6, 37, 155, 157, 159–166, **167**, 188, 190, 193, 196
Epidaurus 81, 103–106, 196
Europe 31, 41, 46, 56, 58
eye contact 62, 67, 128, 131, 141–144, 146, 152

facial expressions 126, 144, 152, 159, 166, 169
Farricelli, Adrienne 78, 196
Federation Cynologique Internationale 14, 54, 56, 196
Festival of Tihar **120**
Fine, Aubrey H. 5, 170, 195–197
Foltz, Richard 93–95
fossils 21, 23–27, 30–31, 35, 37–39, 197
Fox, Michael 178–179, 188, 197
Frydenborg, Kay 15, 19–20, 23, 197
functions of mythology 11, 31–32, 36

gazing cues 141, 148, 150, 152
genetics 57–58, 61–62, 65–66, 68, 70, 198
geometrical gaze following 145, 147, 149–150, 158, 196
German Shepard 168
Germonpré, Mietje 12, 21–24, 26, 197
gestalt 123, 197
Goyet Cave 23–26
Grace, Randolf C. 145, 147–149, 158, 198

Greece 51–53, 55, 70, 75, 81–82, 103–105, 107, 114–115, 198
grey wolf 18, 23, 58, 61
Greyhound 17, 45–46, **50**, 54–55, 70, 198
Grimm, David 12, 15, 20, 26, 27, 38–39, 197
Grout, James 51–53, 70, 197
guard dogs 42–43, 45, 47, 53, 60, 65, 67, 71, 82, 95
Guesser-Knower task 145–149, 196, 198
Gula **100**, 101–102, 199

Hades **84**, 85–88
Hart, Lynette A. 97, 183–184, 189, 197
Hausman, Gerald 68–69, 197
Hausman, Loretta 68–69, 197
healing rituals 5, 89, 105, 108
Heberlein, Marianne T. E. 64–67, 197
Hecate 47, 80–82
hellhound 83–84, 88, 90
Hercules 86–88
Hesoid 197
Hillman, James 5, 109, 114–119, 123, 125, 179, 197–198
Hinduism 90–91, 114
Horace 52
Horowitz, Alexandra 16–17, 29, 127–128, 130–132, 143–145, 152, 160, 197
Huber, Annika 155, 161, 163–165, 197
Huber, Ludwig 64, 145–146, 148–150, 158, 197
human-animal bond 5, 156, 170, 177–178, 195–196
humanistic psychology 5, 29, 174
hunter-gatherers 16, 23, 37–38, 41, 43, 58
Hyatt, Eva M. 186–188, 196

Ikram, Salima 33–35, 91, 197
incubation 104–105, 108, 198
India 33, 51, 82
Indra 92–93, 98, 99
Iran 33, 58, 93
Italy 51, 53, 58, 70, 103, 197

Janssens, Luc 37
Jeffers, Jim 46–47, 49, 54–55, 198
Jung, C.G. 5, 108–114, 116–117, 119–123, 198

Kaminski, Juliane 6, 60–63, 67, 128, 140–142, 198
Kubinyi, Eniko 6, 198

Laelaps 47, **75**, 76
Lanese, Nicoletta 175, 198
Lange, Karen E. 15, 18, 20–21, 28, 38, 198

Index

Larson, Greger 11, 14–15, 23, 198
Leach, Maria 51–52, 73, 75–79, 81–82, 86, 88–89, 91, 97–102, 198
Lindow, John 85, 198
Lonardo, Lucrezia 64, 145–146, 148–150, 158, 197

Maginnity, Michelle E. 145, 147–149, 158, 198
Maltese 52
Maslow, Abraham 5, 163, 172, 174–177, 179, 198
Mastiff 14, 17, 45, 48, 51, 60, 65–66
Mayer, Jennifer 155, 160–162, 165, 196
McCowan, Brenda 124, 129, 132–138, 158, 200
Meier, Carl A. 103–108, 198
Mesopotamia 22, 43, 45–46, 48–50, 7, 100–102, 195
Metamorphoses 47, 86
Miklósi, Ádám 6, 15–16, 19, 22, 41–42, 60, 158, 198
Milky Way 74, 76–77
Miller, Geoffrey David 33, 35–36, 101, 198
Molosser 45, 51, 53
Monash Dog Owner Relationship Scale (MDORS) 185–186, 196
Moore, Thomas 116, 118, 197–198
Morford, Mark 76, 80–81, 87–88, 198
Morton's motivation-structural rules 124, 136, 137
mother-child bond 179, 183, 193
motivations 19, 37, 74, 79–80, 124, 139, 155, 157, 175–177
Müller, Corsin A. 118, 155, 166, 168–169, 198

Native Americans 40, 73–74, 76–77, 79
naturopathy 108, 198
Near East 33, 36, 58, 90, 95, 101, 104
Neolithic 38, 42, 45
North America 17, 32, 41–42, 60, 73

object choice tests 141–142, 152, 158
The Odyssey 47, **75**, 97–98
O'Hara, Sean J. 150–154, 159, 200
Okunishi, Shunsuke 83, 92, 199
Ornan, Tallay 101–103, 199
Orpheus 86–88

pariah dog 45, 60, 199
Parker, Heidi G. 42, 57–60, 65, 67–69, 199
Pekingese 59, 68–69
Perin, Constance 178, 188, 199

perspective-taking abilities 66, 145, 150, 156, 158, 166, 173
phenomenology 124–125
Phoenicia 36, 52, 101
Pinch, Geraldine 91, 199
Piotti, Patrizia 6, 198
planets 72–74
play 6, 118, 127–129, 134, 135–137, 152, 162, 181–182, 187–189
play benefits 183–184
play signals 132–133
Pleistocene 35, 37, 68
Pongrácz, Péter 6, 129, 136–138, 199
Previde, Emanuela Prato 180–181, 199
Psyche 86–87, **115**
psyche 5, 6, 106–112, 114–117, 119–122, 195, 197, 199
psychopomp 5, 77, 82, 91

qualitative research 118, 165, 187, 190
quantitative research 118–119, 165, 187

Range, Friederike 126–130, 145, 155, 160, 199
referential communication 129
referential gestures 129, 150, 153
Ridpath, Ian 72–74, **75**, 76, 199
Ripley, Katherine 72–76, 199
Rooney, Nicola 127–128, 131–133, 145, 189, 195
Rosen, David H. 119–120, 199
Royal Kennel Club 14, 56
Ruffman, Ted 161, 163, 165, 200

safety 5, 93, 172, 174–176
Saint Francis of Assisi **109**
Salmon, Ingrid M. 171–173, 183–184, 187–188, 199
Salmon, Peter W. 171–173, 183–184, 187–188, 199
Saluki 45–46, 49, 54, 59–60, 68, 70
Samarà 92–93
Samoyed 55, 68
sanctuaries 99, 102–108
Saqqara 12, **29**, 33, 35–36, 45
Safameya 88, 92
Saudi Arabia 12, 38–39, 45, 196
Sax, Boria 79, 95, 199
scent hounds 48, 50, 65, 70
self-esteem 5, 172, 176
Serpell, James 28, 195–197, 199
shepherd dogs 42, 45, 51, 53, 55, 58, 60, 65–67, 70–71, 134
Shih-Tzu 59, 68–69, 199

Index

Siberia 23, 41, 55, 60, 68
Siberian Husky 55, 59, 68
sight hounds *44*, 45–46, 49, 54, 59, 65, 68, 70
Sinding, Mikkel-Holger S. 68, 199
Sirius 73–75
sledge dogs 55, 68
social capital 6, 174–175, 177, 179, 181, 183, 185, 187–189, 191, 194–195
social cognition 6, 126, 128, 144, 146, 150, 193, 199
Social Exchange Theory 185–186
social interactions 6, 62–63, 126–127, 155–157, 174, 177, 189, 191
social learning 127–129, 145–145, 147, 153–154, 166, 169
social partners 154, 156
Stahl, Peter W. 4, 13, 16, 27, 199
stars 72–73, 76
Strange Situation test 161, 180–183, 199
sympathy 160, 199
synchronicity 119–122, 195, 199

terrier 48–49, 59, 69–70, 168
Tesem 45–46, 70
"A Theory of Human Motivation" 172, 174–177, 198
Theory of Mind 146–148, 150, 159, 198

Tick, Edward 49, 104–105, 108, 199
Topál, József 118, 158, 180–183, 199

Valsecchi, Paola 180–181, 199
Virányi, Zsófia 126–130, 145, 155, 160, 199
Virgil 51, 86–88
visual perspectives 145, 147–148, 153, 198
vonHoldt, Bridgett M. 13–14, 43, 55, 199

White, David Gordon 13–14, 43, 55, 199
White, Ella 56, 200
Wild Hunt 78–80, 90
wolves 14–16, 18–24, 26–27, 41–42, 45, 51, 53, 55, 61–63, 68, 72, 128, 143, 197
Wood, Lisa 6, 189–191, 200
Worsley, Hannah K. 150–154, 159, 200

Xenophon *50*, 51, 53, 57, 200

Yama 82, 88, 91–92, 97, 183–184, 197
Yamamoto, Mariko 97, 183–184, 189, 197
Yin, Sophia 124, 129, 132–138, 158, 200
Yong, Min Hooi 161, 163, 165, 200
Yudhishthira 96, 97–99

Zeus 47, 74, *75*, 76, 107
Zoroastrianism 92–95, 114, 197

www.ingramcontent.com/pod-product-compliance
Ingram Content Group UK Ltd.
Pitfield, Milton Keynes, MK11 3LW, UK
UKHW042358021025
463558UK00017B/114